FINANCIAL SHENANIGANS

FINANCIAL SHENANIGANS

How to Detect Accounting
Gimmicks and Fraud
in Financial Reports

FOURTH EDITION

Howard M. Schilit

Jeremy Perler | Yoni Engelhart

New York   Chicago   San Francisco   Athens   London   Madrid
Mexico City   Milan   New Delhi   Singapore   Sydney   Toronto

8 LCR 23

ISBN   978-1-260-11726-4
MHID   1-260-11726-X

e-ISBN   978-1-260-11727-1
e-MHID   1-260-11727-8

This publication is designed to provide accurate and authoritative information in regard to the subject matter covered. It is sold with the understanding that neither the author nor the publisher is engaged in rendering legal, accounting, securities trading, or other professional services. If legal advice or other expert assistance is required, the services of a competent professional person should be sought.

—*From a Declaration of Principles Jointly Adopted by a Committee of the American Bar Association and a Committee of Publishers and Associations*

Library of Congress Cataloging-in-Publication Data
Names: Schilit, Howard Mark, 1952– author. | Perler, Jeremy, author. |
   Engelhart, Yoni, author.
Title: Financial shenanigans : how to detect accounting gimmicks & fraud in
   financial reports / Howard M. Schilit, Jeremy Perler, and Yoni Engelhart.
Description: Fourth edition. | New York : McGraw-Hill, [2018]
Identifiers: LCCN 2017051533| ISBN 9781260117264 (alk. paper) | ISBN
   126011726X
Subjects: LCSH: Misleading financial statements. | Fraud.
Classification: LCC HF5681.B2 S3243 2018 | DDC 657/.3--dc23 LC record avail-
able at https://lccn.loc.gov/2017051533

In loving memory of Rob Schilit, Howard's dear brother,
who contributed enormously to prior editions
of *Financial Shenanigans*, and is an ongoing source of inspiration.
He is sorely missed.

Contents

PART THREE
CASH FLOW SHENANIGANS

PART FOUR
KEY METRIC SHENANIGANS

PART FIVE
ACQUISITION ACCOUNTING SHENANIGANS

PART SIX
PUTTING IT ALL TOGETHER

Preface

Reflections on My Last 25 Years
Howard Schilit

Fall 2017

Dear Friends,

Having recently reached my sixty-fifth birthday, I began reflecting on my life and the many changes over the last quarter century since writing the first edition of *Financial Shenanigans*. In short, I feel very blessed. On a personal level, my wife Diane and I love spending time with our three young grandchildren, and are eagerly awaiting our fourth. Professionally, I am enjoying building my second business, a forensic accounting consultancy called Schilit Forensics, with my fantastic partners and coauthors, Jeremy Perler and Yoni Engelhart.

In addition to the research engagements we work on for our clients, we spend a fair amount of time teaching the trade of forensic accounting—to investors, regulators, journalists, and graduate students. After a recent presentation at Stanford's Graduate School of Business, my partners and I realized that seven long years had passed since publication of the last edition of *Financial Shenanigans* and that almost 25 years had passed since the first edition. Over that time, more than 100,000 readers have purchased the book around the globe, including translations in Chinese, Japanese, and Korean. We've learned a lot in the intervening years, and as such we felt it timely to share with you the latest accounting tricks as well as a more considered account of the most important lessons from the last quarter century.

But before turning the pages forward to begin this new edition of *Financial Shenanigans*, let's turn back the clock 25 years to share the beginning of my search for "shenanigans" and the unexpected and exciting journey since 1990.

The Beginning—the Early 1990s

As a professor of accounting at American University in Washington, D.C., I began researching the most prominent accounting frauds over the prior 40 years. Many have been documented in Accounting and Auditing Enforcement Releases (AAER) at the U.S. Securities and Exchange Commission (SEC). I began using many of those interesting vignettes in teaching my Intermediate Accounting and Auditing classes. As I saw that the students found those stories fascinating, I started publishing articles on this subject to share with a larger group. And, of course, the next logical step to reach an even greater audience was to write a book.

Publication of *Financial Shenanigans* and Early Years as Entrepreneur

Shortly after my forty-first birthday, in early 1993 McGraw-Hill published the first edition of *Financial Shenanigans*. The book introduced readers to seven broad categories of earnings misrepresentations, identified 20 discrete techniques that management might employ, and sprinkled in many examples of actual companies that had been sanctioned for tricking investors.

A few pleasant surprises emerged after the book was released. First, lots of readers reached out to thank me for shedding light on the steps that investors could take to safeguard their wealth. Second, the book had made its way into the ranks of big institutional investors, who sought to hire me to train their analysts on how to spot companies playing accounting games. Eventually they began asking me to examine the companies in their portfolios. Fortunately, on several occasions, I was able to use these techniques to alert them of major problems, and they were very thankful for keeping them out of harm's way.

Founding the Center for Financial Research & Analysis (CFRA) in 1994

While 1993 was an eventful year with the publication of *Financial Shenanigans* and my introduction to some influential investors, it would have been impossible to predict the dramatic changes that followed in 1994 as I launched the

Center for Financial Research and Analysis (CFRA). Out of the spare room in my house, I began publishing a monthly newsletter highlighting companies I believed to be struggling but that were using accounting tricks to hide the problems. On the fifteenth of each month, I sent reports via overnight mail to our subscribers. (Remember, we were still living in the "dark ages" before the Internet and e-mail.) Thankfully, the service was well received, and over 60 investment firms became subscribers during our first year.

The Transition from Professor to Full-Time Entrepreneur

In 1995 I resigned my tenured teaching position at American University in order to devote myself fully to the growing business. I leased office space and began hiring a team of analysts; CFRA was off to the races. By 1999, we began posting our warnings for clients online and sending out e-mails. (Yay, no more printing and collating reports and sending them via overnight mail.) Our client count grew substantially as we became a major player on Wall Street and around the world, with clients on five continents and offices in Washington, D.C., London, New York, and Boston.

The Later Years Running CFRA and the Sale

During the early 2000s, accounting scandals proliferated, with frauds revealed at Enron, WorldCom, and Tyco. The Governmental Affairs Committee of the U.S. Senate investigating the Enron fraud asked me to testify in February 2002. I was regularly interviewed on TV and in print about the growing usage of accounting tricks.

In April 2002, the second edition of *Financial Shenanigans* was released, and sales spiked as the stock market was spooked by a seemingly endless parade of companies using accounting tricks.

As you might imagine, those were golden times for CFRA. Over 200 new subscribers signed up for our research product in 2002 alone, and by the end of the year we were serving over 500 clients. Investment firms needed more help in monitoring their portfolio companies, and short sellers were on the prowl for the "next Enron." During this busy period at CFRA, we hired additional analysts, and fortunately, both Jeremy and Yoni joined the firm and quickly became leaders. Jeremy eventually became the global head of research, and Yoni led our quantitative research team and headed business strategy for the company.

In early 2003, several potential acquirers came knocking, and I decided to sell a majority stake to the Boston-based private equity firm TA Associates. Jeremy and Yoni remained at CFRA for several more years, while I left the day-to-day job of running the business and started my "years in hibernation," adhering to a long noncompete, which was in effect until late 2010. Yoni left for Harvard Business School in 2008, and upon graduation, he worked for an investment management firm in Boston. Jeremy remained at CFRA until 2011 and then became a forensic accounting specialist at a prominent hedge fund.

The Quiet Years and the Release of the Third Edition of *Financial Shenanigans*

My retirement years involved a lot of traveling, still giving seminars to investment groups and MBA students. By 2009, I was eager to share some of my new ideas and I approached Jeremy about partnering with me to coauthor a third edition of *Financial Shenanigans*. We worked very closely on the book during the summer and early fall of 2009, and the book was released the following April. Knowing that my noncompete would end later that year, I became much more active on the speaking circuit, giving seminars and interviews and doing in-depth research on companies. I was very excited about coming out of retirement and building a new business from scratch.

Building a Second Business: Schilit Forensics LLC

By late 2010, my noncompete had ended, sales of the third edition of *Financial Shenanigans* were brisk, and the media took note of my return from retirement. *Barron's* published a piece entitled "A Financial Sleuth Finds a World of Abuse."

So in 2011 I founded Schilit Forensics LLC on a small scale, taking on just a few clients to dip my toes in the water. I purposefully took it slow, as going from a life of leisure to a full-time commitment seemed daunting. Clients signed three-month agreements for my help in unraveling complicated accounting-focused problems. In contrast to my first business, Schilit Forensics operates as a consultancy engaged to work on custom research projects, not as a subscription service selling a newsletter.

I was really enjoying the nature of the work and close interactions with a small group of wonderfully appreciative clients. In March 2013, Jeremy surprised me with an auspicious phone call. He was still working at the same hedge fund, and while he was very happy there, he was thinking about more entrepreneurial ways to deploy his forensic accounting expertise. It quickly became clear to both of us that we should team up to further build Schilit Forensics. That weekend, he flew to my winter home in Florida, and we formalized our partnership.

Just a couple of months later, Jeremy and I approached our close friend and former colleague Yoni about joining us as a third partner. He was enjoying great success at a prestigious investment firm but harbored a strong desire to harness his entrepreneurial spirit. Yoni's enthusiasm mirrored ours, and he joined Schilit Forensics in July 2013. The three of us are now into our fifth year of working together, and we have developed an impressive team of analysts and diverse roster of clients. Each and every day we read through the fine print of regulatory filings, investor presentations, and other documents to identify signs of business problems before they surface. In doing so we are able to help our clients make better investment decisions.

My partners and I truly love teaching our clients and eager students about spotting companies trying to hide operating problems by using creative accounting games. And, with this same excitement, we are thrilled to impart our quarter-century of learnings and experiences with you, our readers and friends, in this special new edition of *Financial Shenanigans*. Enjoy reading and feel free to be in touch!

Howard M. Schilit
Founder and CEO
Schilit Forensics LLC
howard@schilit.com

FINANCIAL
SHENANIGANS

PART ONE

ESTABLISHING THE FOUNDATION

1

25 Years of Shenanigans

In early 2001, Joe Nacchio, the CEO of Qwest Communications, stood onstage at a companywide meeting and delivered a rousing speech intended to energize his team and focus them on his priorities for the company. "The most important thing we do is meet our numbers," Nacchio declared. "It's more important than any individual product, it's more important than any individual philosophy, it's more important than any cultural change we're making. We stop everything else when we don't make the numbers." Through his words and deeds, Joe Nacchio created a culture that resulted in $2.5 billion of phantom earnings, landing himself in federal prison and devastating investors who saw the stock price tumble by 97 percent in the 18 months following his speech.

Senior managers at all publicly traded companies yearn to report positive news and impressive financial results that will satisfy investors and drive the share price higher. While most companies act ethically and follow the rules when reporting their financial performance, some take advantage of gray areas in the rules (or worse, ignore the rules altogether) in order to "make the numbers."

Executives' desire to put a positive spin on financial results has been around for as long as corporations and investors themselves. Dishonest companies have long used these tricks to prey on unsuspecting investors, and it is unlikely that will ever change. As King Solomon observed in the book of Ecclesiastes, "What has been will be again, what has been done will be done again." With the never-ending need to please investors, the temptation for management to exaggerate corporate performance by using financial shenanigans will always exist.

The lure of accounting gimmickry is particularly strong at struggling companies that are trying to keep up with their investors' expectations or their competitors' performance. And while investors have become more savvy to these gimmicks over the years, dishonest companies innovate to find new tricks (and recycle old favorites) to fool shareholders.

The Art of Fooling Investors

At its core, this book is about the different ways that corporate management fools investors. The tricks are generally intended to cover up some serious deterioration in a company's business, such as slowing sales, contracting profit margins, or declining cash flow.

While accounting shenanigans have been a scourge to investors since time immemorial, the last quarter century has been particularly brutal. To better arm ourselves for the inevitable challenges of the next 25 years, let's begin by reviewing some of the most significant case studies and key lessons from the past quarter-century.

Waste Management: Investors Cannot Always Rely upon the Auditors

Described by the SEC as "one of the most egregious frauds we have seen," Chicago-based trash hauler Waste Management Inc. (WM) inflated its pretax earnings by $1.7 billion over a six-year period starting in 1992. At that time, it represented the biggest misstatement of income in U.S. corporate history.

Waste Management grew dramatically over the period from 1993 to 1995, spending billions acquiring an unfathomable 441 companies. With these acquisitions came the inevitable special charges against income. These "one-time" charges became so common that during the seven-year period from 1991 to 1997, WM took write-offs in six of those years, totaling $1.6

billion. Since investors typically ignore special charges in evaluating profitability, WM appeared to be in tip-top shape. Also, to keep investors in the dark about what was really happening, WM offset (or "netted") numerous one-time investment gains from asset sales against these special charges.

Waste Management was also notorious for finding ways to inflate profits by deferring expenses to a later period. The company aggressively capitalized maintenance, repair, and interest costs to the Balance Sheet rather than expensing them, and minimized the depreciation expense on its garbage trucks by using inflated salvage values and lengthening their useful lives.

As you will see throughout this book, big accounting problems can be conveniently covered up when companies make many acquisitions. Following Waste Management's July 1998 acquisition of USA Waste Services, the company's newly hired CEO became concerned about internal controls and accounting practices and ordered a special review. One of the most troubling findings of the review was that the company's internal controls were so poor that previously reported financial statements could not be relied upon. WM issued the following warning to investors in its 10-Q report:

> The Company, after consultation with its independent public accountants (Arthur Andersen), has concluded that its internal controls for the preparation of interim financial information did not provide an adequate basis for its independent public accountants to complete its review. . . .

After the SEC sued Waste Management alleging fraud, we later learned in reviewing the legal documents that its auditor, Arthur Andersen, was aware of accounting problems much earlier but chose to "protect" its client. As far back as 1993, Arthur Andersen quantified misstatements totaling $128 million, which, if recorded, would have reduced net income before special items by 12 percent. The Andersen partners, however, determined that the misstatements were "immaterial," and they blessed the 1993 financial reports with a clean opinion.

Indeed, each year when Andersen raised accounting concerns with WM, the proposed adjustments and restatements—not surprisingly—were ignored by management. During the 1995 audit, Andersen clearly disagreed with

WM's approach to netting one-time gains against special charges and the choice not to disclose the practice. Here are excerpts from the auditor's 1995 internal memorandum:

> The Company has been insensitive to not use special charges [to elim-inate Balance Sheet errors and misstatements that had accumulated in prior years] and instead has used "other gains" to bury charges for Balance Sheet clean-ups.

Despite writing in the memo a strong disapproval of this practice, Andersen chose not to issue an adverse opinion for the 1995 report, nor take steps to end this practice in the following years. Was it because Andersen had become too close to WM executives and too economically dependent on the company, preventing Andersen from properly serving investors and warning them of this problem? Indeed, WM was Andersen's largest account in its Chicago office, and Andersen had served as WM's auditor every year since its IPO in 1971.

CUC/Cendant: Acquisitions Cannot Make Business Problems Disappear

Just as at Waste Management, many accounting shenanigans can be found at companies using acquisition strategies to achieve rapid growth. Consider CUC International, a darling stock for much of the 1980s–1990s, run by Walter Forbes. By the mid-1990s, CUC started making acquisitions that should have given investors a wake-up call. In April 1996 the com-pany acquired Ideon Group for nearly $400 million. Through the merger, CUC inherited substantial litigation obligations, and booked a reserve for these costs totaling $137 million. Shortly after Ideon closed, CUC bought Davidson and Sierra On-Line for around $2 billion. These businesses pro-duced educational software games, completely unrelated to CUC's core busi-ness, and also came with significant merger-related reserves.

Cendant was created in December 1997, through the merger of Henry Silverman's HFS and Walter Forbes's CUC International. This practice of creating merger-related reserves continued in late 1997 (when CUC was about to merge with HFS to form Cendant), as CUC set up a reserve to write off a staggering $556 million associated with this deal.

The stock eventually collapsed in March 1998 when accounting problems at CUC were revealed to investors. When the subsequent investigations and litigation concluded, the total costs of the fraud were staggering. Consider that in 1996 and 1997 alone, investigators found more than $500 million of bogus operating income. Walter Forbes was sentenced to 12 years in prison and assessed $3.25 billion in restitution for his crime. And CUC's auditor, Ernst & Young, which failed to perform the appropriate tests to spot the fraud, paid $300 million to settle class-action litigation.

Enron: Numbers That Seem Unbelievable Should Not Be Believed

Unlike acquisition-fueled frauds like Waste Management and CUC, Enron's trickery was entirely organic: it simply changed its business model (and accounting policies) in a dramatic way. Enron, perhaps the most recognizable accounting fraud of the past generation, was a largely unknown producer of natural gas that within a few years morphed into an enormous commodities trading company. This dramatic change in business model was accompanied by a meteoric rise in revenues through the late 1990s. In just five short years, Enron's revenue had increased by an astounding factor of 10, growing from $9.2 billion in 1995 to $100.8 billion in 2000. In 2000 alone, Enron's sales grew a staggering 151 percent, from $40.1 billion to $100.8 billion.

As shown in Table 1-1, despite Enron's dramatic revenue growth, net income grew much more slowly. Specifically, revenue grew 10-fold during this period, and net income struggled to even double.

Table 1-1   Enron's Revenue and Net Income, 1995 to 2000

($ millions)	1995	1996	1997	1998	1999	2000
Revenue	9,189	13,289	20,273	31,260	40,112	100,789
Net income	520	584	105	703	893	979

Curious investors might question how often other companies have managed to grow their revenue from under $10 billion to over $100 billion in just five years. The answer: never. Enron's staggering increase in revenue was unprecedented, and the company achieved this growth without any large acquisitions along the way. Impossible! Underlying the reported revenue growth was the company's unusual treatment of trading activities as sales. These transactions resulted in modest profits, but because the notional values of trades were accounted for as part of revenue (and cost of goods sold), it gave the appearance that the business was in a period of hypergrowth.

WorldCom: Focus on Free Cash Flow in Addition to Earnings

Throughout WorldCom's history, its growth came largely from making acquisitions. (As we will explain later in Part Five, acquisition-driven companies offer investors some of the greatest challenges and risks.) WorldCom's largest deal closed in 1998 with its $40 billion acquisition of MCI Communications.

Almost from the beginning, WorldCom used aggressive accounting practices to inflate its earnings and operating cash flows. Much like CUC, one of its principal shenanigans involved making acquisitions, writing off much of the costs immediately, creating reserves, and then releasing those reserves into income as needed. With more than 70 deals over the company's short life, WorldCom continued to "reload" its reserves so that they were available for future releases into earnings.

This strategy would probably have been able to continue had WorldCom been allowed to acquire the much larger Sprint in a $129 billion deal announced in October 1999. Antitrust lawyers and regulators at the U.S. Department of Justice and their counterparts at the European Union disapproved of the merger, citing monopoly concerns. Without the acquisition, WorldCom was left without the expected infusion of new reserves that it needed, as its prior ones had rapidly been depleted after being released into income.

By early 2000, with its stock price declining and intense pressure from Wall Street to hit earnings targets, WorldCom embarked on a new and far more aggressive shenanigan—moving ordinary business expenses from its Income Statement to its Balance Sheet. One of WorldCom's major operating expenses was its so-called line costs. These costs represented fees that

WorldCom paid to third-party telecommunication network providers for the right to access their networks. Accounting rules clearly required that such fees be expensed and *not capitalized*. Nevertheless, WorldCom removed hundreds of millions of dollars of its line costs from its Income Statement to please Wall Street. In so doing, WorldCom dramatically understated its expenses and inflated its earnings, duping investors.

As earnings were being overstated, investors would have found some clear warning signs in evaluating WorldCom's Statement of Cash Flows, specifically, its rapidly deteriorating free cash flow. WorldCom had manipulated both its net earnings and its operating cash flow. By treating line costs as an asset instead of an expense, WorldCom improperly inflated its profits. In addition, since it improperly placed those expenditures in the Investing section rather than the Operating section of the Statement of Cash Flows, WorldCom similarly inflated operating cash flow. While reported operating cash flow appeared consistent with reported earnings, the company's free cash flow told the real story.

In early 2002, a small team of internal auditors at WorldCom, working on a hunch, were secretly investigating what they thought could be fraud. After finding $3.8 billion in inappropriate accounting entries, they immediately notified the company's board of directors, and events progressed swiftly from there. The CFO was fired, the controller resigned, Arthur Andersen withdrew its audit opinion for 2001, and the SEC launched its investigation.

WorldCom's days were numbered. On July 21, 2002, the company filed for Chapter 11 bankruptcy protection, the largest such filing in U.S. history at the time (a record that has since been overtaken by the collapse of Lehman Brothers in September 2008). Under the bankruptcy reorganization agreement, the company paid a $750 million fine to the SEC and restated its earnings in an amount that defies belief. In total, the company reported an accounting restatement that exceeded $70 billion, including adjusting the 2000 and 2001 numbers from the originally reported gain of nearly $10 billion to an astounding loss of over $64 billion. The directors also felt the pain, having to pay almost $25 million to settle class-action litigation.

The company emerged from bankruptcy in 2004. Previous bondholders were paid 36 cents on the dollar in bonds and stock in the new company, while the previous stockholders were wiped out completely. In early 2005, Verizon Communications agreed to acquire its competitor MCI for about $7 billion. Two months later, former WorldCom chief executive Bernie Ebbers was found guilty of all charges and convicted of committing fraud and conspiracy and filing false documents. He was later sentenced to 25 years in prison.

Lehman Brothers: Balance Sheet May Not Reflect Actual Trends at Business

Just as the 1929 stock market collapse scarred our parents' and grandparents' generations, the 2008 financial markets carnage clearly has left a painful memory for all homeowners and investors. Perhaps no Wall Street brokerage had a worse outcome than Lehman Brothers, as its share price collapsed in September 2008 and will be remembered as the biggest bankruptcy (based on asset size) in U.S. corporate history.

In a report commissioned by the bankruptcy court judge to investigate the Lehman collapse, attorney Anton Valukas alleged that the company had cleverly misled investors and creditors by hiding $50 billion of debt from its Balance Sheet. This deception related to Lehman's aggressive interpretation of an arcane (and since changed) accounting rule known as "Repo 105."

When borrowing cash through very short-term collateralized loans, say for payroll, the cash received should be reflected on the Balance Sheet as a liability, and the assets given in collateral should remain on the borrower's Balance Sheet. The "Repo 105" rule allowed for an exception when the value of the assets given as collateral represented at least 105 percent of the loan value. In these cases, the transaction was no longer accounted for as a loan, rather it was considered a sale and subsequent repurchase of the collateral assets. Lehman seized upon this loophole and in doing so recorded its collateralized borrowings as asset sales. As such, instead of recording a short-term liability for the cash received, Lehman would record a temporary reduction to its assets.

The bankruptcy examiner's report highlighted a suspicious spike in Lehman's Repo 105 transaction balance at the month-ends corresponding with either a quarterly or year-end filing. Since the need for overnight borrowings should remain fairly consistent throughout a quarter, the jump in Repo 105 transactions *only* on dates corresponding to financial filings may suggests that Lehman artificially depressed its liability balance in order to mislead investors into believing that the company's leverage was lower. Table 1-2 shows the monthly trend in Lehman's Repo 105 balance. Note that in May 2008, the Repo 105 balance jumped to $50.8 billion from $24.6 billion in March and $24.7 billion in April 2008. This same suspicious phenomenon is found in the earlier period, as well.

Table 1-2   Lehman Repo 105 Spikes at Quarter End

($ billions)	Q4 '07 11/07	12/07	1/08	Q1 '08 2/08	3/08	4/08	Q2 '08 5/08
Repo 105 Balance	$38.6	N.A.	$28.9	$49.1	$24.6	$24.7	$50.8

Valeant Pharmaceuticals: It's Dangerous to Rely on Management's Favored Performance Metrics

Unlike the more celebrated frauds mentioned at Enron, WorldCom, etc., Valeant is less a story of outright fraud and more of a clever company using misleading metrics to dupe some of the most successful institutional investors. And if it could happen to them, it could happen to all of us, if we let our guards down or grow too close to corporate management.

But oh how investors loved this company. In less than a decade, Valeant's market value elevated from just a few billion dollars to $90 billion by early August 2015. Over the next two years, however, it would fall 96 percent, losing a staggering $87 billion of market value. To give a sense of scale in those numbers, the equity value destruction for investor totaled $74 billion at Enron and $29 billion at Cendant.

Valeant would not have been able to realize or sustain its massive run-up in market value based on its GAAP-compliant earnings; in most years, the company reported steep losses. However, management pointed investors to a misleading non-GAAP "cash earnings" metric as a better measure of performance. Cash earnings scaled up quickly as sales from acquisitions fueled top-line growth, and the amount of expenses excluded from the earnings measure increased. The company had persuaded investors to ignore all expenses that did not manifest as normal, recurring cash outflows during the period, and then the company embarked on a strategy to grow through M&A, which ensured that most costs would come through as either depreciation, amortization, or a one-time acquisition-related charge. During the period 2013–2016, Valeant reported cash earnings totaling $9.6 billion, while its audited GAAP net income amounted to *losses* of $2.7 billion, a whopping difference of $12.2 billion.

Looking Ahead

Our tireless journey over the last quarter century has been driven both to uncover games used by management to trick investors and to share these lessons with our readers. In this special twenty-fifth anniversary of *Financial Shenanigans,* we have added a new category of shenanigans, *Acquisition Accounting Shenanigans,* since acquisitions provide a convenient cover for management to play accounting games.

We hope this new edition provides you the tools to sniff out key warning signs and confidently protect and grow your wealth.

2

Just Touch Up the X-Rays

I can't afford the operation, but would you accept a small payment to
touch up the x-rays?

—WARREN BUFFETT, CEO OF BERKSHIRE HATHAWAY

Legendary investor Warren Buffett generously uses his annual letter to shareholders as a vehicle to educate all interested parties about the art of investing.
In one such letter, the Oracle from Omaha, as he is affectionately known, gave
a particularly poignant lesson concerning a subject that is near and dear to
us: companies that use financial shenanigans to hide unpleasant truths from
investors. This letter described a conversation between a seriously ill patient
and his doctor, just after an x-ray revealed the bad news about his condition.
Rather than accepting the diagnosis of his deteriorating health, the patient
immediately responded to the dreadful news by asking the doctor to simply
touch up the x-rays. Buffett uses this story to warn investors about companies
that try to hide the truth about their deteriorating business's economic health
by *touching up* the financial statements. Buffett then prophetically adds, "In
the long run, however, trouble awaits managements that paper over operating

problems with accounting maneuvers. Eventually, managements of this kind achieve the same result as the seriously-ill patient."

No doubt, a company's use of financial shenanigans to paper over its poor economic health would be no more effective than a doctor touching up x-rays to improve a patient's physical health. Such gimmicks are pointless, as the truth of the company's deterioration will remain unchanged and will ultimately come to light one day.

The chapters ahead provide a wide range of case studies covering companies that have simply papered over their financial performance and economic health problems in order to delay the inevitable bad news, and the techniques to identify them in advance.

What Are Financial Shenanigans?

Financial shenanigans are actions taken by management that mislead investors about a company's financial performance or economic health. As a result, investors are tricked into believing that the company's earnings are stronger, its cash flows more robust, and its Balance Sheet position more secure than they really are.

Some shenanigans can be detected in the numbers presented by carefully reading a company's Balance Sheet (formally called the Statement of Financial Position), Income Statement (Statement of Operations), and Statement of Cash Flows. Signs of other shenanigans might not be as easily seen in the numbers and instead require scrutiny of the narratives contained in Footnotes, quarterly Earnings Releases, and other representations by management. We classify financial shenanigans into four broad groups (discussed in Parts Two to Five in the book): Earnings Manipulation Shenanigans (Part Two), Cash Flow Shenanigans (Part Three), Key Metric Shenanigans (Part Four), and Acquisition Accounting Shenanigans (Part Five).

Earnings Manipulation Shenanigans (Part Two)

Investors judge corporate executives harshly when they fail to meet Wall Street's earnings expectations. Not surprisingly, to steer the share price (and often executives' compensation packages) higher, some companies engage in a variety of shenanigans to manipulate earnings. We have identified the following seven categories of Earnings Manipulation (EM) Shenanigans that result in misrepresentations of a company's sustainable earnings.

EM Shenanigan No. 1: Recording revenue too soon

EM Shenanigan No. 2: Recording bogus revenue

EM Shenanigan No. 3: Boosting income using one-time or unsustainable activities

EM Shenanigan No. 4: Shifting current expenses to a later period

EM Shenanigan No. 5: Employing other techniques to hide expenses or losses

EM Shenanigan No. 6: Shifting current income to a later period

EM Shenanigan No. 7: Shifting future expenses to the current period

---

Cash Flow Shenanigans (Part Three)

The plethora of financial reporting scandals and earnings restatements in recent years has left many investors questioning whether reported earnings can ever be free of management manipulation. Increasingly, investors have expanded their focus to include the Statement of Cash Flows and, more specifically, the section that highlights Cash Flow From Operations (CFFO).

Many investors believe that unlike earnings, cash flow is rock solid and difficult to manipulate. Sadly, this is wishful thinking. The Statement of Cash Flows is not immune to accounting gimmicks, and in many ways, manipulating cash flow can be just as easy as manipulating earnings. We have identified the following three categories of Cash Flow (CF) Shenanigans that result in misrepresentations of a business's real cash profitability.

CF Shenanigan No. 1: Shifting financing cash inflows to the Operating section

CF Shenanigan No. 2: Moving cash outflows from the Operating section to other sections

CF Shenanigan No. 3: Boosting operating cash flow using unsustainable activities

---

Key Metric Shenanigans (Part Four)

So far, we have addressed shenanigans in the traditional financial statements. Increasingly however, business results are presented outside of this format in order to cater to a wider range of company-specific and industry-specific metrics. These include measures such Same-Store-Sales, Bookings, Average Revenue per User (ARPU), Return on Invested Capital (ROIC), Earnings Before Interest, Taxes, Depreciation, and Amortization (EBITDA) and many others. Since they are outside the realm of GAAP, companies have much more latitude in calculating and reporting key metrics. Naturally this creates an opportunity for shenanigans. Part Four introduces two categories of Key Metric (KM) Shenanigans.

> **KM Shenanigan No. 1:** Showcasing misleading metrics that overstate performance
>
> **KM Shenanigan No. 2:** Distorting Balance Sheet metrics to avoid showing deterioration

Acquisition Accounting Shenanigans (Part Five)

Over the last quarter century, we have found some of the most disturbing shenanigans hidden through the complicated acquisition accounting process. We have therefore added this section to this new edition of *Financial Shenanigans* to highlight the complexities inherent in evaluating M&A-driven companies and to identify the common shenanigans that often trip up investors.

> **AA Shenanigan No. 1:** Artificially boosting revenue and earnings
>
> **AA Shenanigan No. 2:** Inflating reported cash flow
>
> **AA Shenanigan No. 3:** Manipulating key metrics

Using a Holistic Approach to Detect Financial Shenanigans

Importance of "Checks and Balances"

What began in June 1972 as a bungled burglary of the Democratic National Committee office located in the Watergate Hotel in Washington, D.C., culminated in the unprecedented resignation of a U.S. president in August 1974. The fact that President Nixon was driven out of office confirmed that the American system of checks and balances really does work. Both the judicial and legislative branches played important roles in stopping a chief executive who abused his constitutional powers. The Supreme Court ruled unanimously that President Nixon could not plead executive privilege to prevent investigators from gaining access to White House tapes that were believed to contain damaging evidence, and the Judiciary Committee of the House of Representatives recommended impeachment to the full House. Facing the likely prospect of losing the impeachment votes in the House and the Senate, Nixon resigned the presidency.

In 1999, President Bill Clinton brought the executive office to the brink with another constitutional crisis over poor presidential behavior. The House of Representatives voted to impeach Clinton for lying under oath about his relations with a White House intern, stating that the president "willfully corrupted and manipulated the judicial process of the United States for his personal gain and exoneration." However, with Supreme Court Chief Justice William Rehnquist presiding, the Senate had trouble finding an impeachable offense under "high crimes and misdemeanors," and Clinton was found not guilty.

Whether the goal is preserving a democracy or upholding the integrity of financial reporting, a system of checks and balances is paramount for preventing, uncovering, and punishing improper behavior. And much like the U.S. government, financial reporting has three distinct "branches," an Income Statement, a Balance Sheet, and a Statement of Cash Flows. When one of these financial statements contains shenanigans, warning signs generally appear on the other ones. Thus, Earnings Manipulation Shenanigans can often be detected indirectly through unusual patterns on the Balance Sheet and the Statement of Cash Flows. Similarly, deciphering certain changes on the Income Statement and the Balance Sheet often can help investors sniff out Cash Flow Shenanigans.

What Environment Breeds Shenanigans?

Companies with structural weaknesses or inadequate oversight provide a fertile breeding ground for shenanigans. Investors should probe a company's governance and oversight by asking these basic questions: (1) Do appropriate checks and balances exist among senior executives to snuff out corporate misdeeds? (2) Do outside members of the board play a meaningful role in protecting investors from greedy, misguided, or incompetent management? (3) Do the auditors possess the independence, knowledge, and determination to protect investors when management acts inappropriately? And (4) has the company improperly taken circuitous steps to avoid regulatory scrutiny?

Management Teams Devoid of Checks and Balances

In the best companies, senior executives can freely criticize and disagree with one another—sort of like in a good marriage. In unhealthy companies, a single dictatorial leader runs roughshod over the others—not unlike in a bad marriage. Investors face great risks if that dictatorial leader is also bent on creating misleading financial reports. Who can stop the CEO when a culture of fear and intimidation exists? It is important for investors that sufficient checks and balances exist among senior management to prevent bad behavior.

Be Alert for Companies That Lack Checks and Balances Among Management
Investors are best served when the senior management team includes strong, confident, and ethical members who will thwart a dishonest CEO or CFO and report improper behavior to the board of directors and the auditor. Too often, though, financial shenanigans arise when no such checks and balances exist. For example, an organizational structure in which a small group of family and friends hold key executive positions may embolden management to engage in financial reporting trickery. Additionally, a powerful and bullying CEO, such as Sunbeam's Al Dunlap or HealthSouth's Richard Scrushy,

along with weak complicit or conflicted underlings, raises the risk profile for bad behavior.

Watch for Senior Executives Who Push for Winning at All Costs

At beginning of the previous chapter, we shared Joe Nacchio's words about the necessity of always "making the numbers" when he spoke to his team at a 2001 company meeting.

With that scary philosophy, no one should have been surprised that Nacchio and six former Qwest executives were sued by the SEC, accusing them of orchestrating a sweeping $3 billion accounting fraud from 1999 to 2002. Nacchio was later convicted and sentenced to almost six years in federal prison.

Be Skeptical of Boastful or Promotional Management

Investors should be particularly careful when management publicly boasts about its long consecutive streak of meeting or exceeding Wall Street's expectations. Invariably, tough times or speed bumps emerge, and management may feel more pressured to use accounting gimmicks and perhaps fraud to keep the streak alive, rather than announcing that its run of success has ended.

Consider the case of Symbol Technologies, the Long Island–based maker of bar code scanners. Symbol seemed to be obsessed with never disappointing Wall Street. For more than eight consecutive years, the company either met or exceeded Wall Street's estimated earnings—32 straight quarters of sustained success. In reality, Symbol was using almost every shenanigan in the book to maintain its "winning streak." The SEC ultimately caught up with Symbol and accused the company of perpetrating a massive fraud from 1998 until 2003.

Companies engaged in many other blockbuster frauds have emphasized similar winning streaks, including supermarket giant Royal Ahold, auto parts maker Delphi Corporation, industrial conglomerate General Electric Company, and doughnut shop Krispy Kreme Doughnuts Inc. Royal Ahold, which later emerged as one of largest frauds in Europe, enjoyed boasting about its streak on its earnings calls with investors:

This is the thirteenth consecutive year in which our net earnings have grown significantly. Ahold has always met or exceeded expectations during this 13-year period and we intend to continue to do so.

Boards Lacking Competence or Independence

It may be the best part-time job in the world. Sitting as an outside director on a corporate board brings prestige, perks, and a nice paycheck, with cash and noncash compensation often exceeding $200,000 per year.

While we know that this situation works out just fine for the lucky directors, often it is less clear whether investors receive the necessary and expected protection from these fiduciaries. Investors must evaluate board members on two levels: (1) do they belong on the board, and are they qualified for the committees on which they sit (e.g., audit or compensation), and (2) are they appropriately performing their duties to protect investors?

Inappropriate or Inadequately Prepared Board Members

Baseball fans (of a certain age) surely remember longtime Los Angeles Dodgers manager and later corporate pitchman Tommy Lasorda. For sure, Tommy possessed talent on the baseball diamond and a personality and charisma that helped companies hawk their products. But as a board member for publicly traded Lone Star Steakhouse, Tommy may have been "out of his league." While his seven decades in baseball are quite impressive, they probably did not provide him with strong financial analysis skills.

Worse yet, former Heisman Award–winning running back and NFL gridiron great (and convicted felon) O.J. Simpson was assigned the duty of faithfully protecting investors' interests by serving on the all-important *audit committee* of Infinity Broadcasting in the 1990s. It is unlikely that O.J. (or frankly, most any professional athlete) would have the necessary expertise and experience to navigate the intricacies of a Balance Sheet, let alone overseeing financial reporting and disclosure processes. Investors should insist that outside board members have the essential knowledge and experience and serve only on appropriate committees that suit their technical skills.

Failure to Challenge Management on Related-Party Transactions

In 2008 executives at India's information technology giant Satyam decided to acquire a company, Maytas, in a transaction that required board approval. The board met and acquiesced to management's request, even though the CEO's sons controlled the target company. Specifically, Satyam's board approved the recommendation to invest $1.6 billion for 100 percent of Maytas Properties and 51 percent of Maytas Infrastructure. (The word *Maytas* is *Satyam* spelled backward—another clue for all you Sherlock Holmeses about the related-party nature of the deal.)

The board should have objected to the acquisition not only because the CEO's sons controlled the target company but also because it made little sense. Any Satyam director should have been puzzled that the company was proposing to invest $1.6 billion in related-party real estate ventures (certainly not its core business) at a time when its core business was under pressure and additional investments would have likely been better directed toward staving off the competition.

While the board agreed to the acquisition, it was aborted the next day after an investor uproar. Satyam's CEO later told authorities that the deal was the last attempt to replace Satyam's fictitious assets with real ones. A sign of a healthy and effective board is when a dissenting view overturns a management-driven consensus. That clearly did not happen at Satyam.

Failure to Challenge Management on Inappropriate Compensation Plans

Setting appropriate compensation falls squarely on the shoulders of outside directors, specifically those who serve on the compensation committee. Management may propose some outlandish scheme that inappropriately rewards executives far beyond reason. For example, in the mid-1990s, Computer Associates instituted a plan that later paid senior executives more than $1 billion in additional stock as a reward for keeping the stock price above a designated threshold for a 30-day period. Shockingly, the board went along with this very strange and reckless compensation plan.

Sometimes, even thoughtful compensation schemes, if taken to an extreme, can lead to very risky behavior by management and disastrous results for investors. Consider Valeant's pay-for-performance agreement with its senior executives. The principal factor used to determine stock-based compensation was the average increase in share price, referred to as "total shareholder return" (or TSR). The higher the TSR, the greater number of additional shares received by these executives. And with annualized returns at Valeant exceeding 60 percent, CEO Michael Pearson's wealth grew beyond anyone's imagination—to over $3 billion at its peak! But, of course, it led to incredibly risky behavior, to the detriment of its long-term investors.

Moreover, in addition to its misguided stock-based compensation based solely on stock price appreciation, its annual cash incentive program (AIP) left much to be desired. Rather than basing this payout on certain reliable, audited GAAP-based results, Valeant used two non-GAAP metrics—adjusted earnings and adjusted revenue. (As we show in Chapter 17 , Valeant's adjusted earnings grossly inflate its true performance.)

Upon reflection, a few important lessons emerge: Too much of a good thing could be very bad. Yes, pay for performance generally is a good thing, *but only if it is applied to sensible metrics and if it encourages prudent risk taking.* The compensation plan at Valeant was irreparably flawed in two fundamental ways: (1) it was based solely on stock price appreciation and unreliable non-GAAP metrics, and (2) its excessive pay for extreme TSR growth encouraged reckless management behavior.

When evaluating outside directors, investors must always ask whose interests they are favoring—management's or investors'. Investors should also always question compensation plans that could easily be abused to improperly inflate executives' wallets.

Auditors Lacking Objectivity and the Appearance of Independence

The independent auditor plays a crucial role in protecting investors from dishonest management and an indifferent and ineffective board of directors. Chaos would ensue if investors ever came to question the competence or integrity of the independent auditors. That is indeed exactly what happened in 2002 after Enron and WorldCom collapsed, Arthur Andersen disbanded, and financial markets nosedived.

The auditor, however, can be either friend or foe to investors: a friend if the auditor is competent, independent, and fastidious in sniffing out problems; a foe if the auditor is incompetent, lazy, or a "rubber stamp" for management. Sometimes the very high fees and close personal relationships built up over years lead to botched audits and big losses for investors. Here are the key factors to consider when evaluating in which camp the auditor falls—friend or foe.

Too Long and Close a Relationship
Prevents a Fresh Look at the Picture

The fraud and collapse of Parmalat, the Italian dairy behemoth, has been referred to as the "Enron of Europe." While the business and accounting issues differ, both Enron and Parmalat had one obvious similarity: independent auditors missed the fraud.

One intriguing fact in this case concerns Parmalat's change in its primary auditor from Grant Thornton to Deloitte & Touche. Indeed, Parmalat's chicanery might have continued longer had it not been for an Italian law that requires companies to switch audit firms every nine years. Deloitte & Touche replaced auditor Grant Thornton in 1999 and may have been the first to scrutinize certain offshore accounts, which turned out not to exist (many of which were still audited by Grant Thornton at the time, as they were not subject to Italian law). As a result, fraudulent offshore entities were exposed, including Bonlat, a Cayman Islands subsidiary of Parmalat and one of the primary vehicles used to hide fake assets.

Like Parmalat, one of the biggest accounting frauds to hit Japan went undetected for far too long because the auditor had a long and cushy relationship with company management. Kanebo, a cosmetic and textile company, had been audited by an affiliate of PricewaterhouseCoopers for *at least 30 years*. When one of the company's consolidated subsidiaries hit a very bad stretch, the auditors allegedly advised management to reduce its shareholding in the subsidiary and deconsolidate it. The auditors also allegedly turned a blind eye to the booking of fictitious sales to pad the revenue numbers during slack periods. Kanebo reported about $2 billion in nonexistent profits from 1996 to 2004. The regulators were so incensed with the treacherous behavior of the auditors that they immediately brought legal action against these auditors and imposed a two-month business suspension.

Incompetent Auditors Can Serve as Shills for Management

Every region seems to have its "Enron." India's is IT consultancy Satyam Computer Services, which earned its dubious distinction as the "Enron of India" in 2009 upon exposure that it was a massive fraud. "Satyam" ironically means "truth" in Sanskrit. But with CEO Ramalinga Raju's admission of the company's bald-faced lies to investors for years, maybe he was a bit confused when he selected the company name. Perhaps he really had planned to use the more apt Sanskrit name "Asatyam," meaning "untruth."

PricewaterhouseCoopers, which had been Satyam's auditor since 1991, failed to detect *inflated cash and bank balances on the order of over $1 billion*, according to Raju's own confession. Allegations claimed collusion between Satyam and its auditor. According to a member who joined Satyam's board after the scandal broke out, the documents were "obvious forgeries" and would have been visible as such to anyone.

Management Schemes to Avoid Regulatory Scrutiny

As we pointed out, shenanigans tend to breed freely in environments in which no checks and balances exist among senior management, when the outside board of directors lacks the skills and the desire to protect investors, and when the auditors fail to detect signs of problems. One other substantial line of defense for investors exists in the form of regulators. In the United States, the SEC oversees the setting of reporting requirements and reviews their content. If the reports don't pass muster, the SEC can prevent the securities from being issued or suspend any future stock trades.

While the SEC has mostly served investors well over the years, it has occasionally failed to catch serious reporting infractions. For this it deserves some criticism. Moreover, some companies truly go out of their way to avoid SEC reviews and scrutiny. The following section shows just how this is done and when investors should be especially cautious.

Lack of Regulatory Scrutiny Before Going Public

If managers really want to avoid serious scrutiny from SEC reviewers, they will first sidestep the normal registration process for an initial public offering (IPO) by merging into an already-public company. This is a backdoor approach to becoming a public company and avoiding the typical detailed review that is part of the normal IPO process. Thus, investors should be particularly wary of companies that avoid SEC review by merging into a shell company using either a "reverse merger" or a "special-purpose acquisition company" partner and immediately becoming a public company.

Looking Ahead

Now you are ready to jump in and learn about the four categories of financial shenanigans: Earnings Manipulation (Part Two), Cash Flow (Part Three), Key Metrics (Part Four), and Acquisition Accounting (Part Five).

Earnings Manipulation Shenanigans highlight tricks used by management to inflate or smooth out earnings and portray a healthy company with predictable profits. Each of the seven EM Shenanigans we have identified is discussed in the next part, so please turn the page to begin the lesson.

PART TWO

EARNINGS MANIPULATION SHENANIGANS

Investors rely on the information that they receive from companies to make informed and rational securities selection decisions. This information is assumed to be accurate, whether the news is good or bad. While most corporate executives respect investors and their needs, some dishonest ones hurt investors by misrepresenting the actual company performance and manipulating the company's declared earnings. Part Two fleshes out the seven categories of Earnings Manipulation (EM) Shenanigans and suggests how skeptical investors can ferret out these tricks to avoid losses.

EARNINGS MANIPULATION SHENANIGANS

EM Shenanigan No. 1: Recording revenue too soon (Chapter 3)

EM Shenanigan No. 2: Recording bogus revenue (Chapter 4)

EM Shenanigan No. 3: Boosting income using one-time or unsustainable activities (Chapter 5)

EM Shenanigan No. 4: Shifting current expenses to a later period (Chapter 6)

EM Shenanigan No. 5: Employing other techniques to hide expenses or losses (Chapter 7)

EM Shenanigan No. 6: Shifting current income to a later period (Chapter 8)

EM Shenanigan No. 7: Shifting future expenses to the current period (Chapter 9)

Management may use a variety of techniques to give investors the mistaken impression that the company is performing better than the underlying economic reality. We have categorized all these earnings manipulation tricks into two major subgroups: inflating current-period earnings and inflating future-period earnings.

Inflating Current-Period Earnings

Quite simply, to inflate current-period earnings, management must either push more revenue or gains into the current period or shift expenses to a later one. Shenanigans Nos. 1, 2, and 3 push revenue or one-time gains into current-period operations, and Nos. 4 and 5 shift expenses to a later period.

Inflating Future-Period Earnings

Conversely, to inflate tomorrow's operations, management would simply hold back today's revenue or gains and accelerate tomorrow's expenses or losses into the current period. Shenanigan No. 6 describes techniques to improperly hold back revenue, and Shenanigan No. 7 accelerates expenses into an incorrect earlier period.

Earnings can be *inflated* by inappropriately including revenues or gains and by excluding rightful expenses or losses of that period. Conversely, earnings can be *deflated* by inappropriately excluding revenues or gains of that period and by including expenses or losses that really pertain to another period. Of course, a scheme to deflate current-period earnings pays off when those benefits are released into a later period.

Of the seven categories of Earnings Manipulation Shenanigans, the first five serve to inflate earnings, and the last two serve to lower profits. For most readers, the use of Shenanigans Nos. 1 through 5 to exaggerate earnings might seem more logical or intuitive. After all, higher reported profits often lead to a higher stock price and higher executive compensation. The logic of using Shenanigans Nos. 6 and 7 may be less obvious, but they do serve a purpose. These schemes serve to shift earnings from one period (with excess profits) to another (in need of profits). Put differently, management may simply be attempting to smooth out volatile earnings to portray a less volatile business.

3

Earnings Manipulation Shenanigan No. 1: Recording Revenue Too Soon

Thirty days has September,
April, June, and November;
Of twenty-eight there is but one,
And all the rest have thirty-one.

—A MODERN VERSION OF THE FIFTEENTH-CENTURY
MEDIEVAL BRITISH RHYME

As young children, many of us were taught this useful rhyme to help remember the number of days in each month. Frankly, it still comes in handy as a reminder well into our adult years. It was much later in life though when we realized that February was not necessarily the only exception to the 30- or 31-day rule. In fact, every month could be the exception for a company that wishes to inflate its revenue. Computer Associates (CA) had become the poster child for this revenue inflation trick, regularly stretching out its months to 35 days on the books in order to capture sales booked after the conventional month-end. That scheme worked well for a while—or at least until the company was caught and CEO Sanjay Kumar was sent to jail.

Stretching out the number of days in a month is but one of the creative techniques that management may use to improperly record revenue too early. This chapter describes a variety of ways in which management attempts to accelerate revenue to earlier periods and how investors can spot signs of this transgression.

Techniques to Record Revenue Too Soon

1. Recording revenue before completing material obligations under the contract

2. Recording revenue far in excess of work completed on the contract

3. Recording revenue before the buyer's final acceptance of the product

4. Recording revenue when the buyer's payment remains uncertain or unnecessary

1. Recording Revenue Before Completing Material Obligations Under the Contract

Riding the Tech Wave at Microstrategy
Who could forget the raging Internet-driven bull market during the late 1990s (with the Nasdaq Index up 94 percent in 1999) and the almost-anything-goes accounting practices used to fuel the stratospheric growth of many tech companies? Perhaps the poster child for this crazy period would be Virginia-based software seller MicroStrategy (MSTR). In less than two years after going public, its market value reached $25 *billion*, a staggering 60-fold increase. A key driver of its growth, it turns out, was a practice of recording sales to parties that MicroStrategy had recently invested in. While it's impossible to know for sure whether these were in fact sham

transactions, the fact pattern raised serious suspicion. In addition to these questionable sales, MSTR pushed customers to sign contracts just before quarter-end, believing that the signing of a contract was the key event to permit recording revenue. As we will discuss later, revenue is recognized when earned, that is, when services have been performed.

Living a Dream—and a Nightmare   Imagine living the American dream during the Internet era. You and your college buddy create a software company. For the first few years, you work around the clock, but you take virtually no cash compensation. Instead, you reward yourself and your valued employees with stock and stock options. You begin meeting with investment bankers to plan your much-anticipated initial public offering (IPO). Then it happens—the bankers successfully peddle your shares to the public. You now have your first few million. But that's only the beginning. The share price of your (now public) company begins to levitate wildly, you become one of the wealthiest people in America, and at age 34, you are not even old enough to run for the presidency. The media treat you like royalty.

This was the real-life dream of MicroStrategy's founder, Michael Saylor. Founded in 1989, MSTR went public in 1998 at a market valuation over $200 million. That was only the beginning of an incredible odyssey. In the last four months of 1999, the share price began to rise dramatically, from $20 to over $100. Over the next 10 weeks, the stock soared incredibly to $333. Michael Saylor's net worth reached an almost inconceivable $14 billion.

Then the dream turned into a nightmare of epic proportions. On March 20, 2000, MSTR disclosed to investors that its financial reports contained material accounting irregularities. The financial reports for 1997 to 1999 had to be restated, resulting in massive losses, rather than the previously reported profits. Shocked investors started dumping the stock, dropping the share price $140 (from $226 to $86) *in a single day*. But that was only the beginning. It didn't bottom out until reaching $1.75 twelve months later. (The share price continued declining through 2002, at which point the company announced a 1-for-10 reverse split [effectively pushing its share price up 10-fold] to avoid being delisted from the stock exchange.)

What Led to the Collapse?   In early March 2000, only weeks after its auditors, PricewaterhouseCoopers (PwC), had blessed MSTR's 1999 financial reports (contained in a prospectus for a proposed stock offering), *Forbes* magazine broke the story that raised troubling questions about the company's revenue recognition practices.

After the *Forbes* article, PwC then conducted an internal investigation and concluded that the company's audited financial reports indeed were false and misleading. The auditor's swift about-face, an extremely rare event, sent the share price into a free fall.

Warning Signs for Investors Found in Odd Press Releases   On October 5, 1999, MSTR announced in a press release that it had signed a deal with NCR Corporation. In the release, MSTR described a $52.5 million licensing agreement and a partnership with NCR Corporation. Under the agreement, MSTR invested in an NCR partnership, and NCR returned the favor and purchased MSTR's products. When money flows in both directions, from seller (MSTR) to customer (NCR) and then from customer to seller, we call it a "boomerang" transaction. As the press release put it:

> Under the terms of the partnership, NCR signed a $27.5 million OEM [original equipment manufacturer] agreement for MicroStrategy's products and personal information services. In addition, MicroStrategy has chosen to purchase an NCR Teradata Warehouse worth $11 million to power the Strategy.com network.
>
> As part of the OEM agreement, NCR will become a master affiliate of Strategy.com. As a master affiliate, NCR will join the network, sell Strategy.com affiliations, and sell MicroStrategy products and services. As part of the agreement, MicroStrategy will provide NCR's future OLAP technology. MicroStrategy has agreed to purchase NCR's TeraCube business and all related intellectual property in exchange for $14 million in MicroStrategy stock.

Then just after the December 1999 quarter ended, on January 6, 2000, MSTR sent out another press release (excerpts shown below), also including a suspicious "boomerang" payment scheme that contributed to reported revenue, likely in the preceding period.

> Under the terms of the agreement, Exchange Applications will pay MicroStrategy an initial $30 million fee, payable through the combination of cash and Exchange Applications stock, of which approximately one-third will be recognized by MicroStrategy as revenue during the fourth quarter of 1999. In addition, MicroStrategy can earn up to an additional $35 million for future eCRM applications over the next two to three years. As part of the agreement, Exchange Applications will become a master affiliate of Strategy.com. As a master affiliate, Exchange Applications will join the network, sell Strategy.com affiliations, and sell MicroStrategy products and services.

Key Lessons for Investors   Two important lessons can be gleaned from the MicroStrategy story: (1) Funds flowing back and forth between a customer and seller should raise suspicions about the legitimacy of both transactions, and (2) the suspicious timing of press releases announcing new sales (just after a period ended) should raise questions about whether revenue might have been recognized too early. Indeed, as we learned from other sources, MSTR regularly rushed to have sales contracts signed and dated *just before a period ended*, with the goal of accelerating revenue into that earlier period. We believe that from an accounting perspective such efforts were all for naught, as revenue should be recognized when earned, not at the point of signing a contract.

Calendar Games

Imagine if you could place a bet on a horse race *after* the race ends. That sounds ridiculous; since you already would know the results beforehand, naturally, you would always win. Well, that approach reminds us of companies in jeopardy of "losing"—that is, failing to meet Wall Street's consensus estimates—those companies that at quarter-end stretch out the end date (like CA using 35 days) to ensure that they also always win by closing their books only *after* reaching the desired sales and profits.

Be Wary of Companies That Extend Their Quarter-End Date   CA was not
alone in improperly inflating revenue by keeping the books open beyond the
prescribed quarter-end. During the mid-1990s, "Chainsaw Al" Dunlap and
his minions at Sunbeam changed the company's quarter-end from March
29 to March 31 to make up for a revenue shortfall. The two additional days
permitted Sunbeam to record another $5 million in sales from its core opera-
tions and $15 million more from its recently acquired Coleman Corporation.

Not to be outdone by CA and Sunbeam, San Diego–based software maker
Peregrine also routinely kept its books open well after the official quarter
ended. The practice became so common at the company that officers joked
about this ploy, characterizing these late transactions as having been completed on "the thirty-seventh of December."

Changing Accounting Policies to Keep the Streak Alive

As we discussed earlier, when senior executives boast about an amazing
record streak of performance, it is more likely that they will resort to financial shenanigans to keep that streak alive.

Consider how the popular coffee seller Keurig Green Mountain (Keurig)
tried to hide its slowing revenue growth from investors. The company whim-
sically changed its decision rules on *when* recognition begins and *where* large-
quantity rebates get categorized on the Income Statement. Keurig was growing very fast in the 2005–2008 period, and CEO Lawrence J. Blanford, proud
of this achievement, regularly boasted to investors in Earnings Releases:

> It is great to be sharing such favorable results again this today. 2007 was
> a year of strong financial returns with net sales and earnings increasing
> 52% over the prior year. It was Green Mountain Coffee's 20th con-
> secutive quarter of double-digit net sales growth and eighth consecu-
> tive quarter with growth in excess of 25%.

As we know, compounding anything at over 25 percent for a long time
produces pretty big numbers. In the case of sales growth, it would be virtu-

ally impossible that a streak at that elevated level could be sustained. So it would be only a matter of time before Keurig would have to either announce that the streak had ended or figure out a way to make it appear that the streak had continued. Unfortunately, Keurig chose the latter approach. Reading the company's 10-K filings for fiscal 2007 and 2008, we came across two subtle (but important) accounting policy changes that management made in 2008 to inflate revenue. First, the company began to recognize some revenue earlier in the sales process—at the point of shipment, rather than delivery. Second, it started to treat incentives or "rebates" to customers as an operating expense rather than a reduction of sales.

**KEURIG GREEN MOUNTAIN FOOTNOTES
DESCRIBING ITS REVENUE RECOGNITION POLICY**

10-K 2007—Revenue from wholesale and consumer direct sales is *recognized upon product delivery*. In addition, the Company's customers can earn certain *incentives, which are netted against sales* in the consolidated income statements. [Italics added for emphasis]

10-K 2008—Revenue from wholesale and consumer direct sales is *recognized upon product delivery, and in some cases upon product shipment*. In addition, the Company's customers can earn certain *incentives, which are netted against sales or recorded in operating and selling expenses* in the consolidated income statements. [Italics added for emphasis]

---

2. Recording Revenue Far in Excess of Work Completed on the Contract

The first section illustrated how companies improperly recognize revenue by recording sales before significant activities by the seller even take place. Next, we discuss revenue recognition when the seller has started to deliver on the contract; however, management records revenue in a far greater amount than is warranted.

Changing Revenue Recognition Policy to Record Revenue Sooner
(and Greater Amounts)

Like Keurig, companies can also change their revenue recognition policy for ongoing projects to inflate sales and operating profits. Consider the plight of Japanese manufacturer Ulvac when its business struggled mightily and management considered ways to "solve" its problems by changing its accounting policies.

Watch for a Change in Revenue Recognition Policy to Hide Collapsing Business What to do when your business is collapsing and you hope to hide that fact from investors? In 2010, Ulvac found a very clever solution, but it involved an outrageous financial shenanigan. Table 3-1 shows the audited results Ulvac reported for the fiscal years ended June 2008, 2009, and 2010.

Table 3-1   Ulvac Results for 2008–2010, as Reported

(Yen million)	FY 2008	FY 2009	Percent Change	FY 2009	FY 2010	Percent Change
Sales	241,212	223,825	–7%	223,825	221,804	–1%
Operating profit	9,081	3,483	–62%	3,483	4,809	**38%**

After a rocky 2009 (with sales plummeting 7 percent and operating profits declining 62 percent), 2010 looked like a successful turnaround period (with sales growth improving to just *negative* 1 percent and operating profits jumping an impressive 38 percent). It certainly appeared that the company had done an excellent job in managing costs in a period of no top-line growth. The problem, however, was that the 2010 results were woefully misleading. Specifically, Ulvac had just changed its revenue recognition approach to percentage-of-completion (POC), and as a result, it began booking sales much earlier than it would with its traditional approach. Table 3-2 shows the results Ulvac would have reported, assuming no change in revenue recognition policies. Sobering and shocking results for investors.

Notice in the right-hand column, "Adjusted Percent Change" in 2010, and compare with the change shown Table 3-1—a decline in sales of 1 percent. Rather than sales basically stabilizing in 2010, after a 7 percent decline the prior year, sales would have plummeted 21 percent, completely freaking out investors. So in order to avoid that disappointment, Ulvac's management found a solution, and its auditors inexplicably approved—changing its revenue recognition policy and hiding its big problems from investors.

Table 3-2   Ulvac Results for 2009–2010, Results Assuming
No Change in Accounting Policy

(Yen million)	As Reported, Jun-09	As Reported, Jun-10	Accounting Adjustment	As Adjusted, Jun-10	Adjusted Percent Change
Sales	223,825	221,804	(44,037)	177,767	–21%
Operating profit	3,483	4,809	(12,033)	**(7,224)**	NM

Changing Estimates and Assumptions When Using POC Accounting

Ulvac provides an illustration of the dramatic jump in reported revenue when a company switches from standard revenue recognition practices to the more aggressive POC approach. Investors also should be alert for companies using POC that simply change some key estimates or assumptions, as those actions can also materially inflate revenue.

Consider solar energy leader First Solar (FSLR) and its accounting changes to hide business setbacks from investors. In 2014, FSLR was building out some of the largest solar-powered power plants in the United States. Since these were long-term construction projects, First Solar applied percentage-of-completion accounting, and it determined the proportion of progress on each contract by calculating the costs incurred on the project as a percentage of the total expected costs. Under this method, any changes in the company's estimate for total project costs would have had an immediate impact on reported revenue since it would have either increased or decreased the estimated progress toward completion.

Accounting Capsule:
Background on Percentage-of-Completion (POC)

POC revenue recognition allows companies to report revenue even before a project has been completed. It was introduced so that firms working on long-term construction-type contracts could report business activity each period even if a product was not delivered to the customer. Under this framework companies are expected to estimate the proportion of the project that has been completed and to recognize a pro rata share of the total project's revenue, expenses, and profits. Investors should be extra vigilant when analyzing companies using percentage-of-completion accounting, since the reported results hinge on the company's estimates about its own progress.

Astute investors would have been tipped off about growing changes in estimates by reading the footnotes in First Solar's 2014 10-K filing. When the company updated its estimates for total project costs in 2014, with one click of the mouse inside a spreadsheet, management immediately recognized an additional $40 million of sales (following a boost of $8.5 million in 2013). Moreover, since no additional costs were associated with this windfall revenue, gross profit and operating income increased by an equal amount.

POC accounting provides management with unusual latitude in its ability to pull forward revenue, but CA, an enterprise software company, took matters much further by pulling forward license revenue on multiyear licenses, which would not actually be earned for many years to come.

Be Alert for Up-Front Recognition of a Long-Term License Contract   CA sold long-term licenses allowing customers to use its mainframe computer software. Customers paid an up-front licensing fee for the software, as well as an annual charge to renew the license in subsequent years. Despite the long-term nature of these agreements (some contracts lasted as long as seven years), the company would recognize the present value of all licensing revenue for the entire contract immediately. Since all licensing revenue was recorded at the beginning of the contract, and cash was not collected for many years to come, CA recorded substantial amounts of long-term receivables on its Balance Sheet.

Regulators Also Strongly Disagreed with the Approach
The SEC charged that from January 1998 through October 2000, CA prematurely recognized *over $3.3 billion* in revenue from at least 363 software contracts with customers.

CA's bulging long-term receivables should have alerted investors to the company's aggressive revenue recognition. A careful review would have alerted investors to the firm's surging long-term and total receivables as early as September 1998. Investors should use a measure called "days' sales outstanding" (DSO) to evaluate how quickly customers are paying their bills relative to how quickly revenue is recorded. A higher DSO could indicate more aggressive revenue recognition in addition to simply poor cash management. With the company's long-term installment receivables soaring at September 1998, its DSO reached 247 days (based on product revenue)—a year-over-year increase of 20 days. Furthermore, total receivables, including both current and long term, increased to 342 days—a jump of 31 days.

3. Recording Revenue Before the Buyer's Final Acceptance of the Product

In the first two sections of this chapter, we focused on the seller's performance of its obligations under the contract. In the next two sections, we shift our focus to the buyer. This section deals with three types of tricks that produce revenue before final acceptance by the buyer, specifically, recording revenue (1) before shipment of product to the buyer, (2) after shipment but to someone other than the buyer, and (3) after shipment but while the buyer still could void the sale.

Seller Records Revenue Before Shipment
One problematic and often controversial method of revenue recognition involves so-called bill-and-hold arrangements. With this approach, the seller bills the customer and recognizes revenue but continues to hold the product. For most sales, revenue recognition requires shipment of the product to the customer. In certain cases, however, accounting guidelines allow revenue to

be recognized under bill-and-hold transactions, provided that the customer requests this arrangement and is the main beneficiary. For example, if the buyer does not have adequate storage space, it may ask the seller to hold on to the purchased goods as a courtesy. Under no circumstances can early recognition of revenue occur under a bill-and-hold arrangement if the arrangement is initiated by the seller for the benefit of the seller (i.e., to record revenue at an earlier date).

Watch for Bill-and-Hold Transactions Initiated by the Seller   If it seems like the seller has initiated a bill-and-hold transaction, investors should assume that the seller has attempted to recognize revenue too early. For example, Sunbeam CEO Al Dunlap used a bill-and-hold strategy to make the company's financial performance appear better than it really was by artificially inflating Sunbeam's revenue.

Sunbeam, anxious to boost sales in its "turnaround year," hoped to convince retailers to buy grills nearly six months before they were needed. In exchange for major discounts and longer payment terms, retailers agreed to purchase merchandise that they would not physically receive until months later. In the meantime, the goods would be shipped out of the grill factory in Missouri to third-party warehouses leased by Sunbeam, where they would be held until the customers requested them.

Nonetheless, Sunbeam booked the sales and profits from all $35 million in bill-and-hold transactions. When outside auditors later reviewed the documents, they reversed a staggering $29 million of the $35 million and shifted the sales to future quarters. In doing the initial audit, Arthur Andersen had questioned the accounting treatment of some transactions. But in almost every case, it concluded that the amounts were "immaterial" to the overall audit. Sometimes detecting signs of aggressive accounting is close to impossible. In the case of Sunbeam, it required nothing more than reading the revenue recognition footnote in the company's 10-K.

> ### SUNBEAM'S 10-K FOOTNOTE DISCLOSURE TOLD THE STORY
>
> The Company recognizes revenues from product sales principally at the time of shipment to customers. In limited circumstances, at the customers' request the Company may sell seasonal products on a bill-and-hold basis provided that the goods are completed, packaged and ready for shipment, such goods are segregated and the risks of ownership and legal title have passed to the customer. The amount of such bill-and-hold sales at December 29, 1997 was approximately 3 percent of consolidated revenues.

Eventually, Dunlap was fired when the board of directors realized that he had done little to improve the company's financial situation and had simply used improper financial engineering to drive the stock price higher.

Seller Records Revenue upon Shipment to Someone Other Than the Customer
Auditors often look to shipping records as evidence that the seller delivered its product to the customer, allowing revenue to be recorded. Management might attempt to trick its auditors (and its investors) into believing that a sale occurred by shipping products to someone other than the customer. Consider the case of Krispy Kreme Doughnuts.

Part of Krispy Kreme's revenue comes from selling doughnut-making equipment to its franchisees. It would certainly be appropriate for the company to record sales revenue upon shipment of a machine to a franchisee—provided, of course, that the machine was received by the franchisee. In 2003, Krispy Kreme went to great lengths to fool its auditors by pretending to ship equipment to franchisees. It shipped the equipment out, but to company-owned trailers to which the franchisees had no access. Krispy Kreme still recorded the revenue, even though the customers had failed to take possession of the machines shipped.

Watch for Shipping Product to an Intermediary, Rather Than the Actual Customer Sometimes a seller will ship out product to a reseller before a deal has been fully completed. Autonomy was one of the largest software companies in the United Kingdom until being acquired by HP. To juice its revenue, it would book sales on software deals still under negotiation with end users (but had not yet closed) and transfer the associated product to resellers, which in turn would take ownership immediately and hold on to the product until the sales process with the end user was finalized. In exchange for "stepping into the transaction" and allowing Autonomy to *recognize revenue immediately*, Autonomy paid commission rates (akin to a bribe) of up to 10 percent, even though the reseller had virtually no role in the underlying sales process and often did not even have any information about the status of the deals.

Be Wary of Consignment Arrangements   Another technique for prematurely recording revenue at the point of shipment involves consignment sales. With such sales, the products are shipped to an intermediary, called a "consignee." Think of the consignee as an outside sales agent who is given the task of finding a buyer. Normally the manufacturer (called the "consignor") should recognize no revenue until the sales agent consummates a transaction with an end customer. Chainsaw Al Dunlap and his minion at Sunbeam, not surprisingly, ignored that standard and recorded $36 million in consignment sales before an end user had even been found.

Who Is the Actual Customer—the Distributor or the End User?   Companies that sell products through a distribution network must decide whether to book sales when they ship to the distributor ("sell-in" approach), or later when the distributor sends goods to the actual user of the product ("sell-through" approach). While both approaches are widely used, the sell-through approach is considered more conservative, as it more directly aligns reported revenue with end-customer demand. More aggressive (and most concerning) is when a company switches from the more conservative sell-through to the sell-in approach, which of course inflates sales. We saw an example of such a change at Medicis, shortly after the company was acquired by Valeant in December 2012.

Valeant cleverly changed the existing revenue recognition policy at the newly acquired Medicis unit in the first quarter after the deal closed, so its sales would be recognized sooner and reported growth would be higher.

Medicis sold product through its distributor, McKesson, which then sold it to physicians. Medicis historically used the more conservative sell-through approach, booking no sales until the distributor sold to the physicians. To goose sales at the Medicis unit after the deal closed, Valeant had Medicis immediately switch to the sell-in approach and started recognizing sales much earlier—when product was sent to the distributor. That brazen change in revenue recognition caught the attention of astute investors and eventually the SEC, which issued a formal letter of reprimand.

Medicis was not the only case of revenue shenanigans in Valeant's M&A path. Salix, acquired by Valeant in early 2015, had a string of even more troubling shenanigans in dealings with distributors. In the last quarter of 2013 and the first three quarters of 2014, it aggressively "stuffed the channel," meaning it shipped much more product to the distributors than they could sell to their customers. And by using the sell-in approach, Salix materially inflated its revenue. When the scheme was detected late in 2014, Salix was forced to restate its previously released financial statements to lower revenue and profits during each of these four quarters.

Since all these details were publicly disclosed in late 2014, we are completely baffled why Valeant would still have closed on the acquisition. (We will have more on this in Part Five.)

Seller Records Revenue, but Buyer Can Still Reject the Sale

The final part of this section discusses revenue that is recorded prematurely even though product was shipped and received by the customer. This may occur if (1) the customer received the wrong product, (2) the customer received the correct product, but too early, or (3) the customer received the correct product at the right time but still reserves the right to reject the sale. When a buyer has received a product but can still reject the sale, the seller must either wait until final acceptance to record revenue or recognize the revenue but record a reserve estimating the amount of anticipated returns.

Be Wary of Sellers Deliberately Shipping Incorrect or Incomplete Products

Sometimes companies scheme to inflate revenue by intentionally shipping the wrong product and recording the related revenue, although they know full well that the product will be returned. Symbol Technologies allegedly shipped incorrect product without customer approval in order to report higher sales. Similarly, at the end of the fourth quarter of 1996, Informix recorded revenue but failed to deliver the required software code prior to year-end. Then in January 1997, Informix delivered a beta version of the software that did not function properly with the hardware. It took the company another six months to deliver usable software code. As it turned out, Informix recorded revenue far too early in the fourth quarter of 1996 rather than when the company had satisfied its obligations in the third quarter of 1997.

Be Alert to Sellers Shipping Product Before the Agreed-upon Shipping Date The fiscal quarter is ending, and profits are sagging. What can a company do? Why not simply start shipping merchandise and recording revenue, thereby boosting sales and profits? Merchandise is rushed out of the warehouse to customers toward the end of the year (even before the sales have taken place), and sales revenue is recorded. Since under this method, revenue is recognized when an item is shipped to retailers or wholesalers, some manufacturers may be tempted to keep shipping their products during slow times—even if the retailers' shelves are overstocked. Automobile manufacturers have been doing this for years, thereby artificially increasing their sales. By shipping a product late in a quarter, rather than during the following quarter when a customer expects to receive it, a seller can improperly record revenue too soon. An increase in DSO can often be an indicator that more products were shipped late in a quarter than usual.

Even if a company ships its products to the actual customer and the customer receives them, the company still may not be permitted to recognize revenue. The final hitch involves terms in many contracts that give the customer the right to return the products within a certain period of time.

Be Mindful of Sellers Recording Revenue Before the Lapse of the Right of Return Many businesses permit the buyer a "right of return" if the customer is not satisfied with the goods. In those cases, companies are required to either delay revenue recognition until the right of return lapses or estimate the amount of expected returns and reduce revenue by that amount. If the actual level of returned products is more than the company's initial estimates, the company may be guilty of having recognized too much revenue up front.

4. Recording Revenue When the Buyer's Payment Remains Uncertain or Unnecessary

Continuing our focus on the buyer, we turn our attention to the revenue recognition requirement concerning customer payment. The seller may be accelerating revenue recognition if it records sales when the buyer lacks the ability to pay (payment remains uncertain) or when the seller aggressively induces the sale by not requiring the customer to pay until long after the sale (payment remains unnecessary).

Buyer Lacks the Ability or the Necessary Approval to Pay
In earlier sections, we discussed the requirement that the seller complete its obligations and the requirement that a buyer convey final acceptance. At Kendall Square Research Corporation, a computer systems maker in Cambridge, Massachusetts, all of that took place—the product was shipped, and the customer accepted it. The final question was whether the customer had the wherewithal and the intention to pay. Many of Kendall Square's customers—mainly universities and research institutions—required a third party to provide the funds. In truth, the sale was contingent on the receipt of outside funding, and thus no revenue should have been recognized until such funding had been secured. Kendall Square must have been aware of those contingencies, since it was later revealed that the company had provided customers with "side letter" agreements that essentially voided the sales if the customers failed to receive funding.

A shareholder lawsuit charged that nearly half of Kendall Square's reported revenue in the first quarter of 1993 had been improperly booked. Most of this revenue came from shipments to the University of Colorado and the Applied Computer Systems Institute of Massachusetts before these customers had received sufficient funding. The company eventually restated its financial statements for fiscal 1992 and the first half of 1993, reversing approximately half of its previously reported revenue.

Watch for Companies That Change Their Assessment of Customers' Ability to Pay Management's assessment of a customer's ability to pay is what determines the estimates used to account for uncollectible receivables. Changes in these assessments may provide companies with a nonrecurring boost to revenue. Consider the revenue recognition policy change made by software company Openwave Systems in December 2005.

Openwave initially waited until the receipt of cash before recognizing any revenue from "deadbeat" customers that it feared might not pay. Under a new policy, Openwave could recognize revenue immediately, simply by concluding that the customer no longer was a deadbeat.

Investors who noticed this subtle change by management would have recognized that Openwave's business was actually growing more slowly than reported. Openwave's change in policy indeed reflected its desperation. Revenue growth slowed dramatically in the following years, and Openwave's stock price, which spent much of the March 2006 quarter above $20, plummeted to $6 in July. Diligent investors who reviewed the company's December 2015 10-Q would have easily spotted this change in the revenue recognition footnote, as shown below. However, investors who relied only on the compa-

---

OPENWAVE SYSTEMS REVENUE RECOGNITION CHANGE DISCLOSURE, 12/05 10-Q

As of the quarter ended December 31, 2005, the Company *revised its policy regarding the determination factor for deferrals of revenue recognition* for arrangements deemed not probable for collection. Prior to the quarter ended December 31, 2005, the Company continued to defer revenue recognition on arrangements originally deemed not probable for collection until the receipt of cash from that arrangement. As of the quarter ended December 31, 2005, the *Company revised its policy such that revenue on arrangements previously deemed not probable for collection, which are subsequently deemed probable for collection, is recognized in the period of the change in the assessment of collectability*, rather than upon receipt of cash, provided all other revenue recognition criteria have been satisfied. This change in policy did not have a material impact for the quarter ended December 31, 2005. [Italics added for emphasis]

ny's quarterly Earnings Release and conference call may have missed the boat, as those disclosures made no mention of the change in accounting.

Seller Induces Sale by Allowing an Exceptionally Long Time to Pay
Rather than using a third-party institution for financing, some cash-strapped customers use financing provided by the seller itself. Investors should be cautious about seller-provided financing arrangements (including very generous extended payment terms), as they may indicate the acceleration of revenue into the current period, tepid customer interest in the product, or the buyer's lack of ability to pay.

Watch for Seller-Provided Financing   To accelerate revenue in recent years, a number of high-tech companies have lent money to customers to enable them to pay for their products. In moderation, customer financing can be considered a sound selling technique; when it is abused, however, it can be a dangerous way to do business. When the dot-com bubble burst, the amount of financing provided by telecommunication equipment suppliers to their customers should have made investors nervous. At the end of 2000, these suppliers were collectively owed as much as $15 billion by customers, a 25 percent increase in a single year.

Watch for Companies That Offer Extended or Flexible Payment Terms
Sometimes companies offer sweet payment terms to entice their customers to purchase additional products earlier than normal. While offering favorable payment terms to customers may be a completely appropriate business practice, it may also add a level of uncertainty to the eventual collectibility of receivables. Moreover, even when extending terms to creditworthy customers, overly generous terms may effectively shift sales that originally were slated for future periods into the current one. This shift would allow for unsustainably high near-term revenue growth and produce pressure to fill the void created in that later period.

Sound the Alarm When New Extended Payment Terms Are Disclosed and DSO Jumps   Investors should be particularly concerned about accelerated (or even improper) revenue recognition when a company begins extending very generous payment terms and DSO spikes, as shown in Table 3-3. The deck materials supplier Trex Company, for example, provided extended payment terms to customers under what it called an "early buy program" in late 2004 and early 2005. As demand declined, it seemed that Trex enticed customers to accept products earlier than normal (without having to pay for them). This arrangement had minimal impact on the buyers' total purchases but allowed Trex to record revenue in an earlier period. Astute analysts would have surmised that extended payment terms were needed to avoid reporting disappointing sales growth. Several months later, Trex announced that its revenue for June 2005 would be much lower than Wall Street expectations. Trex's sharp increase in receivables, together with the company's disclosure of extended payment terms and an early buy program, should have alerted investors to the coming slowdown in sales growth.

Table 3-3   Trex's Extended Payment Terms Cause Receivables to Jump

($ millions, except days)	Q1, 3/03	Q1, 3/04	Q1, 3/05	Q2, 6/03	Q2, 6/04	Q3, 9/03	Q3, 9/04	Q4, 12/03	Q4, 12/04
Accounts receivable	13.9	31.9	68.8	21.9	31.2	13.1	12.8	5.8	22.0
Revenue	68.7	76.3	89.9	59.2	83.4	41.2	64.4	21.9	29.6
DSO	18	38	70	34	34	29	18	24	68

More recently, investors in San Francisco–based Fitbit were jolted during the company's November 2016 conference call when management suddenly lowered guidance for future sales growth by a stunning 15 percent. To put that in some perspective, in Q4 2015 sales grew 92 percent, and now the sales growth estimate in Q4 2016 would be only 2 to 5 percent. Yikes!

That announcement by management marked the end of a period of hypergrowth fueled by new fitness tracking products and geographic expansion. But were there no warnings for investors that business was really starting to struggle? Indeed, signs of a weakening business (obscured by shenanigans) could be found in the second-quarter earnings conference call. In his remarks, the CFO mentioned in passing that Fitbit had just *extended payment terms* to "certain customers in Asia Pac [Pacific], due to the channel

inventory levels previously discussed." In that one cryptic sentence, management signaled serious business challenges in Asia, which had been covered
up by offering distributors there more time to pay. As is often the case when
business problems are being covered up by management, the deceptions tend
to work only for a short period; sure enough, by December 2016, unsuspecting investors were stunned as Fitbit's stock collapsed 50 percent.

Looking Ahead

This chapter addressed accounting tricks involving mainly legitimate sources
of revenue. Chapter 4 describes a more sinister transgression: recording
bogus or fictitious revenue.

4

Earnings Manipulation Shenanigan No. 2: Recording Bogus Revenue

The previous chapter discussed situations in which companies record revenue too soon. While this is clearly inappropriate, the acceleration of legitimate revenue is less audacious than simply making the revenue up out of thin air. This chapter describes four techniques that a company might employ to create bogus revenue and warning signs for investors to spot these nefarious shenanigans.

Techniques to Record Bogus Revenue

1. Recording revenue from transactions that lack economic substance

2. Recording revenue from transactions that lack a reasonable arm's-length process

3. Recording revenue on receipts from non-revenue-producing transactions

4. Recording revenue from appropriate transactions, but at inflated amounts

1. Recording Revenue from Transactions
That Lack Economic Substance

Our first technique involves simply dreaming up a scheme that has the "look and feel" of a legitimate sale, yet lacks economic substance. In these transactions, the so-called customer is either under no obligation to keep or pay for the product, or no product or service was even transferred in the first place.

In his brilliant 1971 hit song, John Lennon challenged us to "imagine" a perfect world. Imagination has undoubtedly helped the world become a better place, as people's creativity has broken boundaries and led to countless innovations. Imagination has inspired talented scientists, for example, to diagnose the unknown and find cures for diseases. Similarly, technology pioneers (like Bill Gates and Steve Jobs) imagined exciting ways to create new products, such as Microsoft's Windows and Apple's iPhone, that enhance our enjoyment of life.

Occasionally, though, imagination can run amok. Many corporate executives have given imagination a bad name when they've used theirs to get too creative with reported revenue. For example, insurance industry leader AIG imagined a perfect world for its clients (and itself), in which they would always achieve Wall Street's earnings expectations. Imagine, AIG must have thought, how happy clients would be if they never had to experience the indignity (and stock price decline) that accompanies an earnings shortfall.

AIG and several other insurers began to market a new product called "finite insurance." This solution would guarantee clients the ability to always produce earnings that were acceptable to Wall Street by "insuring against" earnings shortfalls. In a sense, this product was an addictive drug that allowed companies to cover up quarterly blemishes by artificially smoothing their earnings.

And not surprisingly, customers were hooked. Everybody was happy. AIG found a new revenue stream, and customers found a way to prevent earnings shortfalls. However, there was a big problem: some of these "insurance" contracts were not legitimate insurance arrangements at all; rather, they were complex and highly structured financing transactions.

How Was Finite Insurance Abused?

Let's turn to Indiana-based wireless company Brightpoint Inc. to see how some finite insurance transactions were economically more akin to financing arrangements. It was late 1998 and the bull market was racing, but Brightpoint had a problem: earnings for the December quarter were tracking about $15 million below the guidance given to Wall Street at the beginning of the quarter. As the quarter closed, management feared that investors would be unprepared for this news and, as a result, that the firm's stock price would be hammered.

Enter AIG and its "perfect world" products. AIG created a special $15 million "retroactive" insurance policy that would "cover" Brightpoint's unreported losses. Here's how the policy worked: Brightpoint agreed to pay "insurance premiums" to AIG over the next three years, and AIG agreed to pay out an "insurance recovery" of $15 million to cover any losses under the policy. This sounds like your normal insurance policy, except for one big problem: there was no transfer of risk, since the policy covered losses that had already happened. You can't insure your house after it burns down!

Brightpoint proceeded to record the $15 million "insurance recovery" as income in the December quarter (which netted out its unreported losses). AIG recorded what amounted to bogus revenue on the insurance premiums over the next three years. Economic sense dictates that this transaction was not an insurance contract because no real risk had been transferred. Indeed, the transaction was nothing more than a financing arrangement: Brightpoint deposited cash at AIG, which AIG eventually refunded as purported "insurance claim payments."

Accounting Capsule:
Legitimate Insurance Contracts Require a Transfer of Risk

Just because two parties call an agreement an insurance contract does not mean that they can book it as such in their financial statements. To be considered an insurance policy for accounting purposes, an arrangement must involve a *transfer of risk* from the insured to the insurer. Without this transfer of risk, GAAP treats the arrangement as a financing transaction, with premium payments being treated like bank deposits and recoveries being treated like the return of principal.

Regulators Considered This Scheme to Be a Scam

Brightpoint got into trouble with the SEC for inappropriately masking its problems. AIG found itself in the SEC's crosshairs as well for knowingly structuring the insurance policy in such a way that it allowed Brightpoint to misrepresent its actual losses as "insured losses." In November 2004, AIG agreed to pay $126 million to settle litigation with the Department of Justice and the SEC on charges that it had sold products that helped companies inflate earnings via the use of finite insurance.

Peregrine Dupes Investors with Sales That Lack Economic Substance

Creating bogus revenue from transactions that lack any economic substance extends far beyond insurance companies. Plenty of technology companies apparently got the memo of how easy it is to employ this shenanigan. Take, for instance, San Diego–based Peregrine Systems, which got busted for a massive fraud scheme that involved recognition of bogus revenue.

The SEC charged that Peregrine improperly recorded millions of dollars of revenue from nonbinding sales of software licenses to resellers. The company apparently negotiated secret side agreements that waived the resellers' obligation to pay Peregrine, which means that revenue should not have been recorded. Employees at Peregrine had a great name for the scheme: "parking" the transaction. Sales that were near the finish line were often "parked" to help Peregrine achieve its revenue forecasts. Peregrine engaged in other deceptive practices as well to create bogus revenue, including entering reciprocal transactions in which the company essentially *paid for its customers' purchases* of its software. In 2003, Peregrine restated its financial results for several earlier quarters, reducing previously reported revenue of $1.34 billion by $509 million, of which at least $259 million was reversed because the underlying transactions lacked substance.

Be Aware That with Bogus Revenue Come Those Fake Receivables

Peregrine obviously did not receive cash from customers on these nonbinding bogus revenue contracts, resulting in bogus receivables festering on the Balance Sheet. As we have learned, a rapid increase in accounts receivable is often an indication of deteriorating financial health. Peregrine knew that analysts would naturally begin questioning the "quality of earnings" if the bulging receivables balance remained stubbornly high. To avoid these questions, Peregrine played several tricks that made it seem like the receivables had been collected. These shenanigans inappropriately lowered the receivables balances, and in doing so, improperly inflated cash flow from operations (CFFO). We break down the mechanics of this chicanery and discuss Peregrine's Cash Flow Shenanigans further in Chapter 10.

Symbol Wants in on the Action

Symbol Technologies found a creative way to recognize revenue that lacked economic substance. From late 1999 through early 2001, Symbol conspired with a South American distributor to fake more than $16 million in revenue. It instructed the distributor to submit purchase orders for random products at the end of each quarter, even though the distributor had absolutely no use for those products. Symbol never shipped the products to the distributor or any of its customers. Instead, to fool the auditors into believing that a sale had occurred, Symbol sent the products to its own warehouse in New York; however, it still retained all "risks of loss and benefits of ownership." The distributor, naturally, did not have to pay for the warehoused product and could "return" or "exchange" the goods at no cost when it placed legitimate new orders for any product that it needed. Without a doubt, the only purpose of this charade was to give the appearance of a legitimate sale so that Symbol could record revenue.

Watch for Barter Transactions with Related Parties   Investors should always be wary in seeing sales booked when *no cash is paid* (i.e., a barter transaction). And when such transactions are with a related-party customer, investor concerns should rise to the highest level.

Consider how D.C.-based comScore tried to cover up sluggish 2014 sales growth in its core business of selling web traffic data to advertisers. Management entered into agreements with other data providers to exchange certain "data assets." Because no money changed hands, these transactions were disclosed and described as "nonmonetary" in its Footnotes to the Financial statements. Arrangements in which goods or services are swapped are inherently suspicious, because the amount of sales recorded for the exchange is subject to the company's own estimate of its value, and that amount can easily be inflated, or even conjured up entirely, reflecting no real substantive economic activity.

These nonmonetary (barter) arrangements accounted for $16.3 million of total 2014 sales (5 percent of total sales), representing a big portion of comScore's reported growth. Not only were these transactions suspicious on a stand-alone basis, but almost all (88 percent) of these barter sales were to related parties of comScore. By the third quarter of 2015 the company had already recognized $23.7 million of additional barter revenue (now representing 9 percent of total revenue). And by the end of 2015, investors had raised enough troubling questions about the true nature of these arrangements that management found it impossible to properly file its financial statements. And by failing to file, comScore was eventually delisted from the Nasdaq stock exchange.

> **TIP**
>
> Be extremely cautious when a company reports barter or "nonmonetary" sales, especially when the buyer is a related party.

Failing to Detect Accounting Tricks at Autonomy
Costs Hewlett-Packard Billions

As Hewlett-Packard (HP) tried to jump-start its struggling business, it went shopping in October 2011 for an acquisition across the pond and paid $11.1 billion for software maker Autonomy Corporation. That turned out to be a colossal mistake; one year later, HP took an $8.8 billion impairment charge, recognizing that it had materially overpaid for Autonomy. Worse yet, HP claimed that most of this massive loss was linked to serious accounting improprieties.

When this bad news became public, not only did HP's share price plummet 12 percent in a single day, but HP alleged that Autonomy executives had fraudulently inflated revenue to trick investors. In short, HP's leaders claimed that they were duped by Autonomy.

The SEC investigated these allegations and concluded that Autonomy indeed used a variety of schemes to vastly overstate sales in the years prior to the acquisition. In many cases, these tricks allowed Autonomy to accelerate revenue recognition on software sales earlier in the selling process; in some cases, however, the revenue may have been *completely fabricated* as Autonomy was not ultimately successful in closing a deal with the end user. For example, it not only sold products to a distributor but later repurchased from that same distributor unwanted, unused, or overpriced products, initiating a "round-trip" cash payment that would come back to Autonomy. According to the SEC, this scheme alone inflated Autonomy's reported revenue by nearly $200 million between 2009 and 2011.

2. Recording Revenue from Transactions That Lack a Reasonable Arm's-Length Process

While recognizing that revenue on transactions that lack economic substance should never be considered legitimate, transactions that lack a reasonable arm's-length process are sometimes appropriate. But prudent investors should bet against it. That is, most related-party transactions that lack an arm's-length exchange produce inflated, and often phony, revenue.

Transactions Involving Sales to an Affiliated Party

If a seller and a customer are also affiliated in some other way, the quality of the seller's recorded revenue may be suspect. For example, a sale to a vendor, relative, corporate director, majority owner, or business partner raises doubt about whether the terms of the transaction were negotiated *at arm's length*. Was a discount given to the relative? Was the seller expected to make future purchases from the vendor at a discount? Were there any side agreements requiring the seller to provide a quid pro quo? A sale to an affiliated party or a strategic partner may be an entirely appropriate transaction. However, investors should always spend time scrutinizing these arrangements, as it is important to understand whether the revenue recognized is truly in line with the economic reality of the transaction.

Be Wary of Related-Party Customers and Joint Venture Partners   A representative case in point is the alleged fraud at Syntax-Brillian, the Arizona-based maker of high-definition televisions. In 2007, Syntax-Brillian was flying high. Extraordinary demand in China sent sales of TVs soaring, and the start of a marketing relationship with ESPN and ABC Sports generated a buzz about its Olevia HDTVs. The company more than tripled its revenue in fiscal 2007, with sales approaching $700 million, up from less than $200 million the prior year. Yet one year later, Syntax-Brillian was bankrupt and under investigation for fraud.

Syntax-Brillian's demise was not a surprise to investors who understood the extent to which the company's reported results benefited from transactions with related parties. For example, the company's staggering revenue growth came from a 10-fold increase in sales to a suspicious related party. The sales accounted for nearly half of Syntax-Brillian's total revenue, and the related party was an Asian distributor named South China House of Technology (SCHOT). Syntax-Brillian's relationship with SCHOT was much more incestuous than a typical customer-supplier arrangement. The two companies seemed to be involved in a tangled web of joint ventures (which also, oddly, included Syntax-Brillian's primary supplier). Syntax-Brillian was close enough with SCHOT that it granted it 120-day payment terms and routinely extended those terms even further.

Syntax-Brillian described SCHOT as a distributor that would purchase its TVs and then resell them to retail outlets and end users in China. Many investors failed to question the company's significant uptick in sales to SCHOT, as they believed that demand in China was high, with people upgrading their TV sets heading into the 2008 Summer Olympics in Beijing. Investors were also cheered by reports that the Beijing Olympic Village itself was planning to fit its facilities with Olevia TVs.

Then suddenly, in February 2008, Syntax-Brillian cryptically announced that the Olympic facilities would no longer be installing the TVs that the company had "sold" to South China House of Technology. Even though Syntax-Brillian had already recorded revenue from the sale of these TVs, it agreed to "repurchase" more than 25,000 TVs for nearly $100 million. The company did not need to come up with the cash because the receivable from SCHOT was, of course, still outstanding. With this significant right of return and no receipt of cash, Syntax-Brillian should never have recognized this revenue in the first place!

Syntax-Brillian's elaborate related-party transactions (and many other red flags, such as surging receivables) were in plain sight for any investor who read the SEC filings. Take, for example, the following reference to SCHOT found in Syntax-Brillian's March 2006 10-Q that would have led even the most novice investor to raise questions.

SYNTAX-BRILLIAN'S ACCOUNTS RECEIVABLE DISCLOSURE—MARCH 2006

At March 31, 2006, the accounts receivable balance from one of our Asian customers, that is also a joint venture partner, totaled $9.6 million, or 70.8 percent of the outstanding balance of accounts that had not been assigned to CIT.

Watch for Transactions with Parent Companies   Consider the case of Hanergy Solar, the Chinese manufacturer of clean energy equipment (and dirty accounting tricks). In 2013, business was just starting to heat up as revenue grew 18 percent to HK$3.3 billion. The following year, revenue tripled to HK$9.6 billion. From May 2013 to May 2015, Hanergy's stock surged 1,300 percent, bringing the total market value to a whopping HK$40 billion and making founder and chairman Li Hejun one of China's richest men.

Digging just beneath the surface of reported revenue growth revealed a shocking fact: Hanergy's primary customer also happened to be its majority owner, Hanergy Group Holdings (the same name was no coincidence). In 2013, 100 percent of Hanergy's revenue came from sales to its parent company. Hanergy had other customers in 2014, but the parent still made up 61 percent of revenue. Moreover, Hanergy barely received any cash from sales to its parent, causing accounts receivable to swell to sky-high levels, resulting in DSO ballooning to 500 days at the end of 2014 (with 57 percent of its trade receivables listed as past due). Clearly, these sales were not arm's length in nature.

By May 2015, the gig was up. One morning, when Chairman Li failed to show up for the annual meeting amid investigations of insider trading, Hanergy's stock fell 50 percent before trading was suspended by the Hong Kong Stock Exchange.

Be Alert for Suspicious Revenue from Transactions with Joint Venture Partners   New York–based brand management company Iconix (ICON) was launched in 2004 by Neil Cole, younger brother of the fashion mogul Kenneth Cole. ICON had a relatively straightforward business model: purchase trademarks related to fashion brands and then license out the right to manufacture and sell clothes under these brand names. Customers generally paid ICON royalties based on a percentage of sales for each brand.

Iconix spent its first few years buying up established, but tired, fashion trademarks (such as London Fog, Joe Boxer, Starter, and Umbro). While the company may have generated a positive return on its trademark investments over time, the slow-and-steady business model failed to produce strong organic growth. To jazz up its revenue growth, management resorted to creative accounting games. One trick was to accelerate sales and earnings by carving up its trademark assets into geographic regions and selling certain ones outright. So in 2013, for example, Iconix sold its Umbro trademarks in South Korea for $10 million, recording a gain on sale for the full $10 million. Inexplicably, this gain was recorded as a *component of revenue*—rather than as a one-time gain from an asset sale.

In some cases, Iconix would actually create the customers that would buy these regional trademarks. In 2013, for example, it formed a 50-50 joint venture with supply-chain partner Li & Fung and transferred several trademarks to this JV. Iconix claimed *not to control* this JV (despite it being named Iconix SE Asia), and therefore was also able to record these trademark transfers as part of its total sales. The company disclosed in its September 2014 filing that sales to this JV alone had generated $18.7 million, which accounted for 16 percent of its total revenue for the quarter—essentially out of thin air!

3. Recording Revenue on Receipts from Non-Revenue-Producing Transactions

So far, we have addressed bogus revenue generated from transactions that are completely lacking in economic substance and ones that may have some economic substance but lack a necessary arm's-length process. We now investigate situations in which bogus revenue arises from misclassification of cash received from non-revenue-producing activities.

Investors understand that not all cash received necessarily would be revenue or even directly pertain to the company's core operations. Some inflows are related to financing activities (borrowing and stock issuance) and others to the sale of businesses or other assets. Companies that recognize ordinary revenue or operating income from these noncore sources should be viewed suspiciously.

Question Revenue Recorded When Cash Is Received in Lending Transactions

Never confuse money received from your friendly banker with money from a customer. A bank loan must be repaid and is considered a liability. In contrast, money received from a customer in return for a service rendered is yours to keep and should be considered revenue.

Apparently, auto parts manufacturer Delphi Corporation failed to understand the distinction between a liability and revenue. In late December 2000, Delphi took out a $200 million short-term loan, posting inventory as collateral. Rather than recording the cash received as a liability that needed to be paid back, Delphi improperly recorded it as the sale of goods—as if the inventory posted as collateral had been purchased by the bank. As you will see with Delphi in Chapter 10, not only did this twisted interpretation allow Delphi to record bogus revenue; it also provided bogus cash flow from operations.

Pay Attention to Accounting for Vendor Rebates

When purchasing goods from a vendor, cash normally flows in one direction—from the customer to the vendor. Sometimes, cash will flow in the opposite direction, usually in the form of a volume rebate or refund. Booking these cash rebates as revenue would clearly be inappropriate, as they should be considered an adjustment to the cost of inventory purchased. However, the creative folks at Sunbeam did not see it that way. Sunbeam played a neat trick to boost revenue in which it advanced cash to vendors and then recorded revenue when that cash was repaid. Additionally, Sunbeam would commit to future purchases from a particular vendor in exchange for an immediate "rebate" from that vendor, which Sunbeam, or course, recorded as revenue.

Royal Ahold, owner of U.S. supermarkets Stop & Shop and Giant, played similar games with its vendor rebates. Executives manipulated vendor accounts to create fake rebates that boosted earnings and allowed the company to reach its earnings targets. Overstated rebates totaled over $700 million in 2001 and 2002, which led to massively overstated earnings. The executives who perpetrated this scheme were ultimately found guilty of fraud and sent to prison.

Similarly, in September 2014, British grocer Tesco announced that it had overstated its profits by recording too much income related to supplier discounts and rebates. Turmoil ensued as the stock fell by over 50 percent since the beginning of the year. Tesco's chairman, CEO, CFO, and other key executives and board members left the company. In September 2016, the U.K.'s Serious Fraud Office announced that it would prosecute three former employees for fraud and false accounting.

4. Recording Revenue from Appropriate Transactions, but at Inflated Amounts

The first three sections of this chapter focused on sources of revenue that were wholly inappropriate, as they lacked any economic substance, failed the necessary arm's-length test, or were derived from non-revenue-producing activities. The companies profiled in this section, on the other hand, generally meet the broad guidelines for recognizing revenue. The transgression, however (and not an insignificant one), concerns recording revenue in an amount that seems excessive or misleading to investors. Excessive or misleading revenue might result from (1) using an inappropriate methodology to recognize revenue and/or (2) grossing up revenue to make a company appear much larger than it really is.

Enron Uses an Inappropriate Methodology to Recognize Revenue
As we discussed in Chapter 1, long before Enron became infamous as the "biggest accounting fraud," for many years it operated as a small gas pipeline business in Houston, Texas. During the 1990s, the company gradually transitioned from a producer of energy to a company that facilitated trading in energy and related futures.

To understand Enron's new business, and how it would impact the company's reported financial statements, it's worth considering a simple commodity brokerage transaction. Typically, if a broker facilitates a transaction with a $100 million notional value and a 1 percent commission rate, the broker would recognize just the $1 million commission as its revenue and gross profit. Enron, however, took a much more aggressive (and inappropriate) approach to recording this type of transaction. Enron would have "grossed up" this transaction by recording revenue of $101 million offset by cost of goods sold of $100 million, resulting in the same gross profit of $1 million. This uber aggressive accounting is why Enron showed the odd combination of rapidly growing revenue and puny profit margins.

A Chance Meeting with Enron CFO Andrew Fastow

So that was our working thesis for years, but we were unable to speak to senior management people to confirm this thesis because they were locked up in prison. But in December 2015, Howard's path crossed with that of former Enron CFO Andrew Fastow, as both were invited speakers at a conference in Park City, Utah. During the Q&A of Fastow's presentation, Howard had the opportunity to describe what he believed to be the main accounting fraud (using the same commodity example as above), and he asked Andrew whether the thesis was correct. Was Enron grossing up the notional value of a transaction and counting that amount as its revenue, rather than just counting the commission earned? His first five words to the answer were, "You are fundamentally correct, but . . . ," and he then went on to describe why this underlying accounting rule was not applicable to Enron. Howard just rolled his eyes and smiled, as the thesis had been confirmed.

Watch for Companies Grossing Up Revenue to Appear to Be Much Larger

E-commerce phenom Groupon burst onto the scene in November 2008, and only 17 months later it was privately valued at a billion dollars—the quickest that any company had reached that threshold. Then by its third birthday in November 2011, Groupon went public, raising an astonishing $700 million, becoming the second largest tech IPO at that time (after Google's $1.7 billion raised in 2004). But before its public offering, Groupon had a tough time gaining SEC approval for its IPO, as it had to amend its registration statement eight times. The most consequential restatement pertained to Groupon's revenue recognition, resulting in changes that sliced its revenue by over 50 percent. (See Table 4-1.)

Table 4-1   Groupon's Gross and Net Revenue

($ thousands)	Year Ended		Six Months	
	Dec-09	Dec-10	Jun-10	Jun-11
Initial (gross)	30,471	713,365	135,807	1,597,423
Restated (net)	14,540	312,944	58,938	688,105
Difference	15,931	400,421	76,869	909,318
% inflated	110%	128%	130%	132%

Groupon's main shenanigan was trying to make the business seem larger by booking as sales the gross amount its members paid for a deal, without deducting the sizable portion it owed to the merchants. In the restated registration documents (contained in Form S-1A), the SEC mandated that Groupon change from the "gross" to "net" method, causing revenue to melt down from almost $1.6 billion to only $688 million, a decline of 57 percent during the six months ended June 2011.

Surprisingly, investors seemed to ignore this very ominous development; the November IPO proved to be a major success, with Groupon's share price jumping 31 percent on the first day traded as a public company. It closed at $26.11 on November 4 with a market value of $16 billion. But things began to unravel quickly with another (company-initiated) restatement in early 2012. And by its first anniversary in November 2012, the share price plummeted to $2.76—an astounding 90 percent decline for one of the most anticipated IPOs. Investors had seen enough, and by February 2013, CEO Andrew Mason was dismissed.

When traditional businesses migrate into e-commerce, there are often opportunities to revisit the gross vs. net revenue distinction. Take, for example,the games played by advertising agencies who began placing ads online. These companies typically record revenue for the commission fees that they earn on ads placed by their clients on television or radio spots, newspapers, or billboards. However, most agencies have approached online ads differently, electing to recognize revenue on a gross basis, thereby including the full value of the ads in reported revenue. It might seem simple enough for investors to see through this shenanigan; however, in many cases the online ad revenue is commingled with other agency fees recognized on a net basis, making it quite difficult to assess the true performance of the agency's commissions. Since online advertising tends to grow as a share of the advertising market each year, this revenue treatment has been providing an artificial boost to reported sales growth of the agencies.

Looking Ahead

This chapter and Chapter 3 both addressed techniques for inflating revenue. These tricks included either recognizing revenue too early or recording revenue that, in whole or in part, was bogus. Chapter 5 looks at techniques for inflating income, but it moves further down the Statement of Operation. While they are not part of revenue, one-time gains may create distortions in the operating or net income of a company.

5

Earnings Manipulation Shenanigan No. 3: Boosting Income Using One-Time or Unsustainable Activities

When a magician wants to make a rabbit appear out of thin air, he may tap a wand or say the magic word "abracadabra." Not to be outdone, corporate executives have their own way of creating something out of nothing when it comes to reporting earnings. Executives don't need special props, though, and they don't need to use special words like "abracadabra." All they need is a few simple techniques.

One-time gains are akin to the proverbial rabbit in the hat, magically appearing from nowhere. A struggling company may be tempted to use certain techniques that boost income by using one-time or unsustainable activities. This chapter explores such methods, which, if undetected, might confuse investors. In this chapter we examine the following two techniques used by management to give income a quick, but temporary, "shot in the arm."

Techniques to Boost Income Using One-Time or Unsustainable Activities

1. Boosting income using one-time events
2. Boosting income through misleading classifications

1. Boosting Income Using One-Time Events

Dot-Com Hysteria Had the Blue Chips Feeling Blue

During the late 1990s, "dot-com" technology start-ups captivated investors' attention, while older technology stalwarts yearned to regain their luster. Just the simple act of adding "dot-com" to the end of a company name led investors to immediately pay more for the stock. The actual economic performance and fundamental health of these businesses seemed to be of little interest to investors, who became intoxicated with the potential for insane growth in the new economy or the potential for the company to be acquired at a tremendous premium. Some of these companies flourished (Yahoo!), others joined forces with old-line businesses (AOL merged with Time Warner), and many just went bust (eToys went from a market value of $11 billion in 1999 to bankrupt in 2001). Investors were so focused on these up-and-comers that technology blue chips like IBM, Intel, and Microsoft were often viewed as old fuddy-duddies.

IBM indeed ran into a rough patch during 1999, as the company's costs increased faster than revenue. As Table 5-1 shows, cost of goods and services (COGS) grew 9.5 percent in 1999, while revenue was up 7.2 percent, resulting in a lower gross margin. However, somehow IBM's operating and pretax profits jumped a very impressive 30 percent.

The large discrepancy between revenue and operating income growth should have tipped off diligent investors to do some further digging. Since by reading this book, you are now considered a diligent investor, let's take a close look at the Income Statement found in IBM's 10-K filing (shown in Table 5-1). One thing that should immediately stand out is the 11.6 percent *decline* in "Selling, general, and administrative (SG&A) expenses," in contrast to the 9.5 percent *increase* in the COGS category. Second, the 30 percent growth in both operating and pretax income seems very surprising on just 7.2 percent sales growth, unless the company also either had a large one-time gain that was hidden from view—or had chosen another shenanigan to boost income or hide expenses.

Table 5-1   IBM's 1999 Income Statement, as Reported

($ millions, except %)	1998 Reported	1999 Reported	% Change
Revenue	81,667	87,548	7.2%
Cost of goods and services	(50,795)	(55,619)	9.5%
Gross profit	30,872	31,929	3.4%
Selling, general, and administrative expenses	(16,662)	(14,729)	(11.6%)
Research and development	(5,046)	(5,273)	4.5%
Operating income	9,164	11,927	30.2%
Nonoperating expenses	(124)	(170)	
Net income before taxes	9,040	11,757	30.0%
Income taxes	(2,712)	(4,045)	
Net income	6,328	7,712	21.9%

And that is precisely what happened. A footnote in the 1999 10-K disclosed that IBM booked a $4.1 billion gain from selling its Global Network business to AT&T and curiously included that gain as a *reduction in the SG&A expense*. In so doing, IBM magically hid its deteriorating operations from many investors.

As Table 5-2 illustrates, the results excluding the one-time gain would have appeared dreadful in comparison to IBM's reported numbers. Adjusting IBM's 1999 results by simply removing the gargantuan gain that was improperly bundled into SG&A expense would cause the expense to jump from $14.7 billion to $18.8 billion. Operating income would, in turn, decline by the same amount, from $11.9 billion to $7.9 billion. As a result, both operating and pretax income would be sliced by $4.1 billion.

Now we can compare the results (as reported versus our adjusted figures that excluded the gain) and clearly see the dramatic differences. SG&A expenses really *increased* by 12.7 percent (rather than the reported *decline* of 11.6 percent), and operating and pretax profits *declined* by 14.1 and 14.8 percent, respectively (rather than the reported *increases* of 30.2 and 30.0 percent).

Table 5-2 IBM's 1999 Income Statement, Adjusted to Exclude One-Time Gain

($ millions, except %)	1998 Adjusted	1999 Reported	% Change
Revenue	81,667	87,548	**7.2%**
Cost of goods and services	(50,795)	(55,619)	9.5%
Gross profit	30,872	31,929	3.4%
Selling, general, and administrative expenses	(16,662)	(18,786)	**12.7%**
Research and development	(5,046)	(5,273)	4.5%
Operating income	9,164	7,870	**(14.1%)**
Nonoperating expenses	(124)	(170)	
Net income before taxes	9,040	7,700	**(14.8%)**
Income taxes (at 34.4%)	(2,712)	(2,649)	
Net income	6,328	5,051	**(20.2%)**

Turning the Sale of a Business into a Recurring Revenue Stream

Some companies will sell a manufacturing plant or a business unit to another company and at the same time enter into an agreement to buy back products from that sold business unit. These transactions are common in the technology industry and are often used by companies to quickly "outsource" an in-house process. For example, a mobile phone manufacturer that decides that it no longer wants to make its own batteries may sell its battery manufacturing division to another company. At the same time, since the phone manufacturer still needs batteries for its phones, the two companies may enter into another agreement in which the phone manufacturer purchases batteries from the division that it just sold.

Not surprisingly, such transactions that commingle a one-time event (the sale of a business) and normal recurring operating activities (the sale of products to customers) create opportunities for management to use financial shenanigans. For example, the phone company may take less money for the sale of its battery business if the buyer also agrees to give the company a good deal on future battery purchases. In another type of commingled transaction, a company may sell a business at a deflated price if the buyer also agrees to purchase other goods from the seller at an inflated price.

Consider the structure of a November 2006 deal between semiconductor giant Intel Corporation and fellow chip manufacturer Marvell

Technology Group. Intel agreed to sell certain assets of its communications and application business to Marvell. At the same time, Marvell agreed to purchase a minimum number of semiconductor wafers from Intel over the next two years. A careful reading of Marvell's description of the transaction reveals something odd: Marvell agreed to purchase these wafers from Intel at *inflated* prices. (Interestingly, Intel did not disclose this, perhaps considering the amount to be insignificant.) Why would Marvell agree to overpay for this inventory?

MARVELL'S 10-Q DISCUSSION OF ITS TRANSACTION WITH INTEL

In conjunction with the acquisition of the ICAP Business, the Company entered into a supply agreement with Intel. The supply agreement obligates the Company to purchase certain finished product and sorted wafers at a contracted price from Intel for a contracted period. The contracted period can differ between finished products and sorted wafers. *Intel's pricing to the Company was greater than comparable prices available to the Company in the market in almost all cases.* In accordance with purchase accounting, the Company recorded a liability at contract signing representing the difference between Intel prices and comparable market prices for those products for which the Company had a contractual obligation. [Italics added for emphasis]

TIP

Be sure to always review both parties' disclosures on the sale of businesses to best grasp the true economics of the transactions.

Marvell certainly would not have agreed to pay an inflated price for purchases from Intel unless it was receiving something of equal value in return. Remember that Marvell and Intel negotiated the asset sale and the supply agreement concurrently. To understand the true economics of this arrangement, we must analyze both elements of the transaction together.

Economically, it would make sense for the total cash paid by Marvell for both the business and the future products to correspond with the value that Marvell was receiving from both the business acquired and the products that were later purchased. It follows, then, that if Marvell overpaid for the products, it must have underpaid for the business. In other words, Intel probably received less cash up front from the sale of the business in exchange for more cash later in the form of revenue from the sale of products. This certainly works out well for Intel, as investors are far more impressed with a recurring revenue stream than cash received from the sale of a business.

Of course, Marvell's financial reporting also benefited from paying less for the business and more for the products. (In Chapter 7, we return to Marvell and show how this arrangement provided the company with the opportunity to exert discretion over its earnings each quarter.)

Beware of Commingling the Sale of a Business with the Sale of Product
Certainly, the Intel-Marvell scheme is not a uniquely American phenom-enon. On the other side of the Pacific, Japanese technology conglomer-ate Softbank also reported impressive results from its unusual method of accounting for the sale of a business. Specifically, it seems that rather than including the entire gain in the period of the sale, Softbank deferred some of the gain and used it to benefit future-period revenue and income.

In December 2005, Softbank sold its modem rental business and con-currently entered into an agreement to provide some services to the buyer. Softbank received a total of ¥85 billion, which it split between the sale and the service agreement, allocating ¥45 billion to the business sale and the remaining ¥40 billion to future revenue under the service agreement. By commingling the asset sale with later product sales, Softbank, like Intel, could report a smaller one-time gain and a larger stream of product revenue. As a result, investors might have been tricked into believing that Softbank's sales were growing faster than the underlying economic reality.

Watch for Changes in Accounting Policies That Accelerate Recognition of Income   In 2013 Boston-based Dunkin' Brands (franchisor of Dunkin' Donuts and Baskin-Robbins) got an earnings boost from an unlikely source. Like many other chain retailers, Dunkin' Donuts sold preloaded gift cards that could be used at any national location. At the beginning of the year, the company had an accounting policy that assumed that any card that had not been used for five years was considered lost, and any remaining balance on the card was recognized as income after 60 months of inactivity. However, in the second quarter of 2013 management changed its practice to begin recognizing income for the amount that would likely go unused on an *ongoing basis*, starting from when the card was first used. This change had the effect of accelerating those gains, providing an opportune boost to reported earnings per share. Moreover, it shed a light for investors to see that management had desperately engaged in tricky accounting changes to make up for a softening franchise business.

The second part of this chapter illustrates the techniques that management may use to shift income or losses around to obfuscate any deterioration in a company's recurring operating profits.

2. Boosting Income Through Misleading Classifications

When assessing a company's business performance, it is of course important to analyze the earnings generated by the actual operations of the business (operating income). Gains and losses from interest, asset sales, investments, and other sources unrelated to operating the business (nonoperating income) are important to analyze as well—however, not in a review of a company's operating performance. Some companies will misclassify income or losses and blur the line for investors to make operating income look better.

This section identifies three types of financial statement classifications that could inflate operating (above-the-line) income: (1) shifting normal operating *expenses* (i.e., the "bad stuff") to the nonoperating section, (2) shifting nonoperating or nonrecurring *income* (i.e., the "good stuff") to the Operating section, and (3) using questionable management decisions regarding Balance Sheet classification to help offload the bad stuff or upload the good stuff.

Shifting Normal Expenses Below the Line

The most common way to shift normal operating expenses below the line involves one-time write-offs of costs that would normally appear in the Operating section. For example, a company taking a one-time charge to write off inventory or plant and equipment would effectively shift the related

expenses (i.e., cost of goods sold or depreciation) out of the Operating section to the nonoperating section and, as a result, push up operating income.

Watch for Companies That Constantly Record "Restructuring Charges"
Struggling companies often enter restructuring plans, in which they incur
nonrecurring costs. For example, if a company closes one of its offices, it
may have to pay severance to employees or a fee to break the office lease.
Companies often strip out charges related to a restructuring plan from their
operating income and present them below the line. If done appropriately,
this treatment is helpful for investors, as it provides insight into the performance of the company's recurring operations. In general, with proper disclosure of restructuring charges by management, investors should be better
armed to assess the more important recurring activities of a company.

Some companies, however, abuse this presentation by recording "restructuring" charges in virtually every period. Investors should view these charges
with skepticism, as the company may be bundling normal operating expenses
into these charges and trying to pass them off as one-time in nature. For example, telecom network equipment supplier Alcatel has recorded below-the-
line restructuring charges in just about every quarter since the early 1990s.
Annually, these charges amounted to hundreds of millions of dollars, and
occasionally billions. Whirlpool also recorded restructuring charges nearly
every year since 1990 until present, prompting the SEC, in an October 2016
correspondence letter to the company, to challenge management: "Please
explain to us why these are not normal, recurring cash expenses necessary to
operate your business."

Watch for Companies That Shift Losses to Discontinued Operations An
easy trick that can magically improve a company's operating profit starts
with an announcement of plans to sell off a money-losing division. Consider
a struggling company with three divisions producing the following operating results: Division A, $100,000 income; Division B, $250,000 income;
and Division C, $400,000 *loss*. The company would report a $50,000 net
loss—unless it had decided to put Division C up for sale at the beginning
of the period and account for it as a "discontinued operation." In so doing,

that entire $400,000 loss would be moved below the line and most likely be ignored by investors. Magically, although the company still operates all three divisions at a combined loss of $50,000, it would report headline operating income of $350,000 and an "unimportant" $400,000 below-the-line loss. We consider this trick no different from a dishonest golfer who counts only those shots that he likes and ignores those that wind up in the water or completely off the course. Using that approach, all golfers would shoot under par.

Consider how Sabre Corporation cleverly inflated its income from continuing operations shortly before selling its Travelocity division to Expedia. Once Sabre decided to sell this business, as required by GAAP, it shifted all revenue and expenses of this money-losing business to "discontinued operations." In so doing, Sabre artificially inflated its income from continuing operations since the business that previously deflated the company's earnings (Travelocity) was treated as if it no longer was part of Sabre's business. Of course, this money-losing business had not yet been sold, but it was all but ignored by investors. Astute investors might have noticed that Sabre had increased the historical allocation of costs to the Travelocity segment after it was designated as a discontinued operation, leaving the remaining business segments with lower expenses and higher profits.

Specifically, in its S-1 filing (before the online travel site was designated as "discontinued"), the Travelocity segment reported selling, general, and administrative expenses of $331 million for 2013. Subsequently, when Travelocity was separated out as a discontinued business, the amount of selling, general, and administrative expenses that were removed from continuing operations jumped to $389 million for the same 2013 period. This higher allocation of cost had the effect of making the rest of the business appear more profitable. Sure enough, following the divestiture, Sabre's reported operating expenses increased back to the normal level.

Shifting Nonoperating and Nonrecurring Income Above the Line

As we pointed out, bundling normal operating expenses into a restructuring charge would be a relatively easy game to play. Management would simply need to convince the auditor that a write-off would produce more conservative earnings. Shifting nonoperating income above the line, in contrast, is a bit more complicated and might sometimes be harder for management to put past careful investors. But that won't stop companies from trying. As we illustrated with IBM, inflating operating income by including a one-time gain from selling a business could mislead investors about a company's true underlying economic health.

Watch for Companies That Include Investment Income as Revenue   Investors should be particularly alert when companies include nonoperating gains or investment income in revenue. Boston Chicken, the franchisor of the Boston Market restaurant chain, camouflaged its deteriorating business by including in revenue its interest income and various fees charged to the franchisees. While treating interest income as revenue clearly would be appropriate for banks and other financial institutions, it certainly sounds a bit unusual for a restaurant.

Boston Chicken's inclusion of investment income as part of revenue cleverly hid its dire financial situation. As a result, many investors failed to notice that Boston Chicken had been losing money in its core restaurant operations. Indeed, all the company's profits came from noncore activities, such as interest income on loans or various service fees charged to these same franchisees. One huge (but apparently ignored) warning in the 1996 Annual Report was that franchisee-owned restaurants were losing a ton of money. The losses grew to $156.5 million in 1996 from $148.3 million during the prior year.

With franchisees losing so much money, investors should have wondered how Boston Chicken, the franchisor and owner of some of the restaurants, could be reporting such strong profits itself. A little digging would have answered that question. The main source of revenue and operating income was not restaurant customers but *the franchisees themselves.* Boston Chicken initially raised capital (equity and debt) from the market and lent the money to franchisees. As the franchisees began paying off the loans, Boston Chicken recorded substantial amounts of interest income and other fees and classified such inflows as revenue. Ominously, this ancillary revenue and income was becoming the predominant portion of the company's reported operating

income. Because this income had been bundled with restaurant sales revenue, detection was difficult, but not impossible for careful investors.

Be Suspicious of Inflated Operating Income Related to Subsidiaries
Companies can produce misleadingly strong revenue and operating income
growth simply by benefiting from one of the quirks of consolidation
accounting. Let's look at the accounting if a company decided to form several majority-owned joint ventures, owning 60 percent of each. Accounting
rules require that the units be consolidated and that the "parent" report all
the revenue and operating expenses as operating income (that is, above the
line) as if it were its own; the 40 percent owned by others would be subtracted later on the Income Statement (shown below the line). Consider this
hypothetical situation assuming a subsidiary with total revenue of $1 million
and total expenses of $400,000. Under accounting rules, the parent that
owns 60 percent of the subsidiary still reports 100 percent of the revenue
and operating expenses, or a $600,000 operating profit. Since it owns not
100 but 60 percent, the 40 percent difference, or $240,000 (40 percent of
$600,000), is subtracted below the line. Thus, investors will see an operating
profit of $600,000, not the real economic profit of $360,000 (or 60 percent
of $600,000), which would be less visible. Is it any wonder that so many
subsidiaries are 51 percent owned? Surely, including 100 percent of the revenue above the line and subtracting those 49 percent profits owned by others
below the line seems an awfully enticing outcome.

Using Discretion Regarding Balance Sheet Classification
to Boost Operating Income

The final part of this section discusses how companies might produce misleadingly attractive income by offloading losses to or uploading income from
the Balance Sheet.

If executives of a company believe that they exercise significant influence
over a subsidiary or other entity (but do not control it), a proportionate share
of the entity's income or loss should flow to the Income Statement (under
the equity method of accounting). Conversely, if the company lacks such
influence, the Balance Sheet account related to the joint venture is simply

adjusted periodically to fair value. Thus, shenanigan opportunities abound for people in management who wish to push income onto the Income Statement by asserting that they possess that influence in periods when the income from a subsidiary is strong, or to push losses off to the Balance Sheet by stating that no significant influence exists when the venture's operations are weaker.

Accounting Capsule:
Accounting for Investments in Other Companies

For a small investment in a company (typically under 20 percent), the owner presents the investment at fair value on its Balance Sheet. If the investment is designated as a *trading security*, changes in fair value are reflected on the Income Statement. If it is instead designated as *available for sale*, changes in fair value are presented as an offset to equity, with no impact on earnings (unless permanent impairment exists).

For a medium-sized investment in a company (typically 20 to 50 percent), the owner reports its proportional share of the investment's earnings as a single line on the Income Statement. This is called the "equity method."

For a large investment in a company (typically over 50 percent), the owner fully merges the investment's financial statements into its own. This is called "consolidation."

Enron Boosts Operating Income by Shifting Losses
on Joint Ventures to the Balance Sheet

The executives at Enron understood perhaps better than anyone else the benefit of using nonconsolidated joint ventures to offload debt and losses. In the mid-1990s, Enron began building out a series of new ventures that would require massive infusions of capital and would probably produce large losses during their early years. Management no doubt contemplated the potentially damaging impact of including the debt on the Balance Sheet and the big losses on the Income Statement. Enron knew that lenders and credit rating agencies would blanch if it showed bulging loans payable, and that investors would disapprove of big losses and the earnings dilution that would come from equity financing. Since these traditional forms of financing seemed problematic, Enron developed a somewhat unique and certainly very unorthodox strategy. It created thousands of partnerships (ostensibly under accounting rules) that it hoped would not be consolidated and, as a result, would keep all this new debt off its Balance Sheet. Moreover, Enron believed that this complicated structure would also help hide the expected economic losses (or, whenever possible, pull in gains) from these early-stage ventures.

Interestingly, the capital that Enron contributed to some of these joint ventures turned out to be nothing other than its own stock. In some cases, the partnerships themselves even held Enron stock among their investment holdings. As its stock price jumped over time, the value of the joint venture assets likewise increased, as did Enron's own equity stake in these partnerships. This trick allowed Enron to recognize approximately $85 million in earnings simply because its own stock price increased during a fabulous bull market.

So Enron's rapidly appreciating stock price became the "drug" that drove up the value of its partnership stakes and its income. In one period alone, Enron generated a whopping $126 million from a joint venture. Curiously, when the stock began its rapid descent, Enron must have developed a severe case of amnesia and simply forgot to report the resulting $90 million loss to shareholders. Instead, Enron conveniently announced that the results remained "unconsolidated" and, of course, were not included on the Income Statement. So by Enron's rules, on the very same investment vehicle, gains were included and losses were hidden from investors' view. In other words, for Enron it was—heads I win, tails I still win! Well, we all know how that story ended.

Looking Ahead

Now we can catch our collective breaths for a moment and reflect, as we have reached an important stage in the book. The end of this chapter marks the completion of the third of the three chapters that focus on techniques that inflate current-period profits by recognizing too much revenue or other income, such as one-time gains on events or from questionable management assessments.

The next two chapters complete the lesson on inflating profits, but they focus on reporting too few expenses. Chapter 6 ("Earnings Manipulation Shenanigan No. 4: Shifting Current Expenses to a Later Period") shows how expenses can be hidden on the Balance Sheet and, as a result, shifted to a later period. Chapter 7 ("Earnings Manipulation Shenanigan No. 5: Employing Other Techniques to Hide Expenses or Losses") describes gimmicks for keeping expenses out of investors' view today and, in some cases, forever.

6

Earnings Manipulation Shenanigan No. 4: Shifting Current Expenses to a Later Period

The Texas two-step is a vibrant country and western dance made popular by the 1980s film *Urban Cowboy*. Once a simple barn dance, the version of the two-step that is danced today has evolved to include moves borrowed from the fox-trot and swing. Dancers whirl around the floor and routinely swap partners, providing great entertainment for their fellow dancers and for observers as well.

Companies account for their costs and expenditures in a similar two-step accounting dance. Step 1 occurs at the time of the expenditure—when the cost has been paid, but the related benefit has not yet been received. At Step 1, the expenditure represents a *future benefit* to the company and is therefore recorded on the Balance Sheet as an asset. Step 2 happens when the benefit is received. At this point, the cost should be shifted from the Balance Sheet to the Income Statement and recorded as an expense.

This accounting two-step is danced at different tempos, depending on whether the cost is related to a benefit with a long-term or a short-term horizon. Costs with a long-term benefit sometimes require a slower dance in which the cost remains on the Balance Sheet and is recorded as an expense gradually (e.g., equipment with a useful life of 20 years). Costs that provide a short-term benefit require a fast-paced dance in which the two steps happen virtually simultaneously. Such costs spend no time on the Balance Sheet, but instead they are recorded as expenses (e.g., most typical operating expenses, such as salaries and electricity costs).

Companies can exert their own influence over the speed at which they dance the two-step, and this discretion can have significant implications for earnings. Diligent investors should assess whether management is improperly keeping costs frozen at Step 1 on the Balance Sheet, instead of continuing the dance and moving them to Step 2 as expenses on the Income Statement. This chapter shows four techniques that management uses to exploit the two-step process by improperly keeping costs on the Balance Sheet, thereby preventing them from reducing earnings until a later period.

Techniques to Shift Current Expenses to a Later Period

1. Excessively capitalizing normal operating expenses

2. Amortizing costs too slowly

3. Failing to write down assets with impaired value

4. Failing to record expenses for uncollectible receivables and devalued investments

1. Excessively Capitalizing Normal Operating Expenses

The first section of this chapter focuses on a very common abuse of the two-step process: management's taking only one step when two are required. In other words, management improperly records costs on the Balance Sheet as an asset (or "capitalizes" the costs), instead of expensing them immediately.

Accounting Capsule:
Assets and Expenses

For this discussion, it is helpful to think of assets as falling into one of two categories: (1) those that are expected to produce a future benefit (e.g., inventory, equipment, and prepaid insurance) and (2) those that are ultimately expected to be exchanged for another asset such as cash (e.g., receivables and investments). Assets that are expected to provide a future benefit are actually close cousins of expenses: they both represent costs incurred to grow a business. The key distinction between these assets and expenses is timing.

For example, assume that a company purchases a two-year insurance policy. At its inception, the entire amount represents a future benefit and would be classified as an asset. After one year's benefit has been received, half the costs would be shown as an asset and the other half as an expense. After the second year, none of the costs would remain as an asset, and the remaining half still in the asset group would be expensed.

Improperly Capitalizing Routine Operating Expenses

At the height of the 1990s' dot-com boom, telecom services behemoth WorldCom signed many long-term network access arrangements to lease line capacity from other telecommunication carriers. These agreements included fees that WorldCom paid for the right to use other companies' telecommunication networks. At first, WorldCom properly accounted for these costs as an expense on its Income Statement.

With the technology meltdown beginning in 2000, WorldCom's revenue growth began to slow, and investors started paying more attention to the company's large operating expenses. And line costs were, by far, WorldCom's largest operating expense. The company became concerned about its ability to meet the expectations of Wall Street analysts. Disappointment would surely devastate investors.

So WorldCom decided to use a simple trick to keep earnings afloat. In 2000, it began concealing some line costs through a sudden, and very significant, change in its accounting. (Red flag!) Rather than record these costs as expenses, WorldCom capitalized large portions of them as assets on the

Balance Sheet. The company did this to the tune of billions of dollars, which had the impact of grossly understating expenses and overstating profits from 2000 to early 2002.

Warning Signs of Improper Capitalization of Line Costs

When WorldCom began capitalizing billions in line costs, it clearly continued paying the money out, although the Income Statement reported fewer expenses. As pointed out in Chapters 1 and 2, a careful reading of the Statement of Cash Flows would have flashed a bright light on deteriorating free cash flow (that is, cash flow from operations minus capital expenditures). Table 6-1 shows how free cash flow went from a *positive $2.3 billion* in 1999 (the year before capitalizing the line costs) to a *negative $3.8 billion* (an astounding $6.1 billion deterioration). Well-trained investors should have seen this trend as a sign of trouble.

Table 6-1   WorldCom's Free Cash Flow

($ millions)	1999	2000
Reported cash flow from operations	11,005	7,666
Subtract: Capital expenditures (capex)	(8,716)	(11,484)
Free cash flow	2,289	(3,818)

Specifically, WorldCom's sizable increase in capital spending should have raised questions. It belied WorldCom's own guidance (given at the beginning of the year) for relatively flat capital expenditures, and it came at a time when technology spending, in general, was collapsing. Indeed, this reported increase in capital spending was fiction; in reality, it was largely the result of WorldCom's changing its accounting practices to shift normal operating costs (i.e., line costs) to the Balance Sheet to inflate profits. Diligent investors should have spotted the 32 percent jump (from $8.7 billion to $11.5 billion) in capital expenditures and questioned why this spending made sense during a technology slowdown in which the company's operating cash flow had contracted by 30 percent. Flagging such a massive increase in spending would prove to be an important first step in sniffing out one of the biggest accounting frauds in history.

> ### WARNING SIGNS OF IMPROPERLY CAPITALIZING NORMAL OPERATING EXPENSES
>
> - Unwarranted improvement in profit margins and a large jump in certain assets
> - A big unexpected decline in free cash flow, with an equally sizable increase in cash flow from operations
> - Unexpected increases in capital expenditures that belie the company's original guidance and market conditions

Watch for Improper Capitalization of Marketing and Solicitation Costs
Marketing and solicitation costs are also examples of normal operating expenses that produce near-term benefits to a business. Most companies need to spend money to advertise their products or services. Accounting guidelines normally require that companies expense these payments immediately as normal recurring short-term operating costs. However, certain companies take a more aggressive approach to capitalize these costs and spread them out over several periods. Consider Internet pioneer AOL and its accounting treatment of solicitation costs during its critical mid-1990s growth period.

Until 1994, AOL treated its solicitation costs for new customers as an operating expense. However, in 1994 AOL started recording these costs as assets on its Balance Sheet, called "deferred membership acquisition costs" (DMAC). As shown in Table 6-2, AOL initially capitalized $26 million (representing 22 percent of sales and 17 percent of total assets) and then amortized those costs over the next 12 months.

Table 6-2   AOL's Deferred Membership Acquisition Costs

($ millions)	1993	1994	1995	1996
Revenue	52.0	115.7	394.3	1,093.9
Operating income	1.7	4.2	(21.4)	65.2
Net income	1.4	2.2	(35.8)	29.8
Total assets	39.3	155.2	405.4	958.8
Deferred membership acquisition costs	—	**26.0**	**77.2**	**314.2**

Notice the dramatic increase in the DMAC balance over the next few years. By June 1996, DMAC on the Balance Sheet had ballooned to $314 million, or 33 percent of total assets and 61 percent of shareholders' equity. Had these costs been expensed as incurred, AOL's 1995 pretax loss would have been approximately $98 million instead of $21 million (including the write-off of DMAC that existed as of the end of fiscal year 1994), and AOL's 1996 pretax income of $62 million would have been *transformed to a loss of $175 million*. On a quarterly basis, the effect of capitalizing DMAC was that AOL reported profits for six of the eight quarters in fiscal years 1995 and 1996, rather than reporting losses for each period.

Investors should have been alarmed when reviewing these numbers for several reasons. First, the company made the *change from expensing* these costs to the much more aggressive approach of capitalizing them. Second, the *enormous growth* in the unamortized DMAC represented a material underreporting of expenses and overreporting of profits during these three years. Third, AOL had merely shifted expenses from earlier periods to later periods, and those costs would *materially dampen expected earnings in those future periods*.

AOL naturally tried to justify its accounting choice, asserting that it fell under an exception provided in the accounting rules (SOP 93–7). To qualify for the exception and be permitted to capitalize solicitation costs, a company would have to show *persuasive evidence* that the advertising would result in future benefits *similar* to the effects of the company's prior direct-response advertising activities.

The SEC disagreed with AOL's treatment, stating that the company had failed to meet the essential requirements of SOP 93–7 because "the unstable business environment precluded reliable forecasts of future net revenues." Investors required no basic understanding of this cryptic accounting rule to realize that something smelled funny. AOL's change to a more aggressive accounting policy and the sheer magnitude of that policy's impact on earnings should have been more than enough to give astute investors indigestion.

Watch for Earnings Boosts After Adopting New Accounting Rules
Occasionally, the decision to begin capitalizing operating costs comes not

from a management whim but from compliance with a new accounting rule promulgated by the standard setters. While criticism of management for making such a change would clearly be unfair and unjustified, investors should recognize that any improvement in profit resulting from the change would be ephemeral and unrelated to operational success. For example, Lucent (now part of Alcatel) obtained a nice earnings boost by starting to capitalize internal-use software costs, mandated by a new accounting rule.

> **TIP**
>
> Regardless of the legitimacy of an accounting change, investors should strive to understand the impact that this change had on earnings growth. Simply put: *any growth related to the change will not recur.* To be maintained, the growth must be replaced with improved operational performance.

Be Wary of Unusual Asset Accounts on the Balance Sheet   In the year before its bankruptcy and fraud investigation, Syntax-Brillian began reporting on the Balance Sheet curious new asset accounts called "tooling" and "inventory" deposits. The company provided minimal and confusing details about these assets, stating that they represented deposits to the company's primary supplier of inventory (Kolin), according to reports. Oddly, both accounts dwarfed the total amount of inventory reported on the company's Balance Sheet. Moreover, not only was Kolin Syntax-Brillian's largest supplier, but it also was a related party, owning over 10 percent of the company's stock and serving as a counterparty to several joint ventures.

Investors had reason to be skeptical about these new asset accounts, not only because of their unusual and related-party nature, but also because of the rapidly increasing balances. As shown in Table 6-3, Syntax-Brillian reported a startling $70.0 million in "inventory deposits with Kolin" at June 2007, after having no such deposits in the preceding three quarters. Similarly, "tooling deposits with Kolin" were nonexistent in June 2006 but grew consistently over the next year, reaching $65.3 million at June 2007. A surge in any unusual asset accounts like these, particularly ones that involve a related party, should send investors running for the exits.

Table 6-3   Syntax-Brillian's Unusual Asset Accounts

($ millions)	Q3, 3/06	Q4, 6/06	Q1, 9/06	Q2, 12/06	Q3, 3/07	Q4, 6/07
Inventory deposits with Kolin	8.0	5.1	—	—	—	70.0
Inventory deposits with vendor	—	—	—	—	—	8.3
Tooling deposits with Kolin	—	—	15.2	26.3	39.6	65.3

WARNING SIGN

A new or unusual asset account (particularly one that is increasing rapidly) may signal improper capitalization.

Capitalizing Permissible Items, but in Too Great an Amount

Accounting guidelines permit companies to capitalize some operating costs, but only to a certain extent or if certain specific conditions can be met. We will call these costs *hybrids*—that is, the costs are recorded partially as an expense and partially as an asset.

Capitalizing Software Development Costs   One operating cost that commonly finds its way to the Balance Sheet, particularly at technology companies, is the cost incurred to develop software-based products. Early-stage research and development costs for software would typically be expensed. Later-stage costs (those incurred once a project reaches "technological feasibility") would typically be capitalized. Investors should be alert for companies that capitalize a disproportionately large amount of their software costs or that change accounting policies and begin to capitalize costs, particularly if those costs are out of line with industry practices.

Watch for an Increase in Software Capitalization   An accelerating rate of software capitalization is often a red flag that earnings growth is benefiting from keeping more costs on the Balance Sheet. The Ultimate Software Group (ULTI), a Florida-based developer of human resources software, went from not capitalizing any software costs in 2011 to capitalizing $19 million (22 percent of its total R&D spend) just two years later. The capitalized costs were quite material, amounting to nearly 5 percent of total sales and

44 percent of the company's $43 million in operating income in 2013. This practice shifted significant costs to the Balance Sheet and inflated profits.

Watch for Growing Advances or Prepayments   Consider the case of snack foods company Diamond Foods (DMND), purveyor of Emerald nuts, Pop Secret popcorn, and Kettle Chips. As walnut prices spiked in early 2010, Diamond found itself in a situation where it needed to compensate its walnut vendors for the increase in price for that year's crop. Facing pressure from investors to continue its 11-quarter streak of outperformance, CFO Steven Neil orchestrated a scheme in which the company would pay the walnut growers to make them whole for the 2009 crop, but they would call the payment an "advance" on the next year's crop. This sleight of hand gave Neil the justification he needed to capitalize these payments on the Balance Sheet, rather than expense them in the current year. Despite this sneaky trick, the walnut growers knew that this payment was not really an advance on the 2010 crop; rather it related to the already-delivered 2009 crop.

The truth eventually came out as investor scrutiny led to an internal investigation. DMND wound up restating its results in November 2012 to properly account for the cost of acquiring walnuts, and the company's stock price fell to $17, down from a high of $90 in 2011. The SEC ultimately charged the company and its CFO Neil with fraud.

Improper Capitalization of Costs Also Inflates Operating Cash Flow

While normal operating costs are reflected as an operating cash outflow, capitalized costs are typically presented as capital expenditures in the Investing section of the Statement of Cash Flows. By capitalizing normal operating costs, companies inflate not only earnings, but also operating cash flow. We present this topic in Chapter 11, "Cash Flow Shenanigan No. 2: Moving Operating Cash Outflows to Other Sections."

2. Amortizing Costs Too Slowly

Okay, put those dancing shoes back on as we get ready for the second step in our two-step accounting dance. Now that we have completed Step 1, we have those costs capitalized, but the related business benefit has yet to be realized. Step 2 involves recording those costs as expenses, shifting them from the Balance Sheet to the Income Statement.

The nature of a cost and the timing of its related benefit dictate the length of time that this cost remains on the Balance Sheet. For example, expenditures to purchase or manufacture inventory remain on the Balance Sheet until the inventory is sold and revenue recorded. On the other hand, expenditures to purchase equipment or a manufacturing facility provide a much longer-term benefit. These assets remain on the Balance Sheet for the duration of their useful lives, over which they gradually become expenses through depreciation or amortization.

Investors should raise concerns if costs remain on the Balance Sheet as assets for too long, as evidenced by an unusually long amortization horizon. Additionally, if management decides to lengthen the amortization period, that should raise a loud warning signal.

Be Alert for Boosts to Income by Stretching Out the Amortization Period

Remember how our friends at AOL were spending a boatload of money to solicit new clients (as shown in Table 6-2)? We discussed the 1994 change in accounting, attributing it to an aggressive capitalization of advertising costs and the decision to spread those costs over the following 12-month period. This aggressive capitalization completely misled investors, who believed that the company had been profitable, although it continued hemorrhaging cash and sustaining real economic losses.

Unfortunately for investors, the story did not end with that one trick. Beginning on July 1, 1995, AOL decided to double the amortization period for these exploding marketing costs from 12 to 24 months. Extending the amortization period meant that the costs remained on the Balance Sheet much longer and reduced expenses with only half the impact each period. That change alone inflated profits by $48.1 million (to a *reported profit of $29.8 million from a loss of $18.3 million*). This simple accounting adjustment helped hide AOL's huge losses from investors.

A careful review of the Statement of Cash Flows, however, would have revealed the problem. Indeed, AOL's $29.8 million of net income in June 1996 had been much higher than its operating cash outflow of $66.7 million, a staggering shortfall of $96.5 million. By carefully reading the footnotes, investors would have noticed that the aggressive capitalization of marketing costs inflated operating and net income. (See Table 6-4.) With more typical treatment of solicitation costs as expenses, AOL would have posted huge operating and net losses ($154.8 million and $124.2 million, respectively), which would surely have led to a stock price correction.

Table 6-4   AOL 1996 Results Reported and Adjusted

($ millions)	As Reported	Adjustment	Adjusted
Operating income	82.2	(237.0)	(154.8)
Net income	29.8	(154.0)	(124.2)

Be Particularly Wary of Big Income Boosts from Stretching Out Depreciable Lives

A company that chooses an overly long depreciation or amortization period generally would be considered guilty of using aggressive accounting. A more serious offense, however, is a company's *changing to a longer period*. This often suggests that the company's business may be in trouble and that it feels compelled to change accounting assumptions to camouflage the deterioration. Regardless of how management tries to justify such changes, investors should be wary.

Consider how Intel revised its depreciation schedule for manufacturing equipment in 2015. Based on an internal review, management determined that the assumed useful lives should be extended from four to five years. This change alone lowered the company's depreciation expense by approximately $1.5 billion in 2016, with roughly half the benefit accruing to gross margin, which had come under pressure as competition in the industry intensified.

While Intel may have had good rationale for arriving at the new estimate (management cites longer product life cycles and increased reuse of machinery), the decision to make the change at a particular time often signals an underlying weakness in the business or management's anxiety about the future. Healthy and confident companies are far less likely to tinker with these types of accounting assumptions that only provide optical benefits.

Be Alert for Slow Amortization of Inventory Costs

In most industries, the process of turning inventory into an expense is straightforward: when a sale takes place, inventory is transferred to the expense called "cost of goods sold" (COGS). In certain businesses, though, determining when and how inventory turns into expense can be more complicated.

In the aerospace business, for example, the initial development costs of a new jet fighter, which could be quite substantial, might first be included on the Balance Sheet as inventory and later amortized once customers start taking delivery of the aircraft.

One Classic Example: Lockheed's Ill-Fated TriStar L-1011 Program

Lockheed (which later merged with Martin Marietta to become Lockheed Martin) provides one of the best examples of difficulties in determining how best to amortize development costs for new aircraft. Unlike a traditional retailer, for example, which amortizes inventory costs to COGS quickly when a product is sold, aircraft manufacturers place development costs in inventory on their Balance Sheet for years, as development and manufacturing are a multiyear endeavor.

During the 1970s and early 1980s, Lockheed was pouring billions into developing a new aircraft, called TriStar L-1011. The accounting method used for planes is known as the "program method." As each plane in the program was sold (initial estimated total was 300 aircraft), Lockheed would assign a presumed average cost, regardless of the actual production costs. So any actual costs *greater than the assigned costs* (based on the estimate) would be capitalized until the production cost curve had come down. Since Lockheed expected that costs in producing later planes would be less than the average, the previously capitalized excess costs would be amortized into the costs of these more recent (and profitable) later planes. In theory, this sounds fine—unless, of course, the incremental cost per plane always exceeds the incremental revenue. Unfortunately for Lockheed, that indeed was the case.

By late 1975, Lockheed had accumulated approximately $500 million of costs in its "production costs curve" asset account within inventory, and the ill-fated TriStar program showed no signs of profitability. Indeed, things continued to worsen, as cumulative losses from the period 1975–1981 totaled $974 million. (See Table 6-5.) The handwriting was on the wall, and Lockheed began writing off some of the $500 million "blob." But rather than write off the entire amount when the losses became virtually certain, it used an "installment plan," at the rate of $50 million annually (even though the company continued posting staggering losses on the TriStar program).

Table 6-5   Lockheed: Annual Losses from the TriStar L1011 Program

($ millions)	1975	1976	1977	1978	1979	1980	1981	Total
TriStar Losses	94	125	120	119	188	199	129	974

Program accounting is not just an accounting quirk of the past; it persists today at the largest aviation companies. Just like Lockheed did in the 1970s with its TriStar L-1011 program, Boeing uses program accounting for its state-of-the-art 787 Dreamliner. Boeing started developing the Dreamliner in 2003, but it was not until 2011 that it started delivering planes to customers. There were many production and development issues along the way that wreaked havoc with the company's delivery timeline and, more interestingly, with the program accounting estimates. For example, in 2009, after several failed test flights, Boeing wrote off nearly $2.5 billion in program accounting inventory costs that it no longer expected to recoup. Boeing eventually solved its major development problems, and production accelerated in the early 2010s leading to a substantial amount of program accounting inventory. By December 2015, Boeing had accumulated a whopping $28.5 billion of these production costs on its Balance Sheet to be recognized as cost of revenue in the years ahead.

3. Failing to Write Down Assets with Impaired Value

So far, we have warned about two abuses of our two-step accounting dance. The first section discussed taking only one step when two steps would be required (i.e., improperly capitalizing a cost that should be expensed). The second section discussed taking the second step way too slowly (i.e., amortizing assets over a much longer life than was appropriate). In this section, we warn about a third abuse: freezing the dance between Step 1 and Step 2—that is, failing to record an expense for costs that had been properly capitalized but that diminished in value before the expected benefit was received.

Failure to Write Off Impaired Plant Assets

It is not enough for companies to simply depreciate fixed assets on a rigid schedule and assume that nothing can ever happen to change that plan. Management must continually review these assets for possible impairment and record an expense whenever the assumed future benefits fall below the book value. To illustrate, consider a piece of equipment that management first assumed would last for 10 years but that breaks down permanently during year 5. Once it's out of service, the original depreciation schedule should be abandoned, and the remaining asset balance must be moved to the Expense section immediately. If the company instead chooses to continue depreciating the asset according to the original 10-year plan, it will have failed to write down an appropriately capitalized cost that had later become impaired. Not surprisingly, companies that announce big restructuring charges (EM Shenanigan No. 7) are often trying to "clean house" after failing to write off impaired assets appropriately in earlier periods.

Failure to Write Off Obsolete Inventory

Companies naturally build up inventory in anticipation of selling their products to customers. Sometimes, however, the demand for a product fails to meet a company's expectations. As a result, the company may have to lower its prices to move the less-marketable inventory. Or it may have to write off the inventory completely. Management must routinely estimate its "excess and obsolete" inventory and reduce its inventory balance accordingly by recording an expense (often called "inventory obsolescence expense"). However, unlike the depreciation of fixed assets such as equipment, no predetermined rate would have been established for which inventory would be reduced. Thus, these adjustments are subject to a higher level of management discretion and potential manipulation.

Management can inflate earnings by failing to record a necessary expense for excess and obsolete inventory. However, this omission will come back to bite the company, as earnings will be pressured at the time when the inventory is sold at a deep discount (or thrown on the trash heap). Investors should monitor a company's obsolescence expense (and the related inventory reserve) to ensure that the company does not inflate its profits by changing estimates. Regardless of the justification given by management for recording a lower expense, the impact is an artificial boost to earnings.

Vitesse Semiconductor conveniently decided to record no inventory obsolescence expense in 2003, after recording charges of $30.5 million in 2002 and $46.5 million in 2001. No doubt Vitesse's decision to record no obsolescence expense in 2003 helped its gross profit double (to $83.2 million from $41.6 million the prior year) on a mere 3 percent increase in sales. We'll check back in with Vitesse later in this chapter to see how things worked out for the firm.

Watch for an Unexpected Inventory Buildup   Investors should monitor a company's inventory level by calculating its days' sales of inventory (DSI). Just as days' sales outstanding (DSO), introduced in Chapter 3, standardizes receivables when compared with revenue in a period, DSI standardizes the inventory balance relative to inventory sold (i.e., cost of goods sold) in a period. This calculation helps investors determine whether an increase in the absolute level of inventory is in line with the overall growth of the business or whether it might be a harbinger of margin pressure.

Sometimes a company will stock up on inventory heading into a period of expected increased demand and rapid sales growth. While this may be a perfectly legitimate business strategy, companies use it as a common excuse to justify unwarranted inventory growth. When presented with this reasoning as an explanation for increased inventory, investors should determine whether the strategy had been planned before the inventory buildup or whether the strategy was hatched ex post facto as a defensive response to the inventory buildup. Investors should be skeptical if no mention of this growth strategy had previously been made.

An additional measure can be used to test whether an inventory buildup might be justified by upcoming demand: simply compare the growth in the absolute level of inventory with the company's expected revenue growth. If inventory growth far exceeds the expected sales growth, the inventory bulge is probably unwarranted and a concern for investors.

4. Failing to Record Expenses for Uncollectible Receivables and Devalued Investments

Recall the two broad categories of assets discussed earlier in the chapter: assets created from costs that management expects to produce a future benefit (e.g., inventory, equipment, and prepaid insurance) and assets created from sales or investments that will be exchanged for an asset such as cash (e.g., receivables and investments). The first three sections of this chapter featured games that are played with the flow of the first category of assets to the Income Statement, or as we presented it, manipulating the two-step accounting dance. In this concluding section of the chapter, we focus on games played with the other category of assets. Specifically, we show how companies can inflate earnings by failing to turn these assets into expenses when a clear loss in value has occurred.

Some lucky companies have customers that always pay their bills in full and hold only investments that never decline in value. Such companies are rare indeed. Most companies will have a certain number of deadbeat clients and the occasional clunker in their investment portfolio. Heck, even Warren Buffett strikes out from time to time.

When this happens, companies cannot just close their eyes and pray that all their receivables will eventually be collected. Accounting rules require that certain assets be regularly written down to their net realizable value (accountants' lingo for the actual amount you expect to get paid). Accounts receivable should be written down each period by recording an estimated expense for likely bad debts. Similarly, lenders should record an expense (or loan loss) each quarter to account for the anticipated deadbeat borrowers. Additionally, investments that experience a permanent decline in value must be written down by recording an impairment expense. Failing to take any of these charges will result in overstated profits.

Failure to Adequately Reserve for Uncollectible Customer Receivables

Companies must routinely adjust their accounts receivable balance to reflect expected customer defaults. This entails recording an expense on the Income Statement ("bad debts expense") and a reduction of accounts receivable on the Balance Sheet (the "allowance for doubtful accounts," which offsets gross receivables). Failing to record sufficient bad debts expense, or inappropriately reversing past bad debts expense, creates artificial profits.

Watch for a Decline in Bad Debts Expense   Our friends at Vitesse Semiconductor must have conveniently forgotten what it means to accrue for expenses. In the last section, we saw that Vitesse failed to accrue any inventory obsolescence expense in 2003 after recording a $30.5 million charge the previous year. The company also decided to record just $1.9 million in bad debts expense after incurring $14.3 million in the previous year. Tack on an additional reduction in an expense for estimated sales returns, and Vitesse accrued just $2.2 million in estimated expenses during 2003 versus $49.9 million in such expenses during 2002. Had Vitesse accrued these expenses at the same percentage of revenue as in the previous year, its operating income would have been approximately $50 million lower. All these tricks at a company with only $162 million in annual revenue created a huge distortion for investors. So it should be no surprise that a board investigation in 2006 uncovered a laundry list of accounting problems, many of which involved improper accounting for revenue and receivables.

> TIP
>
> When all reserve accruals are moving in the wrong direction (i.e., declining), head for the hills!

Watch for a Decline in Allowance for Doubtful Accounts   Under normal business conditions, a company's allowance for doubtful accounts (ADA) will grow at a rate like that of gross accounts receivable. A sharp decline in the allowance coupled with a rise in receivables often signals that a company has failed to record enough bad debts expense and has therefore overstated earnings.

Such a decline occurred at publisher Scholastic Corporation. Its accounts receivable balance jumped 5 percent in fiscal 2002, yet the ADA *declined* by 11 percent. On a percentage basis (i.e., ADA as a percentage of gross receivables), ADA dropped to 20.4 percent of receivables in 2002 from 24.1 percent in 2001. Had Scholastic kept the allowance account at 24.1 percent,

2002 operating income would have been $11.3 million lower. Like Vitesse, Scholastic was taking down several other reserves as well, including its inventory obsolescence reserve, royalty advances reserve, and a reserve related to a recent acquisition.

Failure by Lenders to Adequately Reserve for Credit Losses

Financial institutions and other lenders must continually estimate the portion of the loans they make that they expect to never collect (called "credit losses" or "loan losses"). The mechanics of this accrual essentially mirror those that are used when reserving for uncollectible accounts receivable. The lender records an expense on the Income Statement (called a "provision for credit losses" or "loan loss expense") and a reduction in total loans receivable on the Balance Sheet (called "allowance for loan losses" or "loan loss reserve"), shown as an offset to the gross loans asset.

Ideally, the total amount in the loan loss reserve should be enough to cover all loans that the bank believes are now or are likely to be in default based on conditions at the date of the financial statements. The additions to reserves charged against income each year should be enough to maintain the reserves at the appropriate level. When management fails to reserve a sufficient amount for losses, however, profits will be overstated. This overstatement will eventually catch up to the company when the loans go bad, as the company will then be forced to write off bad loans.

Watch for a Decline in Loan Loss Reserves   Heading into the painful real estate collapse of the 2008 financial crisis, many lenders failed to establish adequate reserves for bad loans and consequently hid their losses from investors. Lenders to the riskiest customers, the so-called subprime market, were especially exposed. Subprime borrowers often received substantial loans despite having poor credit histories, no income documentation, and plenty of debt. The subprime market eventually crashed when many of these bad borrowers defaulted on their payments.

As lenders began to see increases in borrower defaults and delinquencies, they should have increased their allowance reserves accordingly. However, these companies were hesitant to record the expenses necessary to increase their reserves (or even maintain them at the same level) because it would have meant showing lower earnings during what by all appearances seemed to be a vibrant bull market.

New Century Financial (the first subprime mortgage company to collapse during the financial crisis) completely defied logic in late 2006 by *reducing* its allowance for loan losses in the face of higher delinquencies and increasing nonaccrual (bad) loans. In the September 2006 quarter, New Century shockingly lowered its loan loss reserve from $210 million (29.5 percent of bad loans) to $191 million (23.4 percent). Management seemed to have understood that this action was inappropriate, as the company obfuscated its presentation of the loan loss reserve in its Earnings Release to make it appear its reserve had increased. (We explore such creative manipulation of important metrics in Part Four, "Key Metric Shenanigans.") Had the company kept its loan loss reserve at a similar percentage of nonaccrual loans as in the previous quarter, earnings per share in September 2006 would have been cut by a *whopping 58 percent*—to $0.47 from the $1.12 reported.

Investors who monitored New Century's loan loss reserve had fair warning of the company's impending demise. In early February 2007, one day before the scheduled release of its fourth-quarter results, the company announced a restatement of earnings for the first three quarters of 2006. The stock went into a free fall, and two months later New Century filed for bankruptcy. Lawsuits ensued, and the SEC charged senior management with securities fraud for misleading investors as the business was collapsing.

> RED FLAG!
> Loan loss reserves decline relative to bad (nonaccrual or nonperforming) loans.

Be Extra Cautious When Companies Lend Money to Their Own Customers
Sometimes companies will lend money directly to their customers through in-house customer financing programs. These arrangements warrant extra scrutiny to ensure that the company is not boosting sales by lending to customers that won't be able to pay back their loans. A struggling company desperate for sales growth, for example, may decide to loosen its lending terms and worry about the bad debts later.

Consider the case of Signet Jewelers, owner of a host of jewelry retailers including Kay, Zales, Jared, and H. Samuel. In fiscal 2015, 61 percent of sales in the company's sterling segment were made using Signet's in-house customer financing. This was a big step up from 58 percent credit participation a year earlier and from the low-to-mid 50 percent range throughout the previous decade. Increases in customer lending helped the company achieve its coveted same-store sales growth targets, but unfortunately that growth proved fleeting. In fiscal 2017, credit participation growth slowed, and Signet reported negative same-store sales growth for the first time since the financial crisis.

Failure to Write Down Impaired Investments

Companies must also review their investment portfolio for clunkers. If an investment in a stock, bond, or other security experiences a permanent decline in value, the company must record an impairment expense. This principle especially pertains to certain industries, such as insurance and banks, for which investments represent a substantial portion of their assets.

Investors should watch for companies that fail to take impairment losses during market downturns, as occurred with the collapse of almost every asset class in the 2008 global financial crisis and the resulting losses across company investment portfolios.

As you might imagine, many companies were in denial about the severe drop in portfolio values and considered impairment unnecessary. At first, many financial institutions barely took any charges for these declines. However, as the downturn deepened, it became more difficult for companies to ignore reality and justify maintaining these assets on their Balance Sheets at inflated values. At that point investors saw enormous write-down charges as their portfolio companies finally took the medicine they had previously avoided.

Watch for Tricks to Make Losses from Impaired Assets Disappear   The massive accounting fraud at Japanese camera maker Olympus started out fairly benign, with the company making risky investments in the 1980s and early 1990s. Initially, these investments were properly shown on the Balance Sheet at their original cost. As the investments declined in value however, Olympus failed to properly impair them. Eventually management decided to hide these losses, using a variety of fraudulent schemes, known as *tobashi* schemes, to make the losses disappear. *Tobashi* is Japanese for "flying away." It describes a practice where a company sells or otherwise takes money-losing investments off its books and moves them to another company to conceal losses from its investors. In that sense, the losses are made to disappear, or "fly away."

In Part Five, "Acquisition Accounting Shenanigans," we present details of the Olympus fraud, outlining the specific techniques the company employed to hide almost $2 billion of losses using acquisitions and divestitures as a cover-up.

Looking Ahead

Unlike this chapter, Chapter 7 discusses costs that use a one-step process. While conceptually all costs incurred logically provide some economic benefit, those with only short-term benefit (like rent) never appear on the Balance Sheet and are immediately shown as an expense. Shenanigan No. 5 shows techniques used by management to hide those expenses from investors.

7

Earnings Manipulation Shenanigan No. 5: Employing Other Techniques to Hide Expenses or Losses

Failing to report all of your expenses when filing your taxes with the Internal Revenue Service would be foolish and pointless because you would only wind up with a higher tax bill. Failing to report all your expenses when filing your financial reports, while also foolish, would be useful if you were running a ruse to trick shareholders into thinking profits were stronger than they really are. Chapter 6 profiled how management can try to hide costs on the Balance Sheet, pretending that they are really assets. This chapter presents a more challenging shenanigan for investors to detect: when management depresses its expenses by failing to record a real cost or by expensing an inappropriately low amount. It's amazing that people would try this trick to begin with; what's even more astounding is that they often get away with it!

In the previous chapter, we discussed how certain costs with long-term benefits are initially recorded as assets on the Balance Sheet, while other costs with short-term benefits are expensed immediately. We showed that monitoring trends in assets, expenses, and capitalization policies is a helpful way to catch companies that are inflating their earnings by improperly keeping costs on the Balance Sheet. In contrast, costs that provide only short-term benefits never appear on the Balance Sheet at all because they are expensed immediately. This chapter focuses on tricks related to those short-term benefits that management simply decides to hide from investors.

Employing Other Techniques to Hide Expenses or Losses

1. Failing to record an expense at the appropriate amount from a current transaction

2. Recording inappropriately low expenses by using aggressive accounting assumptions

3. Reducing expenses by releasing reserves from previous charges

1. Failing to Record an Expense at the Appropriate Amount from a Current Transaction

This first technique aims to lower the period's total expenses by failing to record an actual obligation giving rise to an expense (like rent).

Failure to Record an Entire Transaction Regarding an Invoice
Received Late in the Quarter
One of the simplest ways to hide an expense would be to pretend that you never saw an invoice from a vendor until after the quarter has ended. For example, failure to account for an electricity bill received in late March for that month's service would result in underreported expenses (and the related accounts payable) and would therefore overstate income.

A good example of failing to record end-of-period expenses can be found at Symbol Technologies. Symbol paid bonuses to employees in the March

2000 quarter but failed to record the related obligation to pay $3.5 million in Federal Insurance Contributions Act (FICA) insurance. Instead, the company (inappropriately) decided to record the expense in a later period, when the cash was paid. By failing to properly accrue the FICA expense in March, Symbol overstated its quarterly net income by 7.5 percent.

Getting a Little Help from Your Friends

Sometimes clever management can elicit help from other parties, like vendors, to make reported expenses appear smaller. This ploy to artificially reduce expenses and inflate profits involves receiving sham rebates from suppliers. Naturally, this shenanigan needs the assistance of the supplier. Here's how it works.

Tell a supplier that you will agree to purchase $9 million of office products over the next year and that you will pay an inflated price of $10 million. In exchange for this large order, you ask the supplier to pay you a $1 million up-front "rebate" upon signing the agreement. You then improperly record the rebate as an immediate reduction of your office expenses. By using this trick, you have boosted earnings by the $1 million receipt, which should have been recorded as a reduction of the inflated price of future office supplies purchases.

Consider Sunrise Medical's dealings with a supplier in which the company worked out a deal to receive a $1 million rebate on purchases that had already been made during the year. What was in it for the supplier? Well, Sunrise agreed to a price increase on purchases made in the next year to offset the rebate. A "side letter" was executed to seal this caper. Sunrise recorded the rebate as a decrease in expenses, without disclosing to investors or to the auditor that the supplier had tied the rebate to a price increase on future purchases.

> **TIP**
>
> Always view cash receipts from vendors with suspicion. Cash normally flows out to vendors, not in from vendors, so unusual cash inflows from vendors may signal an accounting shenanigan.

Watch for Unusually Large Vendor Credits or Rebates   Syntax-Brillian took the concept of vendor rebates to a completely different level. The company received various vendor "credits" from its primary supplier (Kolin), which, as we discussed in the previous chapter, was also a significant shareholder of the company. Syntax-Brillian recorded these vendor credits as a reduction in cost of goods sold, which naturally provided a benefit to earnings. The problem was, however, that these were no ordinary credits. The size of these credits was absolutely shocking; it accounted for more than all of Syntax-Brillian's gross profit over its brief history as a public company.

Specifically, between December 2005 and June 2007, the company reported a gross profit of $142.7 million, which included credits from Kolin totaling an astounding $214.7 million. Moreover, the company never received cash for these credits; they were just bookkeeping entries. As a result, Syntax-Brillian showed decent profitability, but it showed severely negative cash flow from operations. Even novice investors could have identified this scheme. A quick quality of earnings check would have revealed a huge disparity between cash flow and net income. Moreover, diligent investors could have found in the footnote disclosures of unusually large vendor credits and significant related-party transactions.

Be Alert for Companies Failing to Accrue Expenses for Loss Contingencies
Occasionally, management may be required to establish a contingency reserve and record an expense (or loss) for outstanding, yet-unsettled disputes. Accounting rules require that losses be accrued for such contingencies (e.g., expected payments related to litigation or tax disputes) when the following two conditions exist: (1) there is a probable loss, and (2) the amount of the loss can be reasonably estimated.

Remember to Review Off-Balance-Sheet Purchase Commitments   Existing obligations that result from past transactions are reported as liabilities on the Balance Sheet. Additionally, as discussed above, liabilities for certain contingent payments sometimes also are accrued as a liability. However, what about *future* obligations and contingencies that companies have? For instance, a company may have agreed to purchase inventory over the following two years. Alternatively, a company may have committed to fund a project or a long-term real estate rental.

While these purchase obligations often cannot be rescinded, they are typically excluded from the Liability section of the Balance Sheet and thus are considered "off-Balance-Sheet" liabilities. However, management is required to disclose significant commitments in the Footnotes to the Financial Statements. Despite not being reflected on the Balance Sheet, these obligations could doom the company. Investors who fail to notice them could be in serious jeopardy.

Accounting Capsule:
Nonaccrued Loss Contingencies

Some obligations require only footnote disclosure and have no impact on reported earnings. However, investors should pay close attention to any commitments and contingencies discussed in the Footnotes or the Management Discussion and Analysis section of the financial report. Sometimes unrecorded liabilities for commitments and contingencies are more significant than the liabilities reported on the Balance Sheet.

---

2. Recording Inappropriately Low Expenses by Using Aggressive Accounting Assumptions

This technique demonstrates how management's flexibility in selecting accounting policies and estimates can be a tool for hiding expenses. Companies that provide pensions and other post-retirement benefits to employees can change their accounting assumptions in ways that reduce the recorded expense. Similarly, companies that lease equipment make a variety of estimates that will have a bearing on the reported liabilities and expenses. Management can manipulate earnings (and reduce liabilities) by changing accounting or actuarial assumptions.

Boosting Income by Changing Lease Assumptions

Lease accounting provides management with another massage parlor in which it can knead estimates to help inflate earnings. When Deere & Company leases its farming equipment to customers in the agriculture industry, it receives agreed-upon rental income, and the main expense recorded is the depreciation of the leased equipment. It sounds simple enough, but here's where the massage starts. The depreciation expense is a function of the value of the asset at the beginning of the lease (initial value) and the expected value of the asset at the end of the lease (residual value). The difference between these two values is divided equally across the rental period.

But accounting games can be played reducing the gap between the initial value and the ending value (that is, total future depreciation expense) simply by arbitrarily increasing the portion assigned to the residual value. Stated simply, since the residual value represents the portion that will not be depreciated, the game is to assign a higher percentage to residual value.

In 2012, Deere estimated that the residual value of its rental equipment would amount to 55 percent of the initial value, leaving 45 percent of the initial cost to be depreciated. However, in each subsequent year, this estimate increased, reaching 63 percent in 2015. By increasing the estimate, the company would now be depreciating only 37 percent (down from 45 percent) of the initial value. Because of this subtle change in estimate of the residual value, Deere materially lowered its depreciation expense and artificially boosted its gross margin and operating income.

Self-Insurance Reserves

Some companies balk at paying expensive business insurance premiums (for example, for employee healthcare or disability insurance), and they decide instead to "self-insure" certain risks. Companies that self-insure essentially operate like mini–insurance companies: they create a fund that they believe will be sufficient to pay out insurance claims, and they record expenses each period for the amount needed.

How large should the self-insurance liability be, and how much self-insurance expense should be accrued each quarter? Well, of course, the answer depends on estimates. With a simple tweak of those estimates or a change in assumptions, management can obtain a nice boost to earnings.

Be Alert for Changes in Self-Insurance Assumptions   Rent-A-Center Inc., a large rent-to-own retail store operator, self-insures for workers' compensation, general liability, and auto liability insurance policies. In June 2006,

Rent-A-Center decided that it would change the actuarial assumptions used to calculate its self-insurance accrual for that year. Rather than the previous approach of using only general industry loss assumptions, Rent-A-Center would now also include internally developed assumptions based on its own loss experience. Regardless of the merits of this change, it provided Rent-A-Center with a nonrecurring boost to earnings. This change alone might have provided virtually all of Rent-A-Center's earnings growth over the subsequent four quarters.

Boosting Income by Changing Pension Assumptions

Companies that provide pensions for employees must record an expense each quarter to account for the incremental costs incurred under the plan. Pension expense generally is not shown explicitly on the Income Statement; instead, it is simply grouped with other employee salary costs (usually as a component of cost of goods sold or selling, general, and administrative expense). Investors should scrutinize the pension accounting assumptions in the footnotes, as they allow for considerable management discretion that might be used to reduce (or even eliminate) the expense.

Watch for Changes in Pension Estimates and Assumptions   Several important actuarial assumptions must be used to calculate pension expense, including discount rates, mortality rates, compensation growth rates, and expected asset return rates, among others. Companies usually disclose changes to these assumptions in their footnotes. Simply read the pension footnote to find the changes. For example, Navistar International Corp. disclosed a restructuring of its pension plan in 2003, in which the company changed its assumption for the remaining life expectancy of plan participants from 12 years to 18 years. By increasing the remaining life expectancy assumption, Navistar spread "unrecognized losses" over a longer period, and in doing so, it reduced its pension expense (and inflated its income) by $26 million.

Watch for Changes in the Measurement Date   Just a simple change in the month designated as the measurement date for the pension plan can inflate profits. For example, in 2004, Raytheon Co. changed the date on which it measured its pension plan from October 31 to December 31. This simple change provided a $41 million ($0.09 bump to earnings per share) bottom-line boost, which accounted for about 10 percent of Raytheon's earnings for the entire year.

Watch for Outsized Pension Income   Sometimes companies wind up with results that seem to make no sense at all—like a *negative pension expense*. This phenomenon arises when expected gains from investing pension plan assets become larger than the incremental annual costs of running the pension plan, resulting in *pension income*. What circumstances would lead to this outcome? Oversized gains for a company with very large plan assets could produce a sizable amount of pension income. Usually, these situations arise at companies with large legacy pension plans and few (or no) new employees entering the plan.

Lucent, for instance, recorded more than $1.1 billion in pension income during 2004, accounting for virtually all (91 percent) of its operating income. Moreover, from 2002 to 2004, Lucent's *pension income* totaled $2.8 billion while it reported a cumulative operating loss of $6.0 billion. Like most companies, Lucent chose to not break out pension expense (or income) separately on its Income Statement. As a result, investors who failed to read the pension footnote would have missed this critically important piece of information.

3. Reducing Expenses by Releasing Reserves from Previous Charges

One benefit of taking a special charge is to inflate future-period operating income because future costs have already been written off through that charge. (This issue is covered in Chapter 9, "Earnings Manipulation Shenanigan No. 7: Shifting Future Expenses to the Current Period.") A second benefit of taking a special charge is that the liability created with the charge becomes a reserve that can easily be released into earnings in a later period.

Reserves come in different shapes and sizes and can be found all over the Balance Sheet. In Chapter 6, we highlighted reserves that are recorded on the Balance Sheet as offsets to assets, including the allowance for doubtful accounts, the allowance for loan losses, and inventory obsolescence reserves.

In this section, we discuss reserves that are recorded as liabilities as they represent obligations to another party. While accrual accounting requires companies to create a reserve for costs incurred but not yet expended (such as warranties), these reserves can easily be abused to manipulate earnings.

Accounting Capsule:
Inflating Liabilities Today May Inflate Profits Tomorrow

Liabilities, like income, typically have credit balances. This is quite important and potentially valuable for a management that is intent on inflating future-period profits. The scheme is really quite simple: create a bogus liability with a desirable credit balance and then, whenever needed, make an accounting entry that moves the credit from the liability to an expense account—reducing the expense and boosting profits.

WorldCom Releases Reserves to Reduce Its Line Costs
In the previous chapter, we discussed how WorldCom inflated its earnings in the early 2000s by aggressively capitalizing line costs rather than recording them as an expense. Well, that was not the only game that management played with line costs. It also reversed various generic reserve accounts and recorded the offset as a decrease to line cost expense.

Watch for Earnings Boosts When a Company Misses Its Bonus Targets
Consider how Baltimore-based athletic apparel company Under Armour tried to hide the full extent of its business slowdown in 2016. While annual sales had grown by an impressive 22 percent over the prior year, they fell short of the 24 percent growth target that investors expected, and perhaps more significantly, gross margin fell by more than 150 basis points.

This disappointment, however, provided a small silver lining for reported profits in the fourth quarter. The company had accrued for year-end bonuses in each of the first nine months of the year; however, by the fourth quarter, management realized that it would miss key performance targets, and bonuses would not be paid. So to correct the accounts and remove those previously recorded expenses, in the fourth quarter management reversed the entire previous bonus expenses. This meant recording $48 million of *negative* selling, general, and administrative (SG&A) expense, which boosted reported earnings per share by $0.07. The reversal was not prominently disclosed, making it seem like lower SG&A in the fourth quarter was the result of effective cost management, when, in reality, it was simply due to a one-time accounting adjustment.

Watch for the Release of Restructuring Reserves into Income   Sunbeam Corporation was the master of this trick. When "Chainsaw Al" Dunlap was brought in as CEO, he embarked on a large restructuring plan. Accordingly, the company recorded huge restructuring charges, thereby creating reserves to be used for future expenditures related to the restructuring plan. However, according to the SEC, Sunbeam recorded many improper restructuring and other "cookie jar" reserves as part of this plan. These improper reserves later were released into income, inflating profit margins and creating the illusion of a successful restructuring.

Accounting Capsule:
Release of a Restructuring Reserve

Assume that the company announces a 1,000-person layoff with a severance package totaling $10 million.

Increase:	Restructuring expense	$10 million
Increase:	Liability for severance	$10 million

Six months later, the layoffs have been completed, and yet only 700 employees lost their jobs. The company eliminates the remaining liability and boosts income by reducing an expense:

Decrease:	Liability	$3 million
Decrease:	Expense	$3 million

Thus, by inflating the estimated restructuring cost, this company created a $3 million profit out of thin air when the unnecessary reserve (and expense) was eliminated. Companies can take great liberties in setting up large restructuring (or other) reserves and later inflate profits when closing out these unnecessary expense accounts.

> **TIP**
>
> Many of these liability reserves (especially the generic ones) are often grouped in a "soft" liability account sometimes called "other current liabilities" or "accrued expenses." Investors should monitor soft liability accounts closely and flag any sharp declines relative to revenue. Often, companies discuss these soft liabilities in a footnote. Make sure to find them and track the individual reserves as well.

Getting a Lot of Help from Your Friends—Marvell Cleverly Lowers Its Expenses
Remember our earlier discussion of the quirky two-part transaction between Intel and Marvell? Intel sold a business to Marvell in 2006 at what seemed to be a discount, while simultaneously Marvell agreed to pay above list price for a certain amount of products later to be purchased from Intel. (See Marvell's footnote shown below.) As explained in Chapter 5, Intel appeared to structure this transaction in a way that understated the gain from the one-time asset sale and overstated the more valuable stream of revenue (by overcharging on the product sales).

**MARVELL'S 10-Q DISCUSSION ABOUT
ITS TRANSACTION WITH INTEL**

In conjunction with the acquisition of the ICAP Business, the Company entered into a supply agreement with Intel. The supply agreement obligates the Company to purchase certain finished product and sorted wafers at a contracted price from Intel for a contracted period of time. The contracted period of time can differ between finished products and sorted wafers. *Intel's pricing to the Company was greater than comparable prices available to the Company in the market in almost all cases.* In accordance with purchase accounting, the Company *recorded a liability at contract signing representing the difference between Intel prices and comparable market prices* for those products for which the Company had a contractual obligation. [Italics added for emphasis]

Now let's look at this same two-way transaction, but from Marvell's perspective. Marvell essentially paid Intel less money up front to purchase the business, and in exchange, Marvell agreed to purchase inventory from Intel at an inflated price. While it sounds as if this transaction would cause Marvell's earnings to be lower in future periods, as it is overpaying for inventory, this is not the case. It appears that Marvell accounted for the entire overpayment by recording a liability (or reserve) on its Balance Sheet, which it would draw down over time as a reduction of cost of goods sold (to offset the inflated prices). There was no need for Marvell to record an expense to create this reserve, since it already had been set up in the purchase accounting for the acquisition. Thus, Marvell created a cookie jar reserve without recording an expense, and it used this reserve to offset overpayments as it saw fit. Indeed, this transaction provided Marvell with more discretion over its earnings each quarter.

Management sometimes fails to record the necessary expense accruals for expected costs. These accruals are generally company estimates of routine liabilities incurred in normal business operations, such as a manufacturer's warranty. Often these costs are estimated and recorded at the very end of a quarter. In the previous chapter, we introduced the concept of expense accruals (reserves) and highlighted reserves that are recorded as reductions to assets, such as the allowance for doubtful accounts and the inventory obsolescence reserve. In this section, we discuss reserves for estimated obligations that are shown as liabilities.

Failing to appropriately record an expense for these costs, or reversing past expenses, will inflate earnings. Since these costs rely on management assumptions and discretionary estimates, all management needs to do to generate more earnings (and achieve Wall Street's targets) is to tweak these assumptions. To illustrate, consider the shenanigans that were used by Dell Computer from 2003 through the beginning of fiscal 2007. The published findings of a special investigation conducted by Dell's audit committee in 2007 (as presented below) provide some fantastic, juicy details about Dell's games with reserves (don't skip reading this; there is some amazing stuff in here).

DELL'S DISCUSSION OF ITS AUDIT COMMITTEE INVESTIGATION FINDINGS IN AN AUGUST 2007 8-K

The investigation raised questions relating to numerous accounting issues, most of which involved adjustments to various reserve and accrued liability accounts, and identified evidence that certain adjustments appear to have been motivated by the objective of attaining financial targets. According to the investigation, these activities typically occurred in the days immediately following the end of a quarter, when the accounting books were being closed and the results of the quarter were being compiled. The investigation found evidence that, in that timeframe, account balances were reviewed, sometimes at the request or with the knowledge of senior executives, with the goal of seeking adjustments so that quarterly performance objectives could be met. The investigation concluded that a number of these adjustments were improper, including the creation and release of accruals and reserves that appear to have been made for the purpose of enhancing internal performance measures or reported results, as well as the transfer of excess accruals from one liability account to another and the use of the excess balances to offset unrelated expenses in later periods.

Watch for Declines in Reserves for Warranties or Warranty Expense   Many companies bundle expensive warranties with their products, covering potential problems that could arise years after the purchase. For example, if you were to purchase a laptop from Dell, it might come with a two-year warranty promising that Dell will replace or repair all defective parts during that period.

Dell cannot just wait and see how much it will wind up spending on warranty costs for your computer before recording the expense. Accounting rules require Dell to record an expense for expected future warranty costs at the time the product is sold. Naturally, management can exercise great discretion in the amount it records as warranty expense each period. If it chooses too little, the profits will be inflated; if it chooses too much, profits will be understated (and perhaps held back for a rainy day).

Indeed, part of Dell's restatement involved improper accounting for warranty liabilities. Again, the audit committee's discussion of its findings is quite revealing and did such an excellent job of explaining the mechanics that we figured we'd let the committee teach you directly.

DELL'S DISCUSSION OF ITS AUDIT COMMITTEE INVESTIGATION FINDINGS IN AN AUGUST 2007 8-K (*Continued*)

There were also instances where warranty reserves in excess of the estimated warranty liability, as calculated by the warranty liability estimation process, were retained and not released to the Income Statement as appropriate. Additionally, certain adjustments in the warranty liability estimation process were identified where expected future costs or estimated failure rates were not accurate.

Looking Ahead

This chapter completes our presentation of how management can improperly inflate *current-period* profits. Management can use two different vehicles to do this: (1) recording too much revenue or one-time gains or (2) recording too few expenses.

Under certain circumstances, management might choose just the opposite strategy—to deflate current-period profits and shift them to a later period. Chapter 8 describes methods used by management to improperly shift revenue to later periods, and Chapter 9 presents methods used to improperly shift expenses to the current period. The results of using these tricks lead investors to believe in "deceptively strong" future-period profit growth concocted by management. Read on and learn how not to be duped by these ploys.

8

Earnings Manipulation Shenanigan No. 6: Shifting Current Income to a Later Period

Here's a quiz. Why would management at a publicly traded company ever mislead its investors by reporting *smaller profits*? You may be thinking that the goal would be to cut taxes. That would be the correct answer for private companies, which care more about shortchanging the tax collector. Publicly traded companies, however, certainly care about reducing taxes, but they often direct more attention toward impressing investors with smooth and predictable earnings growth.

As you may recall from Chapter 3, "Earnings Manipulation Shenanigan No. 1: Recording Revenue Too Soon," management used the techniques in that chapter because it believed that current-period results were more important than future-period ones, and thus it decided to accelerate revenue from a later period to the current one. Let's now turn that picture 180 degrees and try to imagine certain times when management might wish to depress current-period results to benefit a later period.

Consider a company that is growing like gangbusters and is unsure of what tomorrow holds, or one that has benefited from a large windfall gain or a huge new contract. Investors surely would love to see those delicious numbers, but they also would naturally expect management to replicate or even exceed them tomorrow. Meeting these elevated investor expectations may be daunting, leading management to feel compelled to use the techniques discussed in this chapter.

Techniques to Shift Current Income to a Later Period

1. Creating reserves and releasing them into income in a later period

2. Smoothing income by improperly accounting for derivatives

3. Creating reserves in conjunction with an acquisition and releasing them into income in a later period

4. Recording current-period sales in a later period

1. Creating Reserves and Releasing Them into Income in a Later Period

When business is booming and earnings far exceed Wall Street estimates, companies may be tempted not to report all their revenue, but instead to save some of it for a rainy day. Consider a situation in which management fails to record some revenue that was rightfully earned during the current period, instead storing it on the Balance Sheet until it is needed during a later period. This is simple to do, and the auditors may not even question the move, as they may consider it "more conservative." All it takes is a bookkeeping entry to increase a Balance Sheet liability account called "deferred revenue" (or "unearned revenue") in the current period; then when the deferred revenue is needed in a later period (to boost earnings), another entry is made to move it to actual revenue. (The bookkeeping entries are illustrated in the accompanying Accounting Capsule.)

Accounting Capsule:
Creating Deferred (or Unearned) Revenue

Assume a company made a cash sale for $900. The correct journal entry
would be:

| *Increase:* | Cash | $900 |
| *Increase:* | Sales revenue | $900 |

Instead, if management decided to only record $600 of the sale this year and
squirrel away the rest for next year, it would record:

Increase:	Cash	$900
Increase:	Sales revenue	$600
Increase:	Deferred revenue	$300

Then next year, management would simply release that "pent-up" deferred
revenue into sales revenue.

| *Decrease:* | Deferred revenue | $300 |
| *Increase:* | Sales revenue | $300 |

Saving Up for a "Rainy Day"

During the late 1990s, software giant Microsoft faced enormous scrutiny
over its alleged anti-competitive practices by both the U.S. Department of
Justice and its European Union counterpart overseeing antitrust regulation.
Presumably, the last thing Microsoft wanted to showcase was skyrocketing
revenue and profits, as this would have become fodder for regulators. It certainly would have been tempting for the company to delay recognition of
certain revenue by deferring it to a later period and storing it on the Balance
Sheet in the form of unearned revenue.

As shown in Table 8-1, Microsoft's unearned revenue account grew by
hundreds of millions of dollars every quarter from March 1998 to March
1999. Indeed, this reserve more than doubled over this period, from $2.0
billion at the beginning of 1998 to $4.2 billion at March 1999. Then sud-
denly the growth abated in the June 1999 quarter, with the company adding
only as much unearned revenue as it was using.

Table 8-1   Microsoft's Unearned Revenue, Quarterly Trend

($ millions, except %)	Q3, 3/98	Q4, 6/98	Q1, 9/98	Q2, 12/98	Q3, 3/99	Q4, 6/99	Q1, 9/99
Unearned revenue (beginning balance)	2,038	2,463	2,888	3,133	3,552	4,195	4,239
Additions	885	1,129	1,010	1,361	1,768	1,738	1,253
Usage	(460)	(704)	(765)	(942)	(1,125)	(1,694)	(1,363)
Unearned revenue (ending balance)	2,463	2,888	3,133	3,552	4,195	4,239	4,129
Net addition (subtraction)	425	425	245	419	643	44	(110)
% change sequentially	20.9%	17.3%	8.5%	13.4%	18.1%	1.0%	(2.6%)

While several factors probably contributed to this big buildup and then sudden drop in unearned revenue, one theory at the time was that Microsoft was building reserves to save up for a rainy day. When revenue fell by 6.6 percent sequentially in the September 1999 quarter, investors questioned whether that rainy day had arrived. Another factor contributing to the decline in deferred revenue was a June 1999 change in revenue recognition policy that caused Microsoft to recognize more revenue up front on certain software sales. In adopting a new rule (SOP 98–9), Microsoft decided to adjust its estimates to increase the amount of revenue it would recognize upon shipment of the software and reduce the amount it would treat as unearned. (See Microsoft's disclosure.) Regardless of the legitimacy of this policy change, the impact was to release some of Microsoft's pent-up deferred revenue.

Stretching Out Unexpected Gains over Several Years

In reality, few companies have the sort of solid sustained growth that would allow them to confidently squirrel away billions of dollars in revenue earned for a later period and still meet Wall Street targets. More commonly, however, companies use EM Shenanigan No. 6 when they are the recipients of a windfall gain.

> **EXCERPTS FROM MICROSOFT'S REVENUE RECOGNITION DISCLOSURE, 1999 10-K**
>
> Upon adoption of SOP 98-9 during the fourth quarter of fiscal 1999, the Company was required to change the methodology of attributing the fair value to undelivered elements. The percentages of undelivered elements in relation to the total arrangement decreased, reducing the amount of Windows and Office revenue treated as unearned and increasing the amount of revenue recognized upon shipment. *The percentage of revenue recognized ratably decreased from a range of 20% to 35% to a range of approximately 15% to 25% of Windows desktop operating systems. For desktop applications, the percentage decreased from approximately 20% to a range of approximately 10% to 20%.* The ranges depend on the terms and conditions of the license and prices of the elements. The impact on fiscal 1999 was to increase reported revenue $170 million. [Italics added for emphasis]

Shifting Huge Trading Gains to the Future   Enron's infamous manipulation of the California energy markets in 2000–2001 earned the company huge windfall profits in its trading division. The profits were so large that management decided to save some for future quarters, which, according to the SEC, was done to "mask the extent and volatility of its windfall trading profits." Compared with the rest of Enron's shenanigans, this scheme was straightforward: simply defer some of the trading gain by storing it in a reserve on the Balance Sheet. These reserves came in handy and helped Enron avoid reporting large losses during more difficult periods. By early 2001, Enron's undisclosed reserve accounts had ballooned to over $1 billion. The company then improperly released hundreds of millions of dollars of these reserves to ensure that Wall Street's expectations were met. Ironically, there would be no future quarters in which to release unused reserves, as Enron imploded in October 2001 and probably needed to show all the revenue that it had held back for the "rainy day." That rainy day surely had arrived in October 2001—a *Category 5 hurricane for investors!*

Using Reserves to Smooth Income Is a Serious Transgression   Smoothing of income is not an uncommon strategy for management, as Wall Street rewards solid and predictable profit growth. However, the use of reserves to shift income to a later period can be as serious an income manipulation ploy as recording revenue too soon (EM Shenanigan No. 1). In both cases, the effect is misleading financial results. When revenue is recorded too early, future income is recorded in the current period; conversely, with income smoothing, current income is shifted to a future period.

2. Smoothing Income by Improperly Accounting for Derivatives

Companies with healthy businesses can engage in income-smoothing shenanigans to give the illusion of nice, steady, predictable results. Consider mortgage giant Federal Home Loan Mortgage Corporation (Freddie Mac, or Freddie) and its desire to portray very smooth earnings despite a period of volatile interest rate movements. Freddie's attempts to smooth earnings went to the extreme and led to a $5 billion fraud.

Volatile Interest Rate Market Makes "Steady Freddie" Much Less Predictable
Freddie's earnings manipulation was largely related to its incorrect accounting for derivative instruments, loan origination costs, and reserves for losses. When the corrected numbers were released, we learned a fascinating thing about the scandal: the company wound up understating its profits. From 2000 to 2002, Freddie Mac underreported net income by nearly $4.5 billion. As shown in Table 8-2, Freddie's smoothing techniques allowed it to report earnings growth of 63 and 39 percent in 2001 and 2002, respectively, when earnings growth was a much more volatile negative 14 percent in 2001 and positive 220 percent in 2002.

Table 8-2   Freddie Mac Restatements for Errors

($ millions, except %)	2000	2001	2002	Total
Reported net income	2,547	4,147	5,764	**12,458**
Restated net income	3,666	3,158	10,090	**16,914**
Effect of restatement	1,119	(989)	4,326	**4,456**
Reported net income *growth*		63%	39%	
Restated net income *growth*		(14%)	220%	

What could have led Freddie to embark on this course? Well, Wall Street had come to expect steady and predictable earnings from the company. A challenge arose in 2000 with the implementation of a new accounting rule (SFAS 133) that created enormous volatility in the company's investment activities involving derivatives. It quickly became clear to management that the change in accounting would create huge windfall gains for the company. Initial estimates of the gain were in the hundreds of millions, but they soon ballooned to the billions. For most of us, billions of dollars in windfall gains would be great news. To Freddie Mac, however, this was a problem. The company's rock-solid stock price was largely built on its ability to produce steady and predictable earnings. It certainly earned its nickname "Steady Freddie." So, ever conscious of its reputation for pleasing Wall Street, Freddie schemed to hold back a large part of the windfall gain and release portions of it when needed to smooth earnings.

Unlike the frauds at Enron and WorldCom, the focal point of Freddie's fraud was not to mask a deteriorating business, but rather to maintain its image as a predictable earnings generator. In other words, the ultimate gain was not earnings creation but earnings smoothing. Both types of shenanigans clearly violate accounting rules and misrepresent the economic reality to investors. The biggest difference between companies that create earnings out of thin air and those that smooth is that the latter group is likely to consist of healthy companies that are simply attempting to portray a more predictable earnings stream.

General Electric Abuses Derivative Accounting to Keep Its Earnings Streak Alive Like many large companies, General Electric (GE) issues commercial paper, a form of very short-term debt with variable interest rates. To hedge against exposure to changing interest rates, GE uses derivatives agreements, called "interest rate swaps" (named because GE is "swapping" its variable interest payment obligation for a fixed payment obligation). If they are done appropriately, interest rate swaps on commercial paper qualify as effective hedges under SFAS 133 (as discussed previously), which means that earnings would be unaffected by volatility in the value of these derivatives.

A problem arose in late 2002 when GE seemed to have "overhedged," or entered into more swaps than it needed to hedge its commercial paper interest rate risk. Naturally, the amount that GE overhedged should be considered ineffective under SFAS 133, which means that the quarterly changes in value would affect earnings. (These hedges were ineffective because they did not offset anything.) GE quickly realized that it would be required to record a pretax charge of $200 million as a result of these ineffective hedges.

Throughout the December 2002 quarter, GE scrambled to find a way to avoid recording this $200 million charge. In early January 2003, after the quarter closed and just days before the company reported earnings, GE created an entirely new accounting approach for these hedges that provided the desired results. The auditors signed off, and GE kept its streak of meeting Wall Street estimates alive. One not-so-small matter remained: the novel approach was in violation of GAAP. Several years later, the SEC busted GE for accounting fraud.

Watch for Large Gains from Ineffective Hedging   Investors should be cautious when a company reports large gains from hedging activities, as these ineffective (sometimes called "economic") "hedges" may really be unreliable speculative trading activities that could just as easily produce large losses in future periods. In addition, investors should look out for ineffective hedges that produce gains much greater than losses in the underlying asset or liability. Consider Washington Mutual Inc. (WAMU), with its history of presenting large gains on activities that it characterized as hedging. In 2004, the company reported $1.6 billion in gains that were classified as "economic hedges" against a $500 million loss from its unhedged MSR (mortgage servicing rights) asset. In other words, WAMU's hedging activities resulted in gains that were three times the size of the underlying loss. Investors should also be wary of "hedges" that move in the same direction as the underlying asset or liability, as this may signal that management is using derivatives to speculate, not to hedge.

3. Creating Reserves in Conjunction with an Acquisition and Releasing Them into Income in a Later Period

As we have pointed out previously, acquisitive companies create some of the biggest challenges for investors. For one thing, the combined companies immediately become more difficult to analyze on an apples-to-apples basis. Second, as we explore in Part 5, "Acquisition Accounting Shenanigans," acquisition accounting rules create distortions in the presentation of cash flow from operations. And finally, companies that are making acquisitions might be tempted to have the target company hold back some revenue that was earned before the deal closes so that the acquirer can record it in the later period. That is where our next story begins.

Minimizing Revenue During the Acquisition "Stub Period"

Imagine that you recently signed an agreement to sell your business, with it closing in two months. You also receive instructions from the acquiring company's management team to refrain from recording any more revenue until the acquisition is complete. Somewhat baffled, you comply and record no more revenue. In so doing, you have given your new owner a generous (and inappropriate) gift, as the two months of revenue you held back will be counted as revenue by the acquiring company.

Consider the 1997 merger of 3Com with U.S. Robotics. Because the two companies had different fiscal year-ends (3Com's was in May and U.S. Robotics' in September), a two-month "stub period" was created just before the closing. Apparently, U.S. Robotics held back an enormous amount of revenue so that it would be available to 3Com after the merger closed. It appeared that in its August 1997 quarter, 3Com included revenue that U.S. Robotics refrained from booking during the stub period. Here's the "smoking gun": U.S. Robotics reported a minuscule $15.2 million of revenue for the two-month stub period (approximately $7.6 million per month), a tiny fraction of the $690.2 million in revenue that the company had reported during the preceding quarter (approximately $230 million per month). Rather than recognizing the revenue during the normal course of business, U.S. Robotics apparently held back well over $600 million (see Table 8-3).

Table 8-3   U.S. Robotics' Revenue Plummets During Its Preacquisition Stub Period

($ millions)	Q3, 6/96	Q4, 9/96	Q1, 12/96	Q2, 3/97	Two Months, 4/97 and 5/97
Revenue	546.8	611.4	645.4	690.2	15.2

Be Alert for Lower Revenue at a Target Company Just Before Acquisition Closes   Remember how management at CA (Computer Associates) manipulated the numbers to help senior management take home $1 billion in bonuses? We pointed out some of the many tricks the company used to accomplish this feat, including the "35-day" month and immediate revenue recognition on 10-year installment sale contracts. Well, like 3Com, CA may have also benefited from revenue that was held back before an acquisition.

Consider, for example, CA's 1999 purchase of Platinum Technologies. During the March 1999 quarter, the last one before the deal closed, Platinum's revenue plunged to its lowest level in seven quarters, falling by more than $144 million sequentially and by more than $23 million from the year-ago period (see Table 8-4). Platinum attributed the sharp decline to delays in closing customer contracts because of its proposed acquisition by CA. Whatever the real reasons, however, Platinum's failure to close these sales provided its new owner with an artificial revenue boost. Taking the analysis one step further, even if Platinum's revenue drop-off was not the result of holding back revenue, investors should still be concerned that CA was buying a business with rapidly shrinking revenue.

Table 8-4   Platinum Technologies' Revenue Falls Immediately Before Being Acquired by Computer Associates

($ millions)	Q2, 6/97	Q3, 9/97	Q4, 12/97	Q1, 3/98	Q2, 6/98	Q3, 9/98	Q4, 12/98	Q1, 3/99
Revenue	164.2	190.8	242.7	193.4	217.4	250.3	314.7	170.1

4. Recording Current-Period Sales in a Later Period

Imagine that late in a very strong period, management has achieved all the earnings targets needed to reach its maximum bonuses. Sales continue at a brisk pace, and management has an idea that will ensure high bonus payments for the next period as well—stop recording any more sales and shift them to the next quarter. It is simple to do, it is unlikely that the auditors will even know about this trick, and your customers certainly won't object since they will get billed later than they expected. Nonetheless, this practice is dishonest and misleading to investors, as it portrays higher sales in the later period. More important, however, it shows that management makes business decisions that are based not on sound business practices, but on dressing up its financial reports for investors.

Looking Ahead

This chapter showed what management might do to hold back legitimate revenue to recognize it in a later and apparently more desirable period. If the goal is to shortchange the present period and benefit future-period income, accelerating expenses to earlier periods should also do the job. Chapter 9 describes techniques used to accelerate expenses, making the current period seem like a disaster to show beautiful profits tomorrow.

9

Earnings Manipulation Shenanigan No. 7: Shifting Future Expenses to the Current Period

Remember the children's game called "opposite day"? For the kids playing the game, the object is to do things the opposite way from how they normally do them. In this chapter, let us adults have a bit of fun playing the opposite day game with expenses. You recall that the whole point of Earnings Manipulation Shenanigans Nos. 4 and 5 was to either push expenses to a later period or simply make them disappear forever. In the *opposite* scheme, the objective is to find ways to *increase* current period expenses.

Doing this involves two basic principles: (1) rather than keeping costs on the Balance Sheet too long (i.e., EM Shenanigan No. 4), rush them to the trash bin of expenses immediately, and (2) instead of trying to hide expenses by failing to record invoices (i.e., EM Shenanigan No. 5), record them all now (the earlier the better) and then some—even if you literally make up expenses just for the heck of it. Sounds crazy, no? Stay tuned, and soon you will fully understand how management benefits from playing this game—and companies play it more frequently than you would imagine.

Techniques to Shift Future Expenses to an Earlier Period

1. Improperly writing off assets in the current period to avoid expenses in a future period
2. Improperly recording charges to establish reserves used to reduce future expenses

1. Improperly Writing Off Assets in the Current Period to Avoid Expenses in a Future Period

Let's briefly return to our Texas two-step dance for moving assets to expenses. When it is done right, Step 1 requires placing costs on the Balance Sheet as assets, since they represent future long-term benefits. Step 2 involves shifting those costs to the proverbial trash bin (known as expenses) when the benefits are received. Chapter 6, "Earnings Manipulation Shenanigan No. 4," showed the first way to bungle the two-step—by shifting from Step 1 to Step 2 far too *slowly*, or perhaps not at all. This chapter shows another inappropriate way to dance the two-step that is the opposite of the dance discussed in Chapter 6—simply shift costs from Step 1 to Step 2 *immediately*. In other words, write off assets by recording expenses much *earlier* than is warranted.

Typical Costs Under the "Two-Step Process"

Step 1 Asset	Step 2 Expense
Deferred marketing	Marketing expense
Inventory	Cost of goods sold
Plant and equipment	Depreciation expense
Intangibles	Amortization expense

Improperly Writing Off Deferred Marketing Costs
You may recall that when we mentioned AOL in Chapter 6, the company was struggling to show a profit and had begun capitalizing marketing and

solicitation costs to push the company into the black. We criticized AOL for inflating profits by capitalizing normal expenses on the Balance Sheet. We then found fault with the company for stretching out the amortization period for these costs from one to two years, as this further muted the expenses and inflated profits. So where we left the story a few chapters ago, AOL had accumulated more than $314 million in the asset account labeled "deferred membership acquisition costs" (DMAC). (See Table 9-1.) But the company still had a big problem: those costs represented tomorrow's expense, and they would need to be amortized over the next eight quarters—a $40 million hit to earnings each quarter. Considering AOL's modest earnings level ($65.2 million in operating income in fiscal 1996), a recurring $40 million quarterly charge would be quite unwelcome.

Table 9-1　　AOL's Deferred Membership Acquisition Costs

($ millions)	1993	1994	1995	1996
Revenue	52.0	115.7	394.3	1,093.9
Operating income	1.7	4.2	(21.4)	65.2
Net income	1.4	2.2	(35.8)	29.8
Total assets	39.3	155.2	405.4	958.8
Deferred membership acquisition costs	—	**26.0**	**77.2**	**314.2**

So three months later, when its DMAC asset had ballooned to $385 million, AOL shifted to Plan B and started playing its version of the opposite day game. Rather than continuing with the two-step dance and amortizing the marketing costs over the next eight quarters, AOL switched gears by announcing "a one-time charge" to write off the entire amount in one fell swoop. Of course, it had to come up with a justification to convince the auditors that this asset account had suddenly become "impaired" and would provide no future benefit. So AOL claimed that the write-off was necessary to reflect changes in its evolving business model, including reduced reliance on subscribers' fees as the company developed other revenue sources. To say that we were skeptical of this explanation would be an understatement.

Just to be clear about the brazenness and extent of the company's scheme, let's recap. First, AOL decided to push normal solicitation costs onto the Balance Sheet—this was to give investors the impression of its being a profitable company, when in fact the company was unprofitable and burning through a ton of cash. Second, it stretched out the one-year amortization period to two years, further inflating profits by cutting the amortization expense recorded each quarter in half. Of course, at this point, the company knew that it still had a very big challenge. By using aggressive accounting practices, it had successfully pushed more than $300 million of expenses into the future; however, it had failed to make these expenses disappear forever. But not to worry; the AOL magicians still had one more trick up their sleeves—the grand finale. In an illusion for the ages, management used a $385 million charge to eliminate all these looming expenses and downplayed the significance by simply calling it a "change in accounting estimate." Surely you will agree that these actions are the product of major chutzpah.

Improperly Writing Off Inventory as Being Obsolete

Unlike the solicitation costs that AOL had improperly capitalized for years (before it started playing the opposite day game), inventory costs most certainly should be capitalized and then later expensed either when the product is sold (most of the time) or when it is written off as obsolete (less frequently). The most common shenanigans with inventory accounting involve failing to shift costs from the asset account to expense in a timely manner. This trick naturally would understate expenses and inflate profits. Since we are playing the opposite day game here, though, let's assume that management decides to write off the inventory cost as an expense long before any sale takes place.

Watch for Reversals of Prior Inventory Impairment Charges   When chip maker NVIDIA took an impairment charge to write down the value of its 2016 inventory, management cited a new product cycle that would make some of the company's older processors obsolete. Based on those concerns, NVIDIA materially increased its impairment expense to $112 million—up from $59 million in 2015 and $50 million in 2014. Those impairment estimates proved to be too high, since in the following year (2017) NVIDIA reported that it had *sold $51 million of previously written-off goods*. And by reversing the inflated impairment charge in 2017, NVIDIA received a 70-basis-point boost to its gross margin.

Too Many Toys

Toys 'R' Us accumulated excess inventory that it determined it wouldn't be able to sell. The company announced that it would take a $396.6 million (pretax) restructuring charge to cover the cost of a "strategic inventory repositioning" (interpretation: moving slow-selling inventory off the shelves), as well as the closing of stores and distribution centers. The portion of the charge related to repositioning of inventory amounted to $184 million. The company explained that the inventory was removed from the stores and sold at lower prices through alternative distribution channels. Normally, the inventory would be written down to its net realizable value and the difference charged as an operating expense.

Whether we are considering AOL accelerating deferred marketing costs, NVIDIA writing off inventory that it did not throw away (and later sold), or Toys 'R' Us taking large one-time charges, each seemingly had the same ultimate result: accelerating future-period expenses into the current period and, moreover, categorizing the write-off as being unrelated to normal activities and showing it below the line. Such actions inflate future-period profits with no detriment to current-period operating results.

Accounting Capsule:
Restructuring Charges Create Interperiod and Intraperiod Benefits

EM Shenanigan No. 7 creates both *interperiod* and *intraperiod* benefits for management. First, future-period expenses are accelerated to an earlier period, leaving fewer expenses to burden the later one. Second, the accelerated expenses are often classified as "restructuring" or "one-time charges" and presented below the line, creating a win-win situation for the company: operating income (above the line) in the period of the charge is unaffected since the impact is felt below the line; and operating income in the later period is inflated, as some normal expenses have been pulled out and included in the earlier-period charge.

Improperly Writing Off Plant and Equipment Considered Impaired

When we introduced shenanigans involving plant and equipment in Chapter 6, we cautioned about management reporting inflated profits by depreciating these assets over too long a period or failing to write them off completely if their values become permanently impaired. As we continue the opposite game, let's shift gears and think how management can accelerate current-period expenses by curtailing the depreciation period and announcing impairment charges for certain pieces of plant and equipment, even though they may be perfectly fine. Investors should be particularly alert to this type of shenanigan when it corresponds to the hiring of a new CEO with tantalizing stock options or if management uses this ploy with uncommon regularity.

Lesson One for New CEOs   Let's assume you are prepping to become CEO of a struggling company and want to get off to a flying start by showing huge profit improvement almost immediately. Here are a few suggestions, assuming you have no ethical qualms about using some shenanigans to achieve your objective.

During your first few weeks on the job, announce some bold initiatives to clean up the mess left by your predecessor and try to look like a strong, decisive leader with a solid grip on the details. Oh, and be sure to announce a streamlining of operations and a large write-down of assets (often called a "big bath")—the larger the write-down, the better. Investors will be impressed, and of course, it makes showing earnings growth in future periods infinitely easier; you just lowered the bar by shifting those future expenses into today's charge. Include in your announcement the need to write off bloated inventory and plant assets. Investors won't even penalize the company for the near-term loss, since it will all be packaged below the line. When tomorrow comes, you will report much-improved profits, since many of tomorrow's costs have already been written off as part of the special charge.

The Saga of "Chainsaw Al" Dunlap   That's how Sunbeam's infamous "Chainsaw Al" Dunlap managed to look so smart—at least for a while. When Dunlap arrived in July 1996, Sunbeam was a struggling company. Dunlap had a reputation as a turnaround artist.

During his prior 18-month gig leading the Scott Paper Company, Dunlap's shenanigans had helped to drive up the stock price 225 percent, increasing the company's market value by $6.3 billion. The company was then sold to

Kimberly-Clark for $9.4 billion, with Dunlap pocketing $100 million as a going-away present. During his short stay at Scott, Dunlap fired 11,000 employees, slashed expenditures on plant improvements and research, and then sold the company to a major rival. Wall Street cheered as Scott became the sixth company sold or dismembered by Dunlap since 1983.

So, not surprisingly, the day Sunbeam announced that Dunlap would become its new CEO, its share price jumped 60 percent—the largest one-day jump in the company's history. By the following year, the apparent turnaround had begun to impress investors. The stock, which had been $12.50 the day before Dunlap's hiring was announced, peaked at $53 in early 1998. Dunlap was given a new contract, doubling his base salary.

Then the truth came out. On April 3, 1998, the stock plunged 25 percent when the company disclosed a loss for the quarter. Two months later, negative statements in the press about the company's aggressive sales practices prompted Sunbeam's board to begin an internal investigation. The investigation uncovered numerous accounting improprieties and resulted in the termination of both Dunlap and the CFO and an extensive restatement of earnings from the fourth quarter of 1996 through the first quarter of 1998. The restatement wiped out nearly two-thirds of Sunbeam's reported 1997 net income, and the company eventually filed for bankruptcy.

Improperly Writing Off Intangible Assets   In a manner like the accounting treatment of plant and equipment, most intangible assets (with goodwill as a notable exception) will be amortized over a set period established by management. Under EM Shenanigan No. 4, stretching out the time horizon provides an artificial boost to income by lowering the quarterly amortization expense. And of course, curtailing the time horizon serves to mute profits. Since this is the precise objective of EM Shenanigan No. 7, investors should be mindful of such a shortened useful life on intangible assets.

Watch for Restructuring Charges Just Before an Acquisition Closes   Remember in the previous chapter that U.S. Robotics gave its new parent 3Com a gift by holding back hundreds of millions in revenue to be released by 3Com after the merger closed? Well, U.S. Robotics had a second wonderful welcoming gift that was just as simple to create by using one of the techniques under EM Shenanigan No. 7. Just before the merger, U.S. Robotics took a $426 million "merger-related" charge, which prevented 3Com from having to record those costs as part of normal operations after the merger. Of the total charge, $92 million was related to the write-off of fixed assets, goodwill, and purchased technology. Naturally, writing off these assets would reduce future-period depreciation and amortization expense and increase net income.

Be Wary When Restructurings Occur with Uncommon Regularity
Restructuring costs for streamlining operations and cost containment programs often are warranted during tough economic times. However, restructuring events should not become a regular occurrence. As we discussed in Chapter 5, "Earnings Manipulation Shenanigan No. 3: Boosting Income Using One-Time or Unsustainable Activities," some companies abuse the ability to present charges below the line by recording charges for "restructuring costs" or "one-time items" in every single period. We showcased Alcatel and Whirlpool, which posted restructuring charges in just about every quarter for years on end. After a while, investors must question whether companies know the difference between nonrecurring and recurring. If a company incurs a certain type of cost every year, it should be shown with all other recurring operating items.

2. Improperly Recording Charges to Establish Reserves Used to Reduce Future Expenses

In the first section of this chapter, we discussed how companies record an expense today to prevent *past expenditures* (which remain as assets on the Balance Sheet) from becoming future expenses. In this section, we highlight a similar trick in which companies record an expense today to keep *future* expenditures from being reported as expenses. With this trick, management loads up the current period with expenses, taking some from future periods and even making some up. In so doing, when the future period arrives, (1) operating expenses will be underreported, and (2) bogus expenses and related bogus liabilities will be reversed, resulting in underreported operating expenses and inflated profits. Let's examine these two results in more detail.

Using Restructuring Charges Today to Inflate Operating Income Tomorrow
Just as AOL was anxious to remove the $385 million in deferred marketing costs from future periods' amortization expense, any company that is taking a restructuring charge (such as laying off workers) might consider padding the total dollars written off to lower future-period operating expenses. Thus, salary expense to employees who are laid off today will decline in future periods, as any future severance payments received will be bundled into today's one-time charge. The result: future periods' above-the-line operating expense disappears, and the current period's below-the-line restructuring charge increases by that same amount. But remember, investors generally ignore restructuring charges, so the more a company throws into the charge-off, the better. More below-the-line expense and less above-the-line is viewed as a win-win situation.

Watch for Dramatic Improvement in the Numbers Right After the Restructuring Period Let's return to Sunbeam to see the significant impact on future earnings from a prior restructuring charge. As shown in Table 9-2, Sunbeam's operating income surged to $132.6 million in the nine months following the restructuring charge, from $4.0 million in the prior-year period. Consider the impact of Sunbeam's accounting policy changes shortly after Dunlap took the reins. During the December 1996 quarter, Sunbeam recorded a special charge of $337.6 million for restructuring and another $12 million charge for a media advertising campaign and "one-time expenditures for market research." According to the SEC lawsuit, the 1996 *restructuring charge was inflated* by at least $35 million, and Sunbeam also improperly created a $12 million litigation reserve.

Table 9-2　Sunbeam's Operational Performance

($ millions)	9 Months, 9/96	9 Months, 9/97	% Change
Revenue	715.4	830.1	16%
Gross profit	124.1	231.1	86%
Operating income	4.0	132.6	NM
Receivables	194.6	309.1	59%
Inventory	330.2	290.9	(12%)
Cash flow from operations	(18.8)	(60.8)	NM

Watch for "Big Bath" Charges During Tough Times Perhaps there is no better time to record huge charges than when the market is in a downturn. Since during these times investors are more focused on how companies will emerge from the downturn, large charges are less likely to draw ire; indeed, they are often seen as a positive. As we discussed earlier, it is not difficult for management to use these charges to inappropriately write off productive assets or establish bogus reserves.

Creating a Larger-Than-Needed Restructuring Reserve and Inflating Future Earnings by Releasing the Reserve

The previous chapter explained how companies tend to obsess over reporting smooth and predictable earnings. Remember the example of Freddie Mac reserving so much that it got caught before it was ever able to release more than $4 billion that it had squirreled away? Creating and releasing reserves as needed is a technique that works great for management playing the opposite game.

Using a Restructuring Reserve to Smooth Earnings When a company takes an appropriately sized restructuring charge (e.g., when it plans to lay off 100 people and takes a charge for only those 100), future compensation expense will be shifted to the current period and classified as a below-the-line expense. That intraperiod movement to below the line works fine for most, but some executives become too greedy and use a second (and unethical) trick. When management is planning to lay off employees, it instead takes an inappropriately large restructuring charge (e.g., it plans to lay off 100 people but takes a charge for 200). By announcing a 200-person layoff when 100 would be sufficient, management doubles the restructuring expense and liability. Let's assume that management provides a $25,000 severance package for each person who is laid off. That works out to $2.5 million if management acts ethically; alternatively, by doubling the 100 employees to 200, it takes a $5 million charge.

The company then pays out the promised $25,000 to each of the 100 folks who are now out of work. Of course, another $2.5 million remains in the liability, with no more expected severance obligations. So management takes the plunge and releases the bogus reserve in the liability account, reducing compensation expense. This sure seems like an enticing trick for an unethical company that needs a few more pennies to beat Wall Street's estimates. We call this "the gift that keeps on giving."

Watch for Companies That Create Reserves at the Time of an Acquisition   In December 2000, Symbol Technologies recorded $185.9 million in charges related to its purchase of competitor Telxon Corporation. At the time, Symbol justified these charges as being necessary for restructuring of operations, impairment of assets (including inventory), and merger integration costs. It turns out that the charges included fictitious costs that were used to create cookie jar reserves to help inflate earnings in future periods. The charges also overstated inventory write-offs that would provide a boost to future gross margins as the related inventory was sold.

Similarly, in June 1997, Xerox purchased a 20 percent stake in its own European subsidiary that had been owned by the U.K.-based Rank Group. Related to this purchase, Xerox improperly established a $100 million reserve for "unknown risks" arising out of the transaction. In establishing the reserve, Xerox violated generally accepted accounting principles by recording a reserve for an unknown and unquantifiable risk. Nonetheless, Xerox began using this reserve as a type of piggy bank, releasing funds from it into income whenever the company's results fell short of Wall Street's estimates. It continued to draw on the reserve each quarter for things that were completely unrelated to the acquisition until it was fully depleted at the end of 1999. Using this same trick, Xerox fraudulently released into income approximately 20 other excess reserves totaling $396 million to improve earnings from 1997 through 2000.

Building Up Your Reserve During Times of Plenty

The Bible tells the story of Joseph's unique ability to decipher Pharaoh's unsettling dream. After hearing details of the dream, Joseph warned Pharaoh that a famine was coming; seven years of shortages would follow seven years of plenty. Joseph became Pharaoh's chief steward and immediately began a program to set aside a reserve of food and supplies. When seven years later the famine hit, Pharaoh and all of Egypt were ready.

Companies also consider the future and can reasonably predict normal business cycles and, less reasonably well, those occasional sudden jolts to the economy. Smart management today understands what Joseph and Pharaoh learned—lean years invariably follow the good ones. In that context, if a company has already met its income projections for the current period, it may attempt to shift next year's expenses into this earlier period. H.J. Heinz Company had a premonition that one of the lean years was fast approaching and shifted some costs to the earlier period by prepaying expenses to boost the following year's profit. One of its subsidiaries engaged in other ploys as well, such as misstating its cost of sales, improperly soliciting bills from vendors for advertising, and expensing invoices for services that had not yet been received.

Looking Ahead

Chapter 8 and this chapter both illustrated games that management might play to (1) smooth earnings, (2) shift income from a particularly strong period to a weaker one, or (3) clear the decks of troublesome expenses to produce future-period earnings to dazzle investors.

These two chapters complete our discussion of the seven Earnings Manipulation Shenanigans. As EM Shenanigans Nos. 1 through 5 illustrated, management has a large arsenal of techniques that can trick investors into believing that a company has generated more profit than it really has. And if management instead desires to make tomorrow look fantastic, EM Shenanigans Nos. 6 and 7 will get the job done.

Chapter 10 begins Part Three, "Cash Flow Shenanigans." Conventional wisdom for years has been that playing accounting games with earnings is quite easy, but the cash flow numbers are rock solid. In Part Three, we debunk this myth and demonstrate that Cash Flow Shenanigans also are pervasive and just as easy for management to use to trick investors as the earnings manipulation gimmicks we discussed in Part Two.

PART THREE

CASH FLOW
SHENANIGANS

With so many recent financial frauds going undetected, investors have increasingly questioned the value of the accrual-based figures shown on the Income Statement. Time and time again, companies have duped investors by recording revenue too soon or hiding expenses, leading some to conclude that earnings can be manipulated and therefore they should put more faith in the "purer" measure of cash flow from operations.

While that's certainly a step in the right direction, be extra careful to look both ways as you cross the street from accrual-based earnings to the cash flow numbers. The reasons for exercising this caution will become abundantly clear as you read through this part of the book.

In Part Three, we showcase three specific types of Cash Flow (CF) Shenanigans, highlighting techniques that companies have employed to inflate reported cash flow from operations (CFFO). We also present strategies for detecting Cash Flow Shenanigans quickly and offer tips on how to adjust the reported numbers to calculate a more sustainable cash flow metric.

THREE CASH FLOW SHENANIGANS

CF Shenanigan No. 1: Shifting financing cash inflows to the Operating section (Chapter 10)

CF Shenanigan No. 2: Moving operating cash outflows to other sections (Chapter 11)

CF Shenanigan No. 3: Boosting operating cash flow using unsustainable activities (Chapter 12)

Accrual Versus Cash-Based Accounting

Before digging into the specific techniques, it is important to have a firm grasp of accrual versus cash-based accounting as well as the structure of the Statement of Cash Flows (SCF). Accounting rules mandate that a company report its earnings performance using the accrual basis. That simply means you report revenue when it is earned (rather than when cash comes in) and charge expenses when the benefit has been received (rather than when payment occurs). In other words, the significance of cash inflows and outflows is muted under accrual-based accounting. Fortunately for investors, companies must also provide a separate SCF highlighting inflows and outflows from three main sources: operating, investing, and financing activities. The information included in the Operating section can be used as an *alternative performance measure* to the accrual-based earnings.

As discussed in previous chapters, savvy investors often compare net income with CFFO and become concerned when CFFO lags net income. Indeed, high net income along with low CFFO often signals the presence of some Earnings Manipulation Shenanigans.

Let's compare the form and structure of a typical Income Statement with the Operating section of the Statement of Cash Flows. Under accounting rules (SFAS 95), companies can use either the "direct" or the "indirect" method to present CFFO. The direct method simply shows major sources of cash inflows (i.e., from customers) and outflows (i.e., to vendors and employees). The indirect method, in contrast, starts with accrual-based net income and reconciles it to CFFO. The direct method certainly seems more intuitive for investors, and rule makers specifically expressed their preference for companies to use that approach. However, this urging by rule makers has failed to convince companies to go along, as almost all present only the indirect method. Here we present the Income Statement (accrual-based), cash flow from operations (direct method), and cash flow from operations (indirect method).

Income Statement: Accrual-Based

Sales revenue	1,000,000
Less: Operating expenses	(850,000)
Operating income	150,000
Less: Nonoperating expenses	(50,000)
Pretax income	100,000
Less: Income tax @35%	(35,000)
Net income	**65,000**

Cash Flow from Operations: Direct Method

Customer collections	750,000
Less:	
Vendor payments	(550,000)
Employee salaries	(600,000)
Tax payments	(35,000)
Interest payments	(40,000)
Cash flow from operations	**(475,000)**

Cash Flow from Operations: Indirect Method

Net income	65,000
Adjustments to reconcile to net cash	
Depreciation and amortization	40,000
Provision for doubtful accounts	10,000
Changes in working capital	
Accounts receivable	(820,000)
Inventory	(80,000)
Prepaid expenses	50,000
Accounts payable and deferred revenue	260,000
Cash flow from operations	**(475,000)**

Although net income and CFFO represent different measures of a company's performance, investors should generally expect them to move in the same direction. That is, if a company reports growing net income, it would be worth raising questions if cash flow from operations is shrinking. Notice in the example of the indirect method above, CFFO lagged net income by a whopping $540,000 (negative $475,000 less a positive $65,000). As we discussed earlier, such an outcome may have investors worried that the company is employing Earnings Manipulation Shenanigans.

Performance Measures—from Earnings to Cash Flow

Management certainly understands that its investors cherish a high "quality of earnings." Executives know that investors test earnings quality by benchmarking earnings against CFFO, as we did in the previous example. They also know that many investors consider CFFO to be the most important measure of company performance; some investors have even completely turned away from earnings and instead focus primarily on analyzing a company's ability to generate cash.

It should therefore come as no surprise that companies have become more creative in their financial reporting and disclosure practices. Many have found innovative ways to mislead investors, using deceptive practices that may go undetected in traditional quality of earnings analysis. As you will learn in Part Three, many of these shenanigans involve the manipulation of cash flow from operations.

Cash Flow from Operations: The Favored Son

Before diving into these Cash Flow Shenanigans, it is important to understand the basic structure of the Statement of Cash Flows. The SCF shows how a company's cash balance changed over the period. It presents all inflows and outflows of cash, reconciling the beginning to the ending balance. All cash movements can be grouped into one of three categories: operating, investing, and financing activities. Figure P3-1 illustrates the typical inflows and outflows within each section of the SCF.

Figure P3-1 The Statement of Cash Flows is Organized into Three Sections: Operating, Investing, and Financing Activities

	Operating Activities	Investing Activities	Financing Activities
Inflows	Customer collections Interest collections Dividend collections	Investment sales Plant/equipment sales Business disposals	Bank borrowings Other borrowings Stock issuance
Outflows	Vendor payments Employee salaries Tax payments Interest payments	Capital expenditures Investment purchases Property purchases Business acquisitions	Loan repayments Stock repurchases Dividend payments

Investors do not consider the three sections of the Statement of Cash Flows equally important. Rather, they regard the Operating section as the "favored son" because it presents cash generated from a company's actual business operations (i.e., cash flow from operations). Many investors are less concerned with a company's investments or changes in its capital structure, and some even go to the extreme and completely ignore the other sections. After all, the Operating section should fully convey a company's operating activities, right?

Well, not really. Companies can exert a great deal of discretion when presenting cash flows. Many of the Cash Flow Shenanigans can be considered *intraperiod geography games*—under which companies take liberal interpretations of "what goes where" on the Statement of Cash Flows. For example, should an outflow be shown in the Operating or the Investing section? Clearly, management's decision would have a profound effect on the reported CFFO and on an investor's assessment of the company's performance. Other shenanigans involve subjective management decisions that influence the timing of cash flows to portray an overly rosy economic picture.

Robin Hood Tricks

Think of these intraperiod geography games as "Robin Hood" tricks: stealing from the rich sections of the Statement of Cash Flows and giving to the poor one. In these cases, the "poor" section will be the Operating section, which investors follow much more closely, and the "rich" sections will be the Investing and Financing sections, which investors tend to de-emphasize.

As you will see, these Robin Hood tricks are quite simple and more common than you might imagine. It is not that difficult for companies to concoct a reason to move the good stuff (cash inflows) to the most important Operating section and to send the bad stuff (cash outflows) to the less important Investing and Financing sections. Figure P3-2 illustrates some of these tricks, such as improperly moving inflows that really come from bank borrowings to the Operating section or shifting those unwanted outflows out of Operating and labeling them capital expenditures.

Figure P3-2   Cash Flow Shenanigans: Robin Hood Tricks

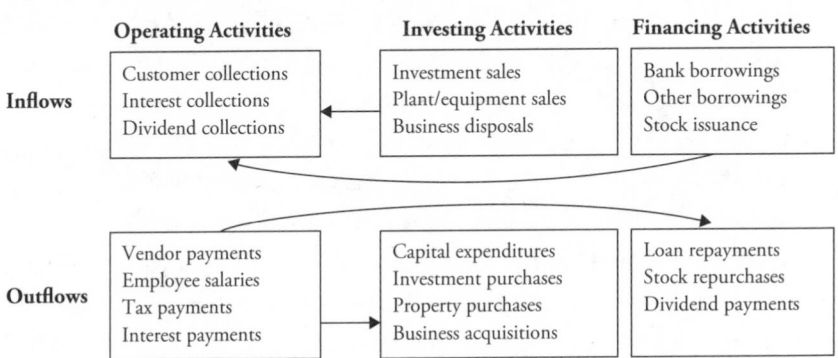

Where Is the Sheriff of Nottingham?

Just as the Sheriff of Nottingham could not prevent Robin Hood from steal-ing from the rich and giving to the poor, the current accounting rules often seem inadequate to prevent companies from engaging in such cash flow she-nanigans. This is because the rule makers failed to adequately address many key issues when they wrote the accounting standards for the Statement of Cash Flows. Indeed, when addressing "what goes where" on the Statement of Cash Flows, the accounting rules are quite vague, providing management with a great deal of discretion.

In fact, occasionally the accounting rules can be considered "accomplices" to Robin Hood's tricks because, as applied, in some cases they fail to capture the true economics of transactions. As a result, even when companies follow the rules, they may still present a CFFO figure that measures the organic growth of the business poorly. Of course, companies that follow the rules should not be accused of chicanery. Nonetheless, playing by the rules does not always result in financial reporting that accurately reflects the underlying economic reality.

Good News and Bad News (but Mostly Good News)

Now it's time for some good news and some bad news. The *bad news* is that there are many techniques that allow companies to portray misleading cash flows. Moreover, many aspects of the rules surrounding the Statement of Cash Flows create confusion about the sustainability of the CFFO reported to investors.

However, the *good news* is that you realize this—indeed, you are reading this book. You are about to learn how to detect these tricks quickly and gain the knowledge and tools necessary to successfully go toe-to-toe with companies that may attempt to mislead you with Cash Flow Shenanigans.

The next four chapters offer a guided tour of four Cash Flow Shenanigans, including techniques used by management to shift undesirable outflows away from the Operating section and push desirable inflows into that section. Naturally, we share our secrets on how to detect signs of these shenanigans. Chapter 10 starts off with shifting the cherished inflows from financing arrangements to the Operating section.

10

Cash Flow Shenanigan No. 1: Shifting Financing Cash Inflows to the Operating Section

Arnold Schwarzenegger and Danny DeVito were an unlikely pair in the 1988 hit comedy *Twins*. The twins were born in a genetics lab as the result of a secret experiment to create the perfect child. Doctors manipulated the fertility process to funnel the desirable traits to one child while sending the "genetic trash" to the other. In so doing, they created an intelligent Adonis (Schwarzenegger), but to do so, the doctors also had to create his gnomish, conniving twin brother (DeVito).

That very same year, new cash flow reporting standards (SFAS 95) took effect, officially formalizing the Statement of Cash Flows and its three sections (Operating, Investing, and Financing). It seems that some corporate executives were reviewing the new rules while they were watching the fertility manipulation in *Twins*. This may be where they got the crazy idea of manipulating the Statement of Cash Flows by sending all the desirable cash inflows to the most important section (Operating) and the unwanted cash outflows to the other sections (Investing and Financing).

In recent years, many companies have seemingly been operating their own *Twins* genetics labs. But rather than attempting to create the perfect child, they are attempting to create the perfect Statement of Cash Flows. In this chapter, we expose one of the most important secret procedures being performed inside those labs: shifting the desirable inflows from a financing transaction to the Operating section.

Techniques to Shift Financing Cash Inflows to the Operating Section

1. Recording bogus CFFO from a normal bank borrowing

2. Boosting CFFO by selling receivables before the collection date

3. Inflating CFFO by faking the sale of receivables

These three techniques all represent ways in which companies inflate cash flow from operations (CFFO) by shifting net cash inflows from financing arrangements to the Operating section, as illustrated in our handy cash flow map in Figure 10-1.

Figure 10-1

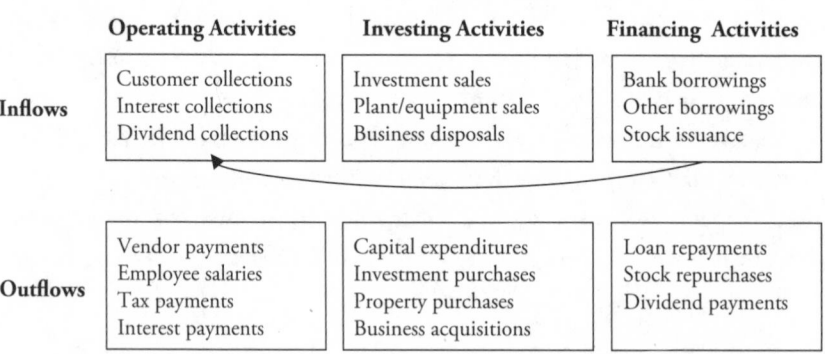

	Operating Activities	**Investing Activities**	**Financing Activities**
Inflows	Customer collections Interest collections Dividend collections	Investment sales Plant/equipment sales Business disposals	Bank borrowings Other borrowings Stock issuance
Outflows	Vendor payments Employee salaries Tax payments Interest payments	Capital expenditures Investment purchases Property purchases Business acquisitions	Loan repayments Stock repurchases Dividend payments

1. Recording Bogus CFFO from a Normal Bank Borrowing

At the end of 2000, Delphi Corporation found itself in a bind. It had been spun out from General Motors a year earlier, and management was intent on showing the company to be a strong and viable stand-alone operation. However, despite management's ambitions, all was not well at the auto parts supplier. Since the spin-off, Delphi had cooked up many schemes to inflate its results. The auto industry was reeling, and the economy was getting worse.

Delphi's operations continued to deteriorate in the fourth quarter of 2000, and the company was facing the prospect of having to tell investors that cash flow from operations had turned severely negative for the quarter. This would have been a devastating blow, as Delphi often highlighted its cash flow in the headline of its Earnings Releases as a key indicator of the company's performance and its (purported) strength.

So, already knee-deep in lies, Delphi concocted another scheme to save the quarter. In the last weeks of December 2000, Delphi went to its bank (Bank One) and offered to sell it $200 million in precious metals inventory. Not surprisingly, Bank One had no interest in buying inventory. Remember, we are talking about a bank, not an auto parts manufacturer. Delphi understood this and crafted the agreement in such a way that Bank One would be able to "sell" the inventory back to Delphi a few weeks later (after year-end). In exchange for the bank's "ownership" of the inventory for a few weeks, Delphi would buy it back at a small premium to the original sale price.

Let's step back and think about what really happened here. The economics of this transaction should be clear to you: Delphi took out a short-term loan from Bank One. As is the case with many bank loans, Bank One required Delphi to put up collateral (in this case, the precious metals inventory) that could be seized in case Delphi decided not to pay back the loan. Delphi should have recorded the $200 million received from Bank One as a borrowing (an increase in cash flow from financing activities). As a plain vanilla loan, this transaction should have increased cash and a liability (loan payable) on Delphi's Balance Sheet. Clearly, borrowing and later repaying the loan produces no revenue.

Rather than recording the transaction in a manner consistent with the economics and intent of the parties, as a loan, Delphi brazenly recorded it as the sale of $200 million in inventory. In so doing, Delphi inflated revenue and earnings, as discussed in EM Shenanigan No. 2. Moreover, it also overstated CFFO by the $200 million that Delphi claimed to have received in exchange for the "sale" of inventory. As shown in Table 10-1, without this $200 million, Delphi would have recorded only $68 million in CFFO for the entire year (rather than the $268 million reported), including a dismal negative $158 million in the fourth quarter.

Table 10-1   Delphi's Cash Flow from Operations,
Adjusted for the Impact of a Sham Loan

($ millions)	FY 2000
Cash flow from operations	268
Less: Borrowed cash improperly recorded as CFFO	(200)
Normalized CFFO	68

Remember That Bogus Revenue May Also Mean Bogus CFFO
In EM Shenanigan No. 2, we discussed techniques that companies use to record bogus revenue, including engaging in transactions that lack economic substance or that lack a reasonable arm's-length process. Some investors become so disillusioned when they read about bogus revenue and other earnings manipulation tricks that they decide to completely ignore accrual-based numbers and, instead, blindly rely exclusively on the Statement of Cash Flows. We consider this decision unwise. Investors should understand that *bogus revenue might also signal bogus CFFO*. This was clearly the case in the Delphi example, as well as in many other so-called boomerang transactions. Thus, as a rule, signs of bogus revenue may portend inflated CFFO as well.

Be Wary Around Pro Forma CFFO Metrics   Delphi steered investors away from its reported CFFO and instead highlighted a cash flow measure that it defined itself and confusingly labeled "Operating Cash Flow." Normally investors use the terms "CFFO" and "operating cash flow" interchangeably; however, Delphi defined them very differently. (More on this in Part Four, "Key Metric Shenanigans.")

In FY 2000, Delphi reported $268 million in CFFO on its Statement of Cash Flows; however, its self-defined "Operating Cash Flow" (reported in the Earnings Release) was $1.6 billion. No, we're not kidding—a differential of an amazing $1.4 billion! Careful investors would have noticed this shenanigan and immediately become skeptical about the company, as the level of trickery was astounding and inexcusable. (Stay tuned for more on this $1.4 billion differential in Chapter 13.) Of course, even the $268 million in reported CFFO was inflated, as it included the sham sale of inventory to the bank discussed previously. The SEC must have had a field day when it sorted through all of Delphi's schemes and charged the company with fraud.

Not only did Delphi create a misleading substitute for CFFO, but it routinely highlighted the strength of this number to investors in the title of its quarterly Earnings Releases. Investors should be cautious whenever management places such an intense focus on a company-created cash flow metric that covertly redefines the very important CFFO. Of course, management's creative use of metrics may not always be indicative of fraud; however, investors should nonetheless ratchet up their normal level of skepticism.

Complicated Off-Balance-Sheet Structures Raise the Risk of Inflated CFFO

We have already outlined several ruses perpetrated by Enron, particularly its use of off-Balance-Sheet vehicles such as special-purpose entities. Some of the schemes that Enron concocted helped it present a misleadingly stronger CFFO. For example, Enron would create such a vehicle and then help it borrow money by cosigning its loans. The Enron-controlled vehicle then used the cash received to "purchase" commodities from Enron. Enron recorded the cash received as an Operating section inflow (CFFO) from the "sale" of the commodities.

The structure of these transactions may seem complicated, but the economics were quite simple: Enron entered arrangements to sell commodities to itself. The problem was that it recorded only half of the transaction—the part that reflected the cash inflows. Specifically, Enron recorded the "sale" of the commodities as an Operating inflow, but ignored the offsetting outflow from the vehicle's "purchase" of these commodities. If Enron had recorded this transaction in line with its economics, the cash inflow would have been deemed a loan and hence recorded as a Financing inflow. This trick allowed Enron to embellish its CFFO by billions of dollars, to the detriment of its Financing cash flow—and, of course, of its investors.

2. Boosting CFFO by Selling Receivables Before the Collection Date

In the previous section, we discussed how Delphi and Enron created dangerous schemes in their *Twins* genetics labs that allowed them to record completely bogus cash flow from operations. In this section, we discuss how companies might boost CFFO with a transaction that is quite popular and considered completely appropriate: selling accounts receivable. However, the way management presents these transactions on its financial statements often leads to a great deal of confusion for investors.

Turning Receivables into Cash Even Though the Customer Has Yet to Pay
Companies often sell accounts receivable as a useful cash management strategy. These transactions are quite simple: a company wishes to collect on its receivables before they come due. The company finds a willing investor (i.e., a bank) and transfers ownership of some receivables. In return, the company pockets a cash payment for the total receivables, less a fee.

Let's think about the underlying transaction, its purpose, and the other party's interest. Does this arrangement sound like a financing transaction or an operating one? Many people would agree that an arrangement in which a bank simply cuts you a check looks strikingly like an old-fashioned loan—nothing more than a form of financing, particularly since management determines the timing and the amount of cash received. They therefore expect that this transaction will not affect CFFO. However, the rules state otherwise. The appropriate place to record cash generated from the sale of receivables would be an Operating inflow, not a Financing inflow. Why Operating? Because the cash received could be viewed as representing collections from past sales. Indeed, this is one of many gray areas that cause confusion among even the savviest investors.

ACCOUNTING CAPSULE: SELLING ACCOUNTS RECEIVABLE

It is important to recognize when a company is selling its receivables, as these transactions are recorded as CFFO inflows. There are a variety of ways in which companies can sell their receivables, including factoring transactions and securitizations. Keep an eye out for these key words in financial statements.

- **Factoring:** The simple sale of receivables to a third party, often a bank or a special-purpose entity

- **Securitization:** The sale of receivables to a third party (often a special-purpose entity) for the purposes of creating new financial instruments ("securities") by repackaging the receivable inflows

---

Selling Accounts Receivable: An Unsustainable Driver of Cash Flow Growth
In 2004, pharmaceutical distributor Cardinal Health needed to generate a lot more cash. So management decided to sell accounts receivable to help the company raise cash very quickly. By the end of the second quarter (December 2004), Cardinal Health had sold $800 million in customer receivables. This transaction was the primary driver of the company's robust $971 million in CFFO growth in December 2004 over the prior-year period.

While Cardinal Health certainly was entitled to any cash received in exchange for its accounts receivable, investors should have realized that this was an *unsustainable* source of CFFO growth. Cardinal Health essentially collected on receivables (from a third party, rather than from its customers) that would normally have been collected in future quarters. By collecting the cash earlier than anticipated, the company essentially shifted future-period cash inflows into the current quarter, leaving a "hole" in future-periods' cash flow. The transfer of cash flow to an earlier period is likely to result in disappointing CFFO in the future—unless, of course, management finds another CF Shenanigan to plug the hole.

Watch for Sudden Swings on the Statement of Cash Flows   Even novice investors could have identified that something important had changed in Cardinal Health's accounts receivable and that CFFO growth was largely driven by this change. Look at the company's Statement of Cash Flows in

Table 10-2. Notice that the $971 million increase (from $548 million to $1.5 billion) in CFFO had been driven primarily by a $1.1 billion "swing" in the impact of receivables. Specifically, in the six months ending December 2004, the change in accounts receivable represented a cash inflow of $622 million, while in the previous year, the change in accounts receivable had contributed a cash *outflow* of $488 million. Without doubt, the massive receivable sale, not an improvement in Cardinal Health's core business, produced the impressive CFFO improvement. To emphasize, investors should focus not only on *how much* CFFO grew, but also on *how* it grew—a very notable difference.

Table 10-2   Cardinal Health's Cash Flow from Operations, as Reported

| | Six Months Ended | |
($ millions)	12/31/03	12/31/04
Earnings from continuing operations	**697.1**	**421.6**
Depreciation and amortization	143.2	198.2
Asset impairments	4.8	155.8
Provision for bad debts	(2.7)	0.8
Decrease/(increase) in trade receivables	**(488.3)**	**622.3**
Increase in inventories	(841.4)	(707.5)
Decrease (increase) in sales-type leases	22.0	(95.3)
Increase in accounts payable	964.3	794.1
Other accrued liabilities and operating items, net	49.4	129.2
Net cash provided by operating activities	**548.4**	**1,519.2**

Sudden swings like these at Cardinal Health signal the need to explore more deeply. In this case, you would have found that the company began selling more accounts receivable. This was fairly easy to find, and the company clearly did nothing improper. In fact, the company was very forthcoming, disclosing the accounts receivable sales clearly in its Earnings Release as well as in the 10-Q filing (although disclosing it on the Statement of Cash Flows would be preferred). While perhaps casual or lazy investors were too easily impressed with Cardinal Health's ability to grow its CFFO, savvy investors would certainly have realized that the growth came from a nonrecurring source.

Stealth Sales of Receivables

Unlike Cardinal Health, which was relatively transparent with its disclosure, some companies try hard to keep investors in the dark when their
CFFO benefits from the sale of receivables. Take, for instance, the case of
a certain electronics manufacturer. Sanmina-SCI Corporation reported
its fourth-quarter results for September 2005 in early November. In the
Earnings Release, Sanmina decided to prominently display its strong CFFO
as one of its fourth-quarter "highlights." Accounts receivable had decreased,
and Sanmina also proudly pointed out the decline in receivables near the top
of the release.

But the Earnings Release didn't tell the whole story. Nearly two months
later, deep in the 10-K filed on December 29, 2005, while many investors
were on holiday, Sanmina disclosed what had really happened: *the primary
driver of CFFO in Q4 was the sale of receivables*. Sanmina reported that $224
million in receivables that it had sold were still subject to recourse at the
end of the quarter. This was quite an increase from the $84 million reported
in the previous quarter. Sanmina had been quietly selling receivables for
the past couple of quarters, but never at this magnitude. As shown in Table
10-3, without this increase in receivables sold, Sanmina's CFFO would have
been $139 million lower, falling to $36 million instead of the reported $175
million.

Table 10-3   Sanmina-SCI's CFFO in Q4, 9/05,
Adjusted to Remove the Impact of Sold Receivables

($ millions)	Q4, 9/05
Cash flow from operations	175
Quarterly change in sold receivables	(139)
Normalized CFFO	36

TIP

When normalizing CFFO to exclude the impact of sold receivables, use the
change in sold receivables *outstanding at the end of the quarter*. In this way,
you could focus on receivables outstanding last quarter but collected during
this one.

Read the Quarterly Filings to Know What to Anticipate Certainly, a full reading of the 10-K would have revealed that sales of receivables drove CFFO. But could you have suspected that this was the case before the 10-K was even filed? Indeed, the answer would be yes. Astute investors would have read the previous quarter's 10-Q and noticed that Sanmina discussed the sale of receivables no fewer than four times. They also would have noted that the company had mentioned the arrangement in passing on its earnings conference call two quarters earlier. These A-plus investors would have known that they should be wary in the fourth quarter when the CFFO suddenly surged because of a significant decline in receivables. They certainly would have been able to connect the dots.

Shun Opacity It is clearly inappropriate for companies to be opaque when reporting sensitive and impactful structured arrangements such as selling receivables. Be wary if companies fail to provide investors with details. Question their reasons for not being transparent about how they monetize their receivables. Perhaps management's objective is simply to window-dress its Statement of Cash Flows. The worst-case scenario would be that the company is trying to hide a real cash crunch from investors. Such a cover-up clearly goes far beyond simple window dressing and points to a company camouflaging a material deterioration in its business. Dot-com high-flyer Global Crossing sold $183 million in receivables just six months before it filed for bankruptcy in 2002. Similarly, Xerox raised the ire of the SEC by silently selling $288 million in receivables at the end of 1999 to report a positive year-end cash balance of $126 million.

3. Inflating CFFO by Faking the Sale of Receivables

In the previous section, we discussed the implications of normal receivable sales for CFFO. We pointed out that in many cases, selling receivables may be not only appropriate, but also a prudent business decision. However, investors also need to understand that the cash flow that was expected in a future period has now been collected, and this inflow should be viewed as unsustainable. In this section, we take a step into more nefarious territory. We will encounter another top-secret procedure being performed in the companies' *Twins* labs: faking the sale of receivables.

Sham Sales of Receivables—the "Watergate" of Shenanigans

President Nixon resigned in disgrace because of trying to cover up the break-in at the Watergate Hotel. The smoking-gun evidence apparently was included on an 18½-minute section of a White House recording that was conveniently erased to cover up the crime. Similarly, Peregrine Systems used a convenient cover-up to hide its accounting fraud. As we discussed in Chapter 4, "Earnings Manipulation Shenanigan No. 2: Recording Bogus Revenue," Peregrine embellished its revenue in the years leading up to its 2002 bankruptcy, using deceptive practices such as recording bogus revenue and entering into reciprocal transactions. This fake revenue resulted in bloated receivables on the Balance Sheet that would never be collected. Peregrine became concerned that these bloated receivables would become the smoking gun of its bogus revenue. So the cover-up began in earnest with *fake sales of accounts receivable.*

In this cover-up, Peregrine transferred its receivables to a bank in exchange for cash; however, the risk of collection loss remained with Peregrine. That collection risk was huge, of course, because *there were no customers*—many of the related sales were bogus. Since the risk of loss had not been transferred, Peregrine remained on the hook to return the cash to the bank when the receivables inevitably were not collected.

Since the receivables had never actually been transferred, the economics of this transaction would be more akin to a collateralized loan, just as we saw with Delphi earlier in this chapter. Peregrine borrowed money from the bank and used receivables as collateral. On the Statement of Cash Flows, this should be presented as a *Financing* inflow. Peregrine, however, ignored the economic reality of the situation. Instead, it recorded the transaction as the sale of receivables and shamelessly reported the cash received as an *Operating* inflow.

Watch Carefully for Disclosure Changes in the Risk Factors   Many investors overlook the "Risk Factor" section of corporate filings because it seems like legal boilerplate. *Warning to investors:* ignore the risk factors at your own peril. While most of the text may be similar from quarter to quarter, investors should carefully try to identify *changes* in the verbiage. If new risks have been added or previously listed ones have been changed, then the change is deemed worthy of disclosure by the company or its auditors, and you need to know about it.

For instance, in 2001, the year before Peregrine imploded in fraud, the company inserted an important new risk factor disclosure that should have awakened investors from their slumber. Peregrine changed its risk factor disclosure twice, first in June 2001 and then again in December 2001. The new disclosure in June 2001 informed readers that Peregrine was engaging in new customer financing arrangements, including loan financing and leasing solutions. It also reported that some customers were failing to meet their obligations. The mere fact that this disclosure found its way into the risk factors tells you it must have been significant.

PEREGRINE'S NEW RISK FACTOR DISCLOSURE IN JUNE 2001

In addition, other factors, including indirect factors resulting from the macroeconomic climate, could have an adverse effect on our operating results in one or over several quarterly periods. For example, in the current economic environment, we have experienced increased demand from some customers for customer financing, including loan financing, and leasing solutions. We expect this demand for customer financing to continue, and we have engaged in customer financing where we believe it is a competitive factor in obtaining business. Although we have programs in place to monitor and mitigate the associated risks, there can be no assurance that such programs will be effective in reducing related credit risk. We have experienced losses due to customers failing to meet their obligations. Future losses, if incurred, could harm our business and have a material adverse effect on our operating results and financial condition.

Then, in December 2001, Peregrine added one small sentence to the end of the new disclosure from the June period. While it was only 12 words, it read like a five-alarm fire:

PEREGRINE'S NEW RISK FACTOR DISCLOSURE IN DECEMBER 2001

The Company may at times market certain client receivable balances without recourse.

Peregrine was doing more than just finding new ways to provide its customers with financing; it was also trying to sell its accounts receivable. The cryptic nature of this new sentence, together with the hush-hush disclosure in the risk factors with no mention of it elsewhere, is extremely concerning. Peregrine was clearly hiding something big from investors and trying to comply with the minimal level of disclosure requirements.

TIP

It is well worth your time to look for changes in disclosure each quarter, particularly in the most important sections of the filings. Most research platforms and word processing software have "word compare" or "blackline" functionality. Reviewing both filings side by side is not as cumbersome as it sounds.

Computer Associates Makes an Accounting "Decision"
Computer Associates' 2000 10-K revealed that one of its primary sources of operating cash flow that year had come from its fourth quarter "decision" to assign accounts receivable to a third party. No other details were provided. Investors were given no insight into the details of the arrangement, the mechanics of the "assignment," or the magnitude of the impact.

COMPUTER ASSOCIATES ACCOUNTS
RECEIVABLE DISCLOSURE 2000 10-K

The primary source of cash for the year was higher net income adjusted for non-cash charges. Other sources of cash included strong collections of outstanding accounts receivable and *the Company's decision, in the fourth quarter, to assign selected existing installment accounts receivable to a third party.* The Company may continue to explore the use of financing companies as a means of expediting debt reduction, mitigating interest rate risk, and reducing installment accounts receivable balances. [Italics added for emphasis]

Recall from Chapter 3, "Earnings Manipulation Shenanigan No. 1: Recording Revenue Too Soon," that the SEC charged Computer Associates (CA) with prematurely recognizing more than $3.3 billion in revenue from 1998 to 2000. Well, like Peregrine, CA needed a cover-up to conceal this bogus revenue. CA found one by offloading receivables, and the company seemed to try to keep that transfer under wraps. Whenever companies disclose that a mysterious new arrangement is a driver of CFFO (or of any important metric, for that matter), investors should seek to understand the mechanics of the arrangement. Only significant changes would require new disclosure, so when you notice something new, consider it a big deal. At the benign end of the spectrum, it may simply be a nonrecurring benefit that might be important to your analysis. However, on the other end of the spectrum (think CA), it may be a red flag signaling a major impropriety.

Recourse or Nonrecourse?

When a company sells its accounts receivable, it typically it does so under a "nonrecourse" arrangement, which means that the risks of customer default are passed on to the buyer (usually a financial institution). In cases where receivables are sold on a "nonrecourse" basis, the cash received is treated as an Operating cash inflow. By contrast, in cases when the seller retains some of the credit risk ("recourse"), the transaction is considered a form of borrowing, and the cash received is classified as a Financing inflow, with no impact on operating cash flow. In these recourse arrangements, Operating cash flow and free cash flow should be unaffected.

Sometimes companies get confused and include cash received as part of cash flow from operations even though credit risks remain and the proper categorization should be in the Financing section. That was the case with Zoomlion, a Chinese manufacturer of construction equipment, when the company claimed to have sold accounts receivables on a nonrecourse basis (thus including the RMB5.2 billion proceeds as part of the operating cash flow), when in fact it still retained some credit risk. Specifically, astute analysts would have noticed that Zoomlion disclosed its obligation to repurchase equipment from financial institutions that repossess equipment as a result of customer defaults. (See the footnote below contained in the company's

2014 Annual Report.) Even though Zoomlion is not directly on the hook for bad debts, the repurchase commitment mandated that the company provide cash should the debts go bad. In our view, this is tantamount to providing recourse, only in a more convoluted way.

ZOOMLION 2014 ANNUAL REPORT

During the year ended 2014, trade receivables of RMB5,197 million (2013: RMB2,021 million) were factored to banks and other financial institutions without recourse, and were therefore derecognized. Under the non-recourse factoring agreement, the Group has *agreed to repurchase equipment at fair value from banks and other financial institutions to which the Group previously factored receivables, upon repossession of the equipment* under the relevant equipment sales contracts by such banks or financial institutions. [Italics added for emphasis]

Looking Ahead

A second clever way in which management may inflate operating cash flows is by pushing some of the "bad stuff" (i.e., the outflows) from the Operating section to another place on the Statement of Cash Flows. The next chapter shows just how easy it is to move these outflows to the less-scrutinized Investing section.

11

Cash Flow Shenanigan No. 2: Moving Operating Cash Outflows to Other Sections

Jimmy Hoffa, corrupt boss of the Teamsters Union, left a Detroit restaurant on July 30, 1975, and vanished without a trace. It is widely believed that he was "whacked" in a mob hit; yet despite having searched for the past 35 years, the FBI has been unable to locate his remains. Urban legends run rampant, providing many different accounts of his final resting place, including a New Jersey landfill, a Michigan sanitation plant, the Florida Everglades, and even (the old) Giants Stadium. Only one thing is for certain: whoever buried Jimmy Hoffa did not want him to be found.

Like Hoffa's handlers, many companies have a secret dumping ground for pesky cash outflows that they don't want anyone to find. It's called the Investing section of the Statement of Cash Flows. Companies have found numerous clever ways to dump normal operating cash outflows into the

Investing section, hoping that those outflows will vanish forever. And most investors, like the FBI in its hunt for Jimmy Hoffa, seem to have very few clues about where to look.

While unfortunately we can be of no help to the FBI in its search for Hoffa, we certainly can help investors find clues to the whereabouts of hidden cash outflows. This chapter will show you exactly where to look. We'll show you how to find these outflows that management loves to bury in the Investing section, even though they seem more like operating-related outflows. And we'll discuss the following four primary techniques that companies use to shift these operating cash outflows to the Investing section.

Techniques to Move Cash Outflows to Other Sections

1. Inflating CFFO with boomerang transactions

2. Improperly capitalizing normal operating costs

3. Recording the purchase of inventory as an investing outflow

4. Shifting operating cash outflows off the Statement of Cash Flows

All four methods are examples of those used by companies that inflate cash flow from operations (CFFO) by dumping normal operating costs into the Investing section, as shown in Figure 11-1.

Figure 11-1

	Operating Activities	**Investing Activities**	**Financing Activities**
Inflows	Customer collections Interest collections Dividend collections	Investment sales Plant/equipment sales Business disposals	Bank borrowings Other borrowings Stock issuance
Outflows	Vendor payments Employee salaries Tax payments Interest payments	Capital expenditures Investment purchases Property purchases Business acquisitions	Loan repayments Stock repurchases Dividend payments

1. Inflating CFFO with Boomerang Transactions

Global Crossing was one of the highest-flying technology companies during the 1990s dot-com bubble. It was building an undersea fiber-optic cable network that would connect more than 200 cities across four continents, and investors appeared thrilled over its prospects. However, as the project neared completion in 2000 and early 2001, critics began to wonder whether Global Crossing would ever sell enough network capacity to recoup the extensive costs of the project and pay down its massive debt.

When questioned, Global Crossing always seemed to have a great rebuttal for these naysayers: "Look at all the cash we are generating." Global Crossing signed many substantial contracts in which it sold future capacity for cash from customers paid up front—and it had the CFFO to prove it. In 2000, despite a negative $1.7 billion in earnings, the company reported to investors a positive $911 million in operating cash flow. (See Table 11-1.)

Table 11-1   Global Crossing's Cash Flow from Operations Versus Net Income

($ millions)	FY 1998	FY 1999	FY 2000	H1, 6/01
Cash flow from operations (CFFO)	349	732	911	677
Net income (loss) (NI)	(88)	(111)	(1,667)	(1,246)
CFFO – NI	437	843	2,578	1,923

Normally, investors would be overjoyed about a company that generates substantially more CFFO than net income. Indeed, some of the differential was legitimately explained by these advances received from customers. However, a sizable portion related to a boomerang scheme to manipulate its CFFO.

As the technology industry was facing a slowdown, Global Crossing and other telecom players came up with a plan to effectively sell products to each other and, in so doing, boost revenue. From a purely economic standpoint, it was like taking money out of your right pocket and putting it into your left: nothing really changed.

Here's how it worked: Global Crossing sold large blocks of future network capacity to telecom customers. At the same time, the company purchased a similar dollar amount of capacity from these same customers. In other words, Global Crossing would sell capacity to a customer and *simultaneously buy a similar amount of capacity* on a different network. This was a classic *boomerang* transaction. You can almost picture some Global Crossing executive telling the company's customers, "You scratch my back, and I'll scratch yours."

So what does this have to do with cash flow? Well, Global Crossing recorded these boomerang transactions in a way that artificially inflated CFFO. The company recorded the cash that it received from its customers in these transactions as an Operating inflow; however, the cash that it paid to the same customers was recorded as an Investing outflow. Essentially, Global Crossing inflated cash flow from operating activities by depressing cash flow from investing activities. This allowed the company to show strong CFFO that clearly exceeded the economic reality of the transaction. It mattered little that the overstated CFFO was offset by understated cash from investing activities, because *CFFO was the key cash flow metric on which investors were focused.* Did we mention the word "chutzpah" before?

Be on the Lookout for Boomerang Transactions

These are very sneaky transactions that make you wonder about the economic substance of the arrangements. Diligent investors should be able to detect these transactions most of the time; look for disclosure of them in 10-Q and 10-K filings, but don't expect that companies will use the term "boomerang." Of course, companies will make investors work to find them, not present them on a silver platter. However, there are often plenty of details about these transactions, particularly when they are substantial in size. Consider Global Crossing's disclosure of its boomerang transactions in its March 2001 10-Q filing.

This disclosure alone should have spooked investors. On page 11, Global Crossing discloses that $375 million of its $441 million in EBITDA came from sales to customers "to whom the Company made substantial capital commitments during the quarter." Page 16 reminds readers that Global Crossing purchased capacity from customers and states that "new capital commitments total an estimated $625 million."

> ## DISCLOSURE OF BOOMERANG TRANSACTIONS IN GLOBAL CROSSING'S MARCH 2001 10-Q FILING
>
> **Page 11:** For the March quarter, $375 in consideration, which is included in the $441 of Recurring Adjusted EBITDA below and in the $1,613 of cash revenue above, *was received from significant Carrier customers who signed contracts during the quarter to purchase $500 of capacity on the Global Crossing Network, and to whom the Company made substantial capital commitments during the quarter.* ([Italics added for emphasis]
>
> **Page 16:** During the quarter, *the Company also entered into several agreements with various Carrier customers for the purchase of capacity and co-location space.* These transactions were implemented in order to acquire cost-effective local network expansions; to provide for cost-effective alternatives to new construction in certain markets in which the Company anticipates shortages of capacity; and to provide additional levels of physical diversity in the network as the Company implements its global mesh architecture. *These new capital commitments total an estimated $625,* including the cost of the possible construction of the Caribbean system. [Italics added for emphasis]

Raise Your Antennae When You See a Boomerang Transaction

Once you identify a boomerang transaction, it is imperative that you dig around and understand the true economics of the arrangement. Look for further disclosure. Call the company and have management explain the arrangement to you. Assess the economics of the transaction and understand how it contributes to the company's results. Consider whether the company has been deliberately avoiding or complicating the disclosure—it may not want you to understand how its boomerang transactions work. If you cannot get comfortable with a boomerang transaction, steer clear of the company.

Key Metric Shenanigans

You may be wondering about the odd metrics that Global Crossing highlighted in the excerpts shown: "cash revenue" and "recurring adjusted EBITDA." The company used these metrics in its communications with investors and advertised them as being better performance measures than

GAAP revenue and earnings. As you might imagine, these metrics were defined in such a way as to circumvent GAAP. The definitions allowed Global Crossing to take credit for cash received in these boomerang transactions that could not legitimately be recognized as revenue until far in the future. The whole concept of management's deliberately sidestepping GAAP to mislead investors is quite alarming and very important to understand. We will pick up on this topic and discuss it much more thoroughly in Part Four, "Key Metric Shenanigans."

2. Improperly Capitalizing Normal Operating Costs

Recording normal operating costs as an asset rather than as an expense sounds simple, and frankly, it is quite easy to do. However, it is one of the scariest and most lethal shenanigans out there. Why? Because it is a simple sleight of hand that does more than just embellish earnings—it inflates operating cash flow as well.

It certainly is no coincidence that WorldCom, the perpetrator of one of the largest and most shocking accounting frauds in history, was a purveyor of this brand of snake oil. By classifying billions of dollars of normal operating costs as capital equipment purchases, WorldCom not only artificially inflated its profits, but it also overstated its CFFO.

> **TIP**
>
> If you suspect a company of receiving an earnings benefit from improper capitalization, don't forget that there may be a boost to operating cash flow as well.

Recording Normal Operating Costs as a Capital Asset
Rather Than as an Expense

Recall our discussion of how WorldCom improperly inflated its earnings by recording its line costs (a clear operating expense) as an asset rather than as an expense? This simple tactic helped the company portray itself as a profitable company rather than tell investors that trouble was stirring.

This move also allowed WorldCom to present strong operating cash flow. Purchases of capital assets ("capital expenditures") are classified on the

Statement of Cash Flows as investing activities. By classifying line costs as a capital asset, WorldCom shifted a very large cash outflow from the Operating to the Investing section.

This line cost scheme artificially inflated WorldCom's CFFO by nearly $5 billion in 2000 and 2001, according to the company's restatement. Together with other improperly capitalized costs and CFFO boosts, WorldCom's operating cash flow was overstated by a whopping $8.6 billion over these two years (as shown in Table 11-2, the difference between $15.7 billion reported and the $7.1 billion restated).

Table 11-2   WorldCom's CFFO, Reported Versus Restated, 2000–2001

($ millions)	FY 2000	FY 2001	Total
Reported cash flow from operations (CFFO)	7,666	7,994	15,660
Improperly capitalized line costs	(1,827)	(2,933)	(4,760)
Other CFFO boosts	(1,612)	(2,216)	(3,828)
Restated CFFO	4,227	2,845	7,072

In Chapter 6 (EM Shenanigan No. 4), we discussed several ways to identify companies that are engaging in aggressive capitalization. Dishonest company executives may find ways to improperly capitalize any normal operating cost; however, the most common ones are generally those related to long-term arrangements, such as research and development, labor and overhead related to a long-term project, software development, and costs to win contracts or customers. Monitor these accounts for the best chance of spotting aggressive capitalization.

> **TIP**
>
> Rapidly increasing "soft" asset accounts (e.g., "prepaid expenses," "other assets") may be a sign of aggressive capitalization.

Pay Attention to Free Cash Flow as Well   When a company improperly records costs as an asset instead of an expense, CFFO will be overstated. However, as we discussed in Chapter 1, free cash flow may not be affected because it is a measure of cash flow after capital expenditures. As shown in

Table 11-3, calculating free cash flow at WorldCom reveals the extent of the company's problems—a $6.1 billion deterioration from 1999 to 2000.

Table 11-3   WorldCom's Free Cash Flow

($ millions)	1999	2000
Reported cash flow from operations	11,005	7,666
Subtract: Capital expenditures (capex)	(8,716)	(11,484)
Free cash flow	2,289	(3,818)

Some very clever companies have figured out how to turn ordinary operating expenses from being a drain on free cash flow to ones that have virtually no cost, either in the present or in the future. In 2013 Salesforce.com, for example, began the unusual practice of accounting for a large multiyear software license as a "capital lease." In all prior years, these types of licenses had been treated as operating expenses, both on the Statement of Operations and within the reported Operating section of the Statement of Cash Flows.

However, by classifying the license agreement as a lease, Salesforce.com moved most of payments to the software vendor from the Operating section of the Statement of Cash Flows to the Financing section under "Principal payments of capital lease obligations." This line item, literally the second-to-last entry of the entire SCF, would be unlikely to draw any attention from analysts, who would have seen reported cash flow artificially inflated by tens of millions of dollars.

Accounting Capsule:
Free Cash Flow

Free cash flow measures the cash generated by a company, including the impact of cash paid to maintain or expand its asset base (i.e., purchases of capital equipment). Free cash flow typically would be calculated as follows:

Cash flow from operations *minus* capital expenditures

---

3. Recording the Purchase of Inventory as an Investing Outflow

Cost of goods sold (COGS) is a very apt name for the direct expenses that companies incur to acquire or produce inventory sold to customers. On the Statement of Operations, COGS are subtracted from revenue to yield a company's gross profit, an important measure of the profitability of the company's products.

The Statement of Cash Flows is sometimes not as straightforward. The economics of purchasing goods to be sold to customers suggests that these purchases should be classified as an operating activity on the Statement of Cash Flows. Normally, this would be the case. Curiously, some companies treat these purchases as an Investing outflow.

Purchase of DVDs: Operating or Investing?

In its early days (before streaming), Netflix Inc. was a mail-based movie-rental company. As you might imagine, one of the company's largest expenditures was purchasing the DVDs that it rented out to customers. DVDs were essentially Netflix's inventory, and therefore the company recorded its DVD library as an asset on its Balance Sheet. This asset was then amortized (over a period of one year for new releases and three years for back catalog), and as you would expect, the amortization cost was presented on the Income Statement as a cost of goods sold. In 2007, Netflix's amortization of its DVD library amounted to $203 million on revenue of $1.2 billion.

While Netflix's Income Statement appropriately reflected the economics of its DVD costs, its Statement of Cash Flows did not. You would think that the purchase of DVDs would have been presented on the SCF as an operating outflow just like the purchase of any inventory (particularly the purchase of the new releases that were amortized for only one year). However, Netflix did not see it that way. Instead, it considered the purchase of DVDs to be the purchase of a capital asset, and therefore the cash outflows were presented in the Investing section. This treatment effectively moved a big cash outflow (payment for DVDs) from the Operating to the Investing section, thereby inflating CFFO.

Interestingly, Netflix's competitor at the time, Blockbuster Inc., a company that is not known for accounting conservatism, changed its accounting for

DVD acquisitions at the end of 2005. Previously, Blockbuster had presented DVD purchases as an investing outflow, just like Netflix. However, after consultation with the regulators at the Securities and Exchange Commission, Blockbuster began classifying DVD purchases as an operating outflow and restated its historical numbers.

Consider Differences in Accounting Policies When Comparing Competitors Since Netflix put DVD purchases in the Investing section and Blockbuster put them in the Operating section, investors had little ability to compare the CFFO of the two companies without making an adjustment. As shown in Table 11-4, Netflix's cash flow from operations was much stronger than that of Blockbuster in 2007; however, the difference was much less pronounced after adjusting for the DVD purchases.

Table 11-4   CFFO for Netflix and Blockbuster (FY 2007), as Reported and as Adjusted to Remove DVD Purchases from Netflix's CFFO

($ millions)	Netflix	Blockbuster
Cash flow from operations (CFFO), as reported	291.8	(56.2)
SCF treatment of acquiring DVD library	Investing outflow	Operating outflow
Acquisitions of DVD library	(223.4)	(709.3)
Apples to apples (Blockbuster's treatment)	68.4	(56.2)

Question Any Investing Outflow That Sounds like a Normal Cost of Operations   While many analysts claim that reading the Statement of Cash Flows is an integral part of their analysis, many of them fail to read carefully below the Operating section. Simply scanning Netflix's Investing section would have revealed that the company classified "Acquisitions of DVD library" as an investing activity. Even investors with only a basic knowledge of Netflix's business would know enough to realize that acquisition of DVDs represents a normal cost of operations for Netflix.

Purchasing Patents and Newly Developed Technologies

Some professional sports franchises fill their team rosters with players whom they scouted, drafted, and developed within their own organizations. Others rely on the "free agent" market to sign proven players (albeit normally at a much higher price). In the same way, some companies rely on their own internal research and development projects to grow their businesses organically, while others choose to grow inorganically by acquiring development-stage technologies, patents, and licenses. While these different business strategies are means to the same end, the expenditures are often treated differently on the Statement of Cash Flows. Specifically, cash paid to employees and vendors for internal research and development would be reported as an operating outflow. However, some companies report cash paid to acquire already researched and developed products as an Investing outflow.

In certain industries, acquiring development-stage technologies is considered commonplace. For example, small biotechnology research companies often develop new drugs and then sell the rights to these drugs to larger pharmaceutical companies once FDA approval is near. The larger pharmaceutical companies then, as owner of the drug, reap all the profits. When analyzing the pharmaceutical company's business, you certainly should consider the cash paid to acquire the drug rights. However, since the payment will be classified in the Investing section, many investors will have no idea it even exists.

Consider the case of biopharmaceutical company Cephalon. Looking to continue its rapid pace of growth, Cephalon went on a $1 billion shopping spree in 2004 and 2005, snapping up patents, rights, and licenses related to several newly developed drugs. Cephalon presented these cash payments as "acquisitions" and dumped them into the Investing section of the Statement of Cash Flows. Had they been classified in the Operating section, CFFO instead would have been severely negative in both years. (See Table 11-5.)

Table 11-5 Cephalon's Cash Flow from Operations
(Adjusted to Subtract Drug Purchases)

($ millions)	2003	2004	2005
Cash flow from operations, as reported	200.2	178.6	185.7
"Acquisition" of drug patents, rights, and licenses	—	(528.3)	(599.7)
Cash flow from operations, as adjusted	200.2	(349.7)	(414.0)

Similarly, Nuance Communications, a speech recognition software company, acquired a substantial amount of a development-stage technology. In

2014, Nuance showed $253 million in "payments for business and technology acquisitions" as an Investing outflow on its Statement of Cash Flows. This was a very large outflow for the company, especially in relation to the $358 million in operating cash flow generated that year. However, despite spending this large amount, Nuance deemed each of its acquired entities to be immaterial and provided little detail about what it actually bought. Certainly, the cash spent on these assets should be considered when analyzing Nuance's cash flow, as it likely relates to acquired technology and other development spending.

I'll Gladly Pay You Tuesday for a Hamburger Today

In an interesting twist, Biovail Corporation, which merged with Valeant in 2010, gained ownership of certain drugs by purchasing the rights through noncash transactions. Instead of paying cash at the time of the sale, Biovail compensated the sellers by issuing a note—essentially, a long-term IOU under which the company would pay cash in the future. Since no cash changed hands at the time of the sale, there was no impact on the Statement of Cash Flows. And as Biovail paid down the notes over time, the cash payments were presented on the SCF as the repayment of debt—a financing outflow.

Biovail's noncash purchases of product rights can be thought of in the same light as Cephalon's patent purchases and Netflix's DVD purchases. The economics suggests that these purchases relate to normal business operations, and yet they are reflected very differently on the Statement of Cash Flows. When analyzing Biovail's ability to generate cash, these purchases should certainly not be ignored.

Look for "Supplemental Cash Flow Information" Companies frequently provide information about noncash activities in disclosures called "Supplemental Cash Flow Information." This disclosure is sometimes found immediately after the Statement of Cash Flows; however, occasionally companies will bury this disclosure deep in the footnotes. For example, Biovail provided the disclosure about its noncash purchases in a supplemental cash flow footnote that came 30 pages after the Statement of Cash Flows.

BIOVAIL'S SUPPLEMENTAL CASH FLOW DISCLOSURE

In 2003, *non-cash investing and financing activities* included the long-term obligation of $17,497,000 related to the acquisition of Ativan® and Isordil®, and the subscription to $8,929,000 Series D Preferred Units of Reliant in repayment of a portion of the loan receivable from Reliant. In 2002, non-cash investing and financing activities included long-term obligations of $99,620,000 and $69,961,000 related to the acquisitions of Vasotec® and Vaseretic®, and Wellbutrin® and Zyban®, respectively, as well as a long-term obligation of $80,656,000 related to the amendments to the Zovirax distribution agreement. [Italics added for emphasis]

---

4. Shifting Operating Cash Outflows off the Statement of Cash Flows

The final section of this chapter shows how creative management found ways to move the undesirable operating cash outflows far away from the Statement of Cash Flows.

Most companies with an employee pension plan fund those plans with cash that is invested to grow and meet the company's projected long-term obligations. These contributions have the unfortunate effect of reducing reported cash flows. What if pensions could be funded without depleting precious cash flow?

In 2011 Diageo (maker of spirits including Johnnie Walker, Smirnoff, and Guinness) funded its U.K. pension scheme with GBP535 million of whiskey. As the whiskey ages, its value would increase, improving the funded status of the plan. All the while, reported cash flows remain unaffected. Similarly, in 2016 IBM contributed $295 million of U.S. Treasury securities to its defined benefit plan, saving that much in reported cash flow.

Looking Ahead

As this chapter showed, shifting operating cash outflows to the Investing section can be quite enticing for management that hopes to impress investors with stronger cash flow. Well, it seems that management cannot get enough of a good thing.

12

Cash Flow Shenanigan No. 3: Boosting Operating Cash Flow Using Unsustainable Activities

With local versions in more than 100 countries, the hit game show *Who Wants to Be a Millionaire?* has been one of the most successful television franchises of all time. The game is alluringly simple: contestants are asked up to 15 trivia questions. Answering all the questions correctly will win the grand prize; however, if the contestant gives one wrong answer, he or she goes home.

If a contestant is struggling with a question, the rules allow for the use of a "lifeline." For example, one lifeline allows the contestant to ask a friend for help, and another lets the contestant poll the studio audience for its opinion. These lifelines can prove very valuable and often keep struggling contestants afloat. However, they must be used judiciously, since there are just three of them, and once they're gone, they're gone.

Similarly, struggling companies often use valuable "lifelines" to help them keep their cash flow afloat. Just as in the game show, it is often wise and certainly legitimate for companies to use these lifelines. Unlike in the game show, however, companies may fail to disclose the use of these nonrecurring cash flow lifelines. It is up to you to spot them, because once they're gone, they're gone.

In this chapter we discuss four unsustainable lifelines that companies use to boost their cash flow from operations.

Techniques to Boost Operating Cash Flow Using Unsustainable Activities

1. Boosting CFFO by paying vendors more slowly

2. Boosting CFFO by collecting from customers more quickly

3. Boosting CFFO by purchasing less inventory

4. Boosting CFFO with one-time benefits

1. Boosting CFFO by Paying Vendors More Slowly

Want to save a little more cash this year? Use your "delay-payments" lifeline: wait until the beginning of January to pay your December bills. If you push your payments out a month, your end-of-year bank balance will be higher, and it will cosmetically seem as if you generated more cash this year. However, you certainly would not be under the delusion that you had found a recurring way to grow your cash flow each year; rather, you would realize that this was a one-time benefit. To grow your cash flow again next year, you would have to push two months' worth of payments into the following January.

Your "delay-payments lifeline may be a helpful cash management strategy, and there is certainly nothing wrong with holding your money a month longer. In the same way, it is completely appropriate for a company to take longer to pay back its vendors and reap the immediate cash management benefits. However, just like you, companies cannot continue to delay payments into eternity. The cash benefit from pushing out payments (i.e., an increase in payables) should be considered a one-time activity, not a sign that the company has found a lasting way to generate more cash. While this may seem like common sense, you would be surprised at how many companies tout their CFFO strength and forget to mention their little secret: that they increased CFFO by stringing out vendors and not paying them in a timely fashion.

Home Depot Squeezes Its Vendors

Just days after losing an internal management succession battle to replace the legendary Jack Welch at GE, Bob Nardelli earned a consolation prize: the top job at Home Depot. Appointed in December 2000, Nardelli immediately was hailed as the master operating executive that the struggling home improvement retail chain desperately needed. The board loved his GE pedigree and rewarded him right off the bat with an extremely generous compensation package. And Nardelli certainly knew how to please. In his first year on the job, he more than doubled CFFO—from $2.8 billion to nearly $6 billion. Investors who were not too worried about the details of its climb were thrilled.

This cash flow growth, however, would prove to be unsustainable and unrelated to increasing sales at the business. In that first year, Nardelli did a masterful job of redefining the way Home Depot did business with its vendors. Specifically, the company started treating suppliers very badly by paying them much more slowly. By the end of fiscal 2001, Home Depot had successfully stretched out accounts payable to 34 days from 22 the year earlier. The company's Statement of Cash Flows (shown in Table 12-1) reveals that this seemingly minor change in accounts payable was the primary driver of the company's impressive cash flow growth. Another large component of CFFO growth was a decrease in the amount of inventory held at each store (as we will discuss later in this chapter).

Table 12-1   Home Depot Statement of Cash Flows, 2000–2002

($ millions)	Fiscal Year 2000	Fiscal Year 2001	Fiscal Year 2002
Net earnings	2,581	3,044	3,664
Depreciation and amortization	601	764	903
Increase in receivables, net	(246)	(119)	(38)
Increase in merchandise inventories	**(1,075)**	**(166)**	**(1,592)**
Increase in accounts payable and accrued liabilities	**268**	**1,878**	**1,394**
Increase in deferred revenue	486	200	147
Increase in income taxes payable	151	272	83
Increase (decrease) in deferred income taxes	108	(6)	173
Other	(78)	96	68
Net cash provided by operations	**2,796**	**5,963**	**4,802**

Okay, mission accomplished for 2001. The next year, Home Depot was faced with the challenge of improving upon an incredible 2001. To grow CFFO again, however, the company first would have to replicate the 2001 boost it would no longer receive in 2002. The company could stretch payables again in 2002, but not to the extent of the prior year (as payables reached 41 days from 34 days). CFFO for 2002 fell to $4.8 billion from $6.0 billion in 2001.

Accounting Capsule:
Days Payable Outstanding

Days payable outstanding (DPO) is generally calculated as follows:

DPO = accounts payable/cost of goods sold × number of days in the period
         (for quarterly periods, 91.25 days is a normal approximation)

Investors should analyze payables in terms of days outstanding in much the same way that they analyze receivables (days' sales outstanding, or DSO) and inventory (days' sales of inventory, or DSI). An increase in DPO means that the company is paying off its payables over a longer period. A decrease in DPO means that the company is paying its bills more quickly.

Investors should note that Nardelli's cash management techniques certainly were not inappropriate and seemed beneficial to the company's operations. The takeaway here, however, is that the $3 billion increase in CFFO during 2001 should have been viewed as nonrecurring. Alert investors would have correctly anticipated that CFFO would shrink in 2002.

Watch for Large and Suspicious Increases in Payables   An increase in payables relative to cost of goods sold tells you the company has probably stretched out its payments to vendors. Assess the extent to which CFFO growth is derived from stretching out payments to vendors and consider that amount an unsustainable boost that is unrelated to improved business activities.

Look for Large Positive Swings on the Statement of Cash Flows   A quick review of Home Depot's CFFO in 2001 shows that improvements in accounts payable and inventory were the primary drivers of CFFO growth. (See Table 12-1.) In the following year, it is evident that Home Depot's inability to sustain that improvement was the primary source of CFFO deterioration.

Be Alert When Companies Use Accounts Payable "Financing"   Some companies choose to "finance" their accounts payable by getting a bank involved in their transactions with vendors. In these so-called vendor financing arrangements, a company does not pay its vendors directly; rather, a bank pays off the vendor invoice, and the company reimburses the bank at a later date. These transactions result in the creation of bank debt on the company's Balance Sheet in place of accounts payable. Since the repayment of bank debt is categorized on the Statement of Cash Flows as a financing activity, the cash paid for this inventory would never be shown as an operating outflow.

Wireless carrier T-Mobile, for example, offered vendor financing arrangements for its handset and network equipment suppliers. In 2015 alone, T-Mobile repaid $564 million in short-term debt that was used for purchases of handset inventory and network equipment. Conveniently, this cash outflow was buried on T-Mobile's Statement of Cash Flows as a financing activity.

This anecdote shows the enormous management discretion available in classifying a straightforward transaction on the Statement of Cash Flows. To properly compare cash flow generation at these competitors, investors must adjust for this difference in policy. Each company provided sufficient disclosure to understand its SCF classification. Diligent investors would have used these disclosures to reflect both sides of the loan transaction (inflows and outflows) as financing, not operating.

> **TIP**
>
> Accounts payable is a relatively straightforward account. If you see a discussion of accounts payable that is longer than a couple of sentences, there is probably something in there that you want to know (for example, accounts payable financing arrangements).

Watch for Swings in Other Payables Accounts   Accounts payable is not the only obligation that companies can use to manage their cash flow. CFFO can be influenced by the timing of payments on many liability accounts, including tax payments, payroll or bonus payments, and pension plan contributions. Consider how Callaway Golf Company's tax situation resulted in unsustainably strong CFFO in 2005.

Callaway spent the off-season working on its long game. The dedication seemed to pay off. In 2005, Callaway drove its CFFO up to $70.3 million—quite an improvement from the meager $8.5 million reported in 2004. A quick check of the Statement of Cash Flows reveals that CFFO growth came from an improved swing—that is, a $55.8 million "swing" in the impact of tax payables and receivables (apparently because of net tax refunds and settlements). It should not have been too rough for investors to spot this tax swing on the Statement of Cash Flows and deduce that Callaway's strong CFFO growth would not recur.

2. Boosting CFFO by Collecting from Customers More Quickly

Another way in which companies can generate a nonrecurring CFFO boost would be to convince customers to pay them more quickly. This certainly would not be considered a bad thing, and it may even speak well of a company's significant leverage over its customers. However, as in our discussion about stretching out payables, companies cannot continue to collect at a faster rate in perpetuity. As a result, the growth in CFFO that results from accelerated collections should be deemed unsustainable.

Watch for CFFO Boosts from Higher Prepayments

For high-end electric automaker Tesla Motors, liquidity and cash flow have been particularly important metrics for investors and lenders. Since its founding in 2003, Tesla had never posted a full year of positive free cash flow, and therefore the company had become entirely reliant on debt financing and equity issuances to continue funding its operations. In 2016, Tesla's operating cash outflows appeared to have improved, amounting to net outflows of $124 million, down from outflows of $524 million in 2015. However, what changed most significantly in terms of cash flow that year was that the company *began accepting orders and refundable customer deposits* for its Model 3 sedan, which had been introduced only in concept. These deposits accounted for $350 million of additional inflows, or 88 percent of the reported improvement in 2016. Skeptical investors would have noted that fundamentally the business continued to burn cash at historical rates, but because of a successful marketing campaign, it was able to "borrow" from future periods and accelerate customer payments to report better results.

Watch for Elaborate Strategies to Influence the Timing of Cash Flow

Warning signs about accelerated collections could certainly have been spotted at Silicon Graphics several quarters before its May 2006 bankruptcy. The company was burdened with debt and did everything in its power to portray a stronger liquidity position to investors. Unlike companies that may use a position of power with customers to accelerate collections, Silicon Graphics' diminished health compelled it to offer discounts to induce early payments. Consider the disclosure shown here from the company's September 2005 10-Q. Also, notice another cash management trick that Silicon Graphics was playing—holding vendor payments and buying inventory at the end of the quarter—to show cash on its Balance Sheet at its highest point on the last day of the quarter. Diligent investors would have noticed these issues and known that disaster was not far away.

SILICON GRAPHICS INC. SEPTEMBER 2005 10-Q

During the first quarter of fiscal 2006, we maintained our focus on customer cash collections and *offered certain customers discounted terms for early payment.* As a result, our days' sales outstanding were 37 days at September 30, 2005, down from 49 days at June 24, 2005 and 39 days at September 24, 2004. We expect that days' sales outstanding will be more in line with historical levels in the second quarter of fiscal 2006.

We also experience significant intra-quarter fluctuations in our cash levels, with the result that *our cash balances are generally at their highest point at the end of each quarter and significantly lower at other times.* These intra-quarter fluctuations reflect our business cycle, with significant requirements for inventory purchases in the early part of the quarter and most sales closing in the last few weeks of the quarter. *To maintain adequate levels of unrestricted cash within each quarter, we offer certain customers discounted terms for early payment and hold certain vendor payments to the beginning of the following quarter.* [Italics added for emphasis]

Be Wary of Dramatic Improvements in CFFO

Chinese telecom equipment manufacturer UTStarcom reported markedly improved CFFO in early 2008. After a dismal 2007, in which it logged four consecutive quarters of negative CFFO (for a total cash burn of $218 million), the company suddenly reported positive cash flow of $97 million in March 2008. Investors could have readily noticed that the cash flow turnaround resulted from a variety of particularly aggressive working capital actions. A quick peek at the Balance Sheet revealed a $65 million drop in accounts receivable and a $66 million increase in accounts payable. The 10-Q gave more insight and mentioned one of those "management decisions" we warned you about in Chapter 10, "Cash Flow Shenanigan No. 1, Shifting Financing Cash Inflows to the Operating Section," with the infamous Computer Associates. (See the accompanying disclosure from UTStarcom's March 2008 10-Q.)

UTSTARCOM'S MARCH 2008 10-Q DISCLOSURE TOLD THE STORY

The decrease in accounts receivable was primarily due to strong customer collections in our PCD business segment. The increase in accounts payable was due to the substantial inventory purchasing activity late into the first quarter of 2008, as well as a *management decision to forgo early payment discounts with a significant vendor.* [Italics added for emphasis]

UTStarcom proceeded to report negative operating cash flow throughout the rest of 2008. Despite the $97 million in positive CFFO during the first quarter, the company ended the year in a hole, having burned through $55 million in operating cash flow.

> **TIP**
>
> While many investors are pleased when management says that it is "aggressively managing working capital," you should take this as a warning sign that recent CFFO growth may not be sustainable.

3. Boosting CFFO by Purchasing Less Inventory

Home Depot, as you recall, received an unsustainable CFFO boost in 2001 from stretching out payments to vendors. Well, the company had another CFFO-improving trick up its sleeve: purchasing less inventory.

Earlier in this chapter, we discussed how Bob Nardelli doubled Home Depot's operating cash flow in his first year on the job by stretching out vendor payables and reducing the amount of inventory at each store. Home Depot lowered its inventory levels simply by not restocking shelves after goods had been sold. In other words, the company just did not purchase as much inventory from vendors as in previous years.

In much the same way that Nardelli's Home Depot "cosmetically" improved CFFO (by paying vendors more slowly), a company choosing to purchase less inventory would also provide an artificial and unsustainable boost to CFFO. Let's revisit Home Depot's Statement of Cash Flows in Table 12-1 to see the inventory swing from an outflow of $1.1 billion in 2000 to an outflow of only $166 million in 2001 (and then back to an outflow of $1.6 billion in 2002 as the benefit reversed).

To be fair, Home Depot was very clear in its disclosure under the Liquidity and Capital Resources section of its 10-K filing, stating that CFFO growth primarily had been driven by an extension of payables and a decrease in inventory per store (see the disclosure in the accompanying box). Investors would be well served by reading through the entire document, because such important nuggets of information can be found deep inside the filing.

HOME DEPOT 2002 10-K

For fiscal 2001, cash provided by operations increased to $6.0 billion from $2.8 billion in fiscal 2000. The increase was primarily due to significant growth in days payable outstanding from 23 days at the end of fiscal 2000 to 34 days at the end of fiscal 2001, a 12.7% decrease in average inventory per store as of the end of fiscal 2001 and increased operating income.

In the next year, Home Depot did not benefit from a decrease in inventory. However, it provided a good spin on this in the Liquidity and Capital Resources section, suggesting that it had pared back inventory too much in the previous year.

HOME DEPOT 2003 10-K

For fiscal 2002, cash provided by operations decreased to $4.8 billion from $6.0 billion in fiscal 2001. The decrease was primarily due to a *7.9% increase in average inventory per store resulting from our focus on improving our in-stock position in fiscal 2002.* [Italics added for emphasis]

TIP

Buried in the 10-Qs and 10-Ks is some extra insight about the drivers of cash flow. It is one of the most important sections of the filing, but many investors don't know it exists. To find it, turn to the Management Discussion and Analysis (MD&A)—in a section often called "Liquidity and Capital Resources." This section is a must-read for every company you analyze.

Watch for Disclosure About Timing of Inventory
Purchases Within Each Quarter

Silicon Graphics purchased inventory at the very beginning of each quarter and then worked it down as much as possible by the end of the period, only to purchase more once the quarter closed. (See the 10-Q disclosure in our earlier discussion on Silicon Graphics.) As with its receivables and payables management schemes, the company used this strategy to manipulate investor perceptions that its liquidity was adequate while it was teetering on the brink of bankruptcy.

4. Boosting CFFO with One-Time Benefits

Microsoft doled out billions of dollars to settle antitrust litigation between 2004 and 2007. One of the largest recipients, Sun Microsystems, pocketed nearly $2 billion from Microsoft in 2004 ($1.6 billion of which was immediately recognized as income). Sun presented this large one-time item in plain view on its Statement of Operations, listing it separately as "settlement income." Sun's disclosure made it very easy for investors to understand that the income from this settlement was nonrecurring and unrelated to its normal operations; it was reported "below the line" as nonoperating income.

Sun's Statement of Cash Flows, however, was less clear. The company recorded the $2 billion in cash as an operating inflow (as is appropriate under the indirect method), but it was not listed separately on the SCF; rather, it was simply bundled with net income. As you would imagine, a $2 billion settlement was quite material to Sun's results—CFFO for all of 2004 was $2.2 billion, up from $1.0 billion in 2003. Diligent investors would have noticed this settlement reflected on the Statement of Operations and immediately realized that it was an unsustainable source of CFFO.

> **TIP**
>
> Nonrecurring boosts to CFFO often are not plainly disclosed on the Statement of Cash Flows. Whenever you spot any kind of one-time earnings benefit, ask yourself, "How does this boost affect the Statement of Cash Flows?"

Looking Ahead

This completes our unit on Cash Flow Shenanigans—techniques used to inflate operating cash flows. In aggregate, Parts Two and Three focused on gimmicks that impress investors with either higher reported earnings or operating cash flows. In Part Four, we show how accounting tricks may also contaminate management's non-GAAP metrics and key performance indicators.

PART FOUR

KEY METRIC SHENANIGANS

We have climbed the first two mountains in our quest to conquer financial she-nanigans, with two still to come. Until now, we have focused on assessing the performance of companies using two separate metrics: earnings and cash flow.

Part Two, "Earnings Manipulation Shenanigans," discussed techniques for manipulating accrual-based performance numbers by playing around with revenue and expenses or shifting them to the wrong section or the wrong financial statement entirely. We pointed out the limitations of accrual-based performance metrics like net income, and we suggested that investors should expand their analysis to evaluate cash flow performance metrics such as cash flow from operations and free cash flow.

Part Three, "Cash Flow Shenanigans," addressed a relatively new and trou-bling phenomenon: management's propensity to use Cash Flow Shenanigans to give a company the misleading appearance of having strong operating and free cash flow. We also presented strategies that investors can use to detect Cash Flow Shenanigans and to adjust the reported numbers to remove these unsustainable boosts.

At this point, you can take a deep breath and feel good about your abil-ity to evaluate a company's "economic" performance through accrual-based (Income Statement) and cash-based (Statement of Cash Flows) models, even when management employs shenanigans to hide the true story from investors. You have also learned how to uncover dozens of tricks used by management.

However, your quest is only half over. In Part Four, "Key Metric Shenanigans," we discuss the importance of using other "key metrics" to eval-uate a company's performance and economic health, and we expose tricks that companies could use to cloud the picture and mislead investors.

Two Key Metric Shenanigans

KEY METRIC SHENANIGANS

KM No. 1: Showcasing misleading metrics that overstate performance (Chapter 13)

KM No. 2: Distorting Balance Sheet metrics to avoid showing deterioration (Chapter 14)

Successful investing requires a rigorous analysis of a broad array of financial performance and economic health metrics for a company. Some pertinent information can be found easily by reading the Income Statement, the Statement of Cash Flows, and the Balance Sheet. Other vital information may be gleaned from supplementary documents (company press releases, Earnings Releases, footnotes, and Management Discussion and Analysis included with the financial reports). In addition, investors should study the financial reporting of competitors, not only to compare performance and health measures, but also to assess the application of accounting standards and disclosure.

Now you have reams of data to read and analyze. Great, but before digging in, remember to ask these two important questions:

1. What are the *best metrics of that specific company's performance*, and does management highlight, ignore, distort, or even make up its own version of these metrics?
2. What are the *best metrics that would reveal a specific company's deteriorating economic health*, and does management highlight, ignore, distort, or even make up its own version of these metrics?

Investors are increasingly evaluating companies using both performance-related and economic health–related metrics. Not surprisingly, with so much riding on pleasing investors, management is providing much more information, but it often tries to camouflage any deterioration in the business. We label this group of tricks Key Metric (KM) Shenanigans. They can be grouped as (1) performance metrics and (2) economic health metrics.

Evaluation of Financial Performance and Economic Health Metrics

For a given industry or company, start out by learning the very best metrics for evaluating economic performance and health—both past and expected in the near term. (Longer-term performance predictions tend to be woefully inaccurate and provide little value for investors.)

Let's consider a subscription-based business. Start with the traditional performance metrics reported on the Income Statement (revenue, operating earnings, net income, and earnings per share [EPS]) and on the Statement of Cash Flows (cash flow from operations and free cash flow). Nothing would be wrong with any of these—provided that *no* Earnings Manipulation or Cash Flow Shenanigans exist. But this list would lack at least one enormously important piece of information—recent developments in the business. Have recent subscriber counts been falling? Has the amount of revenue earned from each subscriber declined over the last few quarters? Since both accrual-based revenue and cash flow–based CFFO focus on *past, not expected, revenue or cash flows*, investors should be keen on receiving and evaluating subscriber-based metrics. This information would be extraordinarily valuable.

Categories of Performance Metrics

Think of our traditional financial performance metrics (e.g., revenue, net income, and cash flow) as being like the *box score* of yesterday's baseball game. While the information reflects past performance, it can often provide very relevant indicators about the strength of the team, and in many cases, it can shed light on what to expect tomorrow. However, other supplementary pieces of information exist or can be derived that are excluded from the box score, yet would be essential for an analysis of the team. As baseball historian Bill James realized when he pioneered a new form of baseball statistical analysis (and as Michael Lewis illustrated beautifully in his book *Moneyball*), many unconventional baseball statistics can be more revealing than the traditional metrics listed in the box score.

The best supplementary financial performance metrics should provide additional insight into a company's recent operational performance (good or bad) to go with that conveyed by traditional financial statement metrics based on generally accepted accounting principles. We highlight ways in which management presents (1) surrogates for revenue, (2) surrogates for earnings, and (3) surrogates for cash flow.

Surrogates for Revenue

Management often tries to clarify and expand its disclosures on customer sales and provide insight into future demand and pricing power. A broadcast cable operator, for example, may disclose its subscriber count, an airline its "load factor" (the percentage of total seats filled), an Internet portal its number of "paid clicks," and a hotel operator its "revenue per available room." Industries and companies often produce their own unique metrics to help investors get a better grasp of a company's performance. Some common metrics that would be considered revenue surrogates include same-store sales, backlog, bookings, subscriber count, average revenue per customer, and organic revenue growth.

Surrogates for Earnings

Management sometimes tries to present a "cleaner" version of earnings to convey the true operating performance of the business. A chemical manufacturer, for example, may remove a large one-time gain from selling real estate when presenting earnings to convey its performance in a way that is comparable with that used in past and future periods. Companies often have similar names for these non-GAAP earnings surrogates, even though each company may define them differently. Some common metrics used include pro forma earnings, EBITDA, non-GAAP earnings, constant-currency earnings, and organic earnings growth.

Surrogates for Cash Flow

As with earnings surrogates, management may also try to present a "cleaner" version of its cash flow, although this may be a bit trickier and is often more controversial. For example, a retail chain may present cash flow excluding a substantial one-time cash payment for a legal settlement. Some common metrics used include pro forma operating cash flow, non-GAAP operating cash flow, free cash flow, cash earnings, cash revenue, and funds from operations.

Accounting Capsule:
Pro Forma Numbers—Apples-to-Apples Comparison

Whenever management makes significant accounting or classification changes, or even makes an acquisition, comparisons with earlier-period results may become difficult, if not impossible, for investors to make. Thus, to provide an apples-to-apples comparison for investors, companies include pro forma ("as if") adjusted financial statements as supplementary information.

For example, let's assume that a company changes its revenue recognition policy. The GAAP-based numbers would naturally show current-period results with the new accounting policy but would still report alongside them the earlier-period results using the old accounting policy, no doubt creating confusion. To help investors make a sensible comparison, a pro forma presentation would include the results of both periods under the new revenue recognition policy.

Categories of Economic Health Metrics

Continuing our baseball analogy, if analyzing performance metrics can be considered akin to reviewing yesterday's *box score*, then analyzing economic health metrics would be like reviewing today's baseball *standings* that show a team's cumulative performance (wins and losses for the season). The Balance Sheet can be thought of as a company's present, up-to-the-minute record that reflects its cumulative performance since its inception. (For some long-standing companies, that could be a very long "season.") While the Balance Sheet reflects the accumulation of all past performance, it can shed light on what to expect tomorrow. A baseball team that is at the top of the win-loss standings and is leading the league in runs scored for the season is usually in excellent health. On the opposite side of the spectrum, a team that is near the bottom of the standings, has a miserable cumulative batting average, and is letting more runs score than any other team can be in poor health and relatively unstable.

As with the approach described for performance, for a given industry, start out by learning the very best metrics for evaluating economic health and stability—both past and expected in the near term. The best supplementary economic health metrics should provide added insight into the strength of a company's Balance Sheet, including how well the company (1) manages customer collections, (2) maintains prudent inventory levels, (3) maintains financial assets at their appropriate value, and (4) keeps liquidity and solvency risks in check to prevent a devastating cash crunch.

Evaluation of Accounts Receivable Management

Investors worry if collection of customer receivables begins stretching out. Analysts use a days' sales outstanding (DSO) metric to catch signs of collection problems. Higher DSO (as discussed earlier) typically suggests that customers have been paying more slowly. Or worse, perhaps management has used Earnings Manipulation Shenanigans to inflate revenue and profits. Now if management wants to hide these problems from investors, it may distort the true accounts receivable balance. Investors should evaluate accounts receivable to gauge whether the DSO metric provided by management fairly presents the underlying economics of the business. Remember, distorting accounts receivable metrics could indeed be an attempt to hide revenue problems.

Evaluation of Inventory Management

A healthy and prudent level of inventory is essential for a well-run business. Holding an inventory of undesirable products leads to write-downs, and not having enough of the "hot" ones will lead to missed sales opportunities. Naturally, investors monitor inventory levels closely and use a metric called days' sales of inventory (DSI). Management may create misleading inventory metrics to hide profitability problems. Or it may simply classify inventory incorrectly on the Balance Sheet to trick investors into using the wrong input when computing DSI.

Evaluation of Asset Impairments for Financial Companies

Financial institutions provide metrics that give investors insight into the quality or strength of their financial assets. Companies may disclose, for example, delinquency rates on mortgage loans or the fair value of their investments. Investors must monitor this supplementary data to ensure that proper reserves and impairments are being recorded. With the 2008 financial crisis, investors unable to spot lax impairment decisions took big hits.

Evaluation of Liquidity and Solvency Risks

Investors can face devastating losses, often with little warning, if they fail to monitor imminent threats of a massive cash crunch. Enron's demise came

very rapidly when credit rating agencies swiftly downgraded its bonds to
"junk" status and the company's liquidity sources immediately dried up.
Similarly, any company that fell out of compliance with its debt covenants
could face unpleasant consequences. If a company fails to provide data on
such threats (or worse, if it intentionally covers up them up), investors will
be in serious jeopardy.

The next two chapters cover two Key Metric Shenanigans. Investors
should be delighted if management provides additional useful information
to help them better assess the company's performance and economic health.
Unfortunately, management might provide information that not only adds
no value, but might be misleading. Chapter 13 highlights metrics that hide
revenue, earnings, or cash flow problems or simply put an overly positive
spin on modest achievements. Chapter 14 describes misleading economic
health metrics that hide problems.

13

Key Metric Shenanigan No. 1: Showcasing Misleading Metrics That Overstate Performance

Above all, do no harm.

—HIPPOCRATES, THE FATHER OF WESTERN MEDICINE

Newly minted doctors are required to take the Hippocratic oath and pledge their commitment to practice medicine ethically. This oath is widely attributed to Hippocrates, the father of Western medicine, in the fourth century BC, and the gist of it can be boiled down to "Above all, do no harm."

Perhaps corporate managers should be made to study this solemn oath taken by physicians and apply it in earnest when they communicate with investors. In so doing, they would pledge to never knowingly harm investors and always refrain from showcasing metrics that misrepresent performance. Based on what you have already seen in this book, that day seems way off in the horizon. Well, we can only dream that such a day will eventually come! Until it arrives, however, investors must be alert to the following three techniques that management can use to obfuscate company performance.

Techniques to Showcase Misleading Metrics That Overstate Performance

1. Highlighting a misleading metric as a surrogate for revenue

2. Highlighting a misleading metric as a surrogate for earnings

3. Highlighting a misleading metric as a surrogate for cash flow

1. Highlighting a Misleading Metric as a Surrogate for Revenue

Many people consider revenue growth to be an important and straightforward measure of the overall growth of a business. Companies also frequently provide additional data points to supplement revenue, providing investors with more insight into product demand and pricing power. As discussed in the previous chapter, investors should welcome this additional information and analyze these supplemental non-GAAP revenue metrics to better assess the sustainable business performance. However, sometimes these revenue surrogates provided by management can be misleading and can harm investors if they have not put appropriate safeguards in place. In this first section, we highlight ways in which companies can be less than honest using common revenue surrogates and how careful investors can protect themselves.

Same-Store Sales
Revenue growth at retailers and restaurants is often fueled by the opening of additional stores. Logically, companies that are in the middle of a rapid store expansion show tremendous revenue growth, since they have many more stores this year than they had the prior one. While total company revenue growth may give some perspective on a company's size, it gives little information on whether the individual stores are performing well. Investors should

therefore focus more closely on a metric that measures how the company's stores have been performing.

To provide investors with that insight, management often reports a metric called *same-store sales* (SSS) or *comparable-store sales*. This metric establishes a comparable base of stores ("comp base" for short) with which to calculate revenue growth, allowing for more relevant analysis of true operating performance. For example, a company may present its revenue growth for stores that have been open for at least one year. Companies often prominently disclose SSS in their Earnings Releases, and investors use it as a key indicator of company performance. Many consider same-store sales to be the most important metric in analyzing a retailer or restaurant. We agree that if it is reported in a logical and consistent manner, SSS is extremely valuable for investors.

However, because same-store sales (and the other metrics discussed in Part Four) fall outside of GAAP coverage, no universally accepted definition exists, and calculations may vary from company to company. Worse, a company's own calculation of SSS in one quarter may differ from the one used in the previous period. While most companies compute their same-store sales honestly and disclose them consistently, "bad apples" try to dress up their results by routinely adjusting their definition of SSS. Investors, therefore, should always be alert to the presentation of same-store sales to ensure that it fairly represents a company's operating performance.

Compare Same-Store Sales to the Change in Revenue per Store   When a company experiences consistent growth, same-store sales should be trending up consistently with the average revenue at each store. By comparing SSS with the change in revenue per store (i.e., total revenue divided by average total stores), investors can quickly spot positive or negative changes in the business. For example, assume that a company's SSS growth has been consistently tracking well with its revenue per store growth. If a material divergence in this trend suddenly appeared, with SSS accelerating and revenue per store shrinking, investors should be concerned. This divergence indicates one of two problems: (1) the company's new stores are beginning to struggle (driving down revenue per store, but not affecting SSS because they are not yet in the comp base), or

(2) the company has changed its definition of same-store sales (which affects the SSS calculation but not total revenue per store).

Watch for Changes in the Definition of Same-Store Sales   Companies usually disclose how they define same-store sales. Once the definition is disclosed, investors should have little difficulty tracking it from period to period. Companies can manipulate same-store sales by adjusting the comp base in two possible ways. The first involves simply changing the length of time before a store enters the comp base (for example, requiring a store to be open for 18 months, versus 12 months previously). The second trick involves changing the types of stores included in the comp base (for example, excluding certain stores based on geography, size, businesses, remodeling, and so on).

Coach Inc., the New York City–based fashion company, made such a change in 2013. Historically, when Coach expanded a store's square footage by at least 15 percent, it excluded these stores' sales from the comp base until one year after completing the expansion. This made sense since larger stores generally have higher sales, and any growth related to a large store expansion should not really be considered same-store sales. Yet Coach decided that beginning in 2014 it would no longer exclude these store expansions from its comp base, meaning its same-store sales metric would include an unsustainable benefit related to growth in store size. Not surprisingly, this change came just as same-store sales was slowing and the company was embarking on a multiyear plan to expand some of its most productive stores.

Pay Close Attention to Which Parts of the Business Reported Growth Reflects In 2013, Thomson Reuters, the Toronto-based media juggernaut, reported "revenue growth before currency" of 2 percent. This figure stood in contrast to the more standard rate of change in reported sales versus the prior year, which was *negative* 3 percent. Which measure was more accurate? It turns out that not only did the headline figure adjust for the effects of currency, but it also only considered "ongoing businesses"; this was not a legal or accounting distinction the way that a "discontinued operation" is, but rather one that management made subjectively. The curious thing about this methodology was that in the 2013 Annual Report, the revenue from "ongoing businesses" in 2012 had fallen by almost $500 million compared with the revenue from "ongoing businesses" originally reported in 2012. It was only the retroactive recategorizing of certain businesses as non-"ongoing" that allowed Thomson Reuters to report positive sales growth in 2013, a period where by all objective measures the company declined. This clever scheme provided similar benefits in 2011 and 2012.

Average Revenue per User

When comparing key non-GAAP metrics across a peer group, it is important to ensure that these metrics are being calculated in the same way. For example, in the broadcast industry, a common metric analyzed is average revenue per user (ARPU), calculated as total subscription revenue divided by average subscribers. Calculating the average revenue per subscriber sounds like it should be simple; however, varying definitions of ARPU abound. Consider, for example, the different definitions at competitors Sirius Satellite Radio Inc. and XM Satellite Radio Holdings Inc. (before they merged in 2008). Sirius's calculation of ARPU included revenue from subscriptions, advertising, and activation fees. XM Radio, on the other hand, calculated ARPU using only revenue from subscriptions; advertising revenue and activation fees were excluded. (See the accompanying box.) To compare ARPU at the two companies on an apples-to-apples basis, investors would have had to either adjust Sirius's ARPU calculation to exclude advertising revenue and activation fees or adjust XM's ARPU calculation to include these revenue sources.

AVERAGE REVENUE PER USER (ARPU) DIFFERENCES AT SIRIUS AND XM RADIO

Sirius's ARPU calculation: Subscriber (including offset for sales rebates) *activation* and *advertising revenue* divided by the daily weighted average number of subscribers for the period. [Italics added for emphasis]

XM Radio's ARPU calculation: Total monthly earned subscription revenue net of promotions and rebates divided by monthly weighted average number of subscribers for the period reported.

Subscriber Additions and Churn

Let's go back to our discussion of subscription-based businesses from earlier in this chapter. Since these types of companies (e.g., research providers, telephone companies, newspapers, fitness clubs, and so on) rely on new subscribers for growth, it is helpful for investors to monitor subscriber levels to get a sense of the latest trends in the business. Logically, the number of new subscriber additions each quarter is often a good leading indicator of upcoming revenue. Similarly, the level of cancellations (called "churn") is important to know when assessing the business. If a company shows a healthy subscriber base with growth in new subscribers and shrinking churn, investors can expect strong revenue growth ahead. That is, unless the company is manipulating these metrics.

In the late 1990s, AOL, for example, found a clever way to inflate the number of subscribers to its online Internet service. One of the ways in which AOL sold subscriptions was to sell "bulk subscriptions" to corporations, which would then distribute these subscriptions to employees as a perk. AOL did not include these bulk subscription sales in its subscriber count because it knew that many of these subscriptions would never actually be activated. When employees did sign up, however, they rightfully entered the subscriber count.

In 2001, AOL was struggling to meet its subscriber targets. So the company began including the number of bulk subscriber sales in its subscriber count, even though most of these subscriptions were never activated. Moreover, AOL would ship these bulk subscription membership kits to customers immediately before the quarter end to meet targets for subscriber count.

Bookings and Backlog

Many companies disclose their quarterly "bookings" or "orders," which are supposed to represent the amount of new business *booked during the period.* Companies may also disclose their backlog, which essentially represents their outstanding book of business or, in other words, all past orders that have yet to be filled (and recognized as revenue). "Book to bill" is also a common disclosure that compares current-period bookings to current-period revenue and is calculated as bookings divided by revenue.

If they are presented accurately, bookings and backlog are important indicators, as they provide investors with extra insight into upcoming revenue trends. However, since they are non-GAAP metrics, companies have plenty of leeway in how they define and disclose bookings and backlog. You would think the calculations would be straightforward, but indeed there are plenty of nuances in what should and should not be included. For example, different companies include the following types of orders differently in their presentation of bookings and backlog: cancelable orders, orders in which the quantity purchased is not defined, bookings for longer-term service or construction contracts, contracts with contingencies or extension clauses, bookings on noncore operations, and so on.

The varying definitions of bookings and backlog across companies make it extremely important for investors to understand exactly what the metric represents before putting any faith in it. Moreover, if the metric is a key performance indicator, investors should use extra diligence to ensure that the company does not change its own definition of bookings in a way that flatters the metric.

Accounting Capsule:
Bookings and Backlog

The following formula shows the general relationship between bookings, backlog, and revenue (for all revenue streams that run through backlog). This formula is very helpful when analyzing companies, as it can be used to test the veracity or consistency of these non-GAAP metrics. It can also be used to calculate bookings when only backlog is given.

Beginning backlog + net bookings − revenue = ending backlog

where net bookings are total bookings minus cancellations.

Some companies will present booking and backlog metrics that do not seem to accurately represent the underlying business economics. For example, First Solar, whose percentage-of-completion shenanigans you may remember from Chapter 3, played tricks with its bookings presentation as well. In its

March 2014 earnings presentation, First Solar presented a "quarterly" bookings figure that included much more than a quarter's worth of bookings. A close read of the fine print revealed that the bookings metric included all new bookings from the beginning of the quarter all the way through the date of the Earnings Release—a full 36 days after the quarter ended.

Consider also the unusual definition of backlog employed by electronic payments company ACI Worldwide. ACI presents a 60-month backlog metric in which all nonrecurring license arrangements are assumed to renew as recurring revenue streams. A better name for this metric would be "wishful thinking backlog."

2. Highlighting a Misleading Metric as a Surrogate for Earnings

Warren Buffett has long poked fun at management teams that create dishonest pro forma metrics. He memorably compared this practice to an archer who shoots an arrow into a blank canvas and *then* draws a bull's-eye around the implanted arrow.

EBITDA and Its Variations

Consider the bull's-eye drawn by the archers at Global Crossing. The company reported a net loss of $120 million in the March 2007 quarter. Desperate to show a profit, however, management removed expenses using a pro forma concoction reminiscent of its misdeeds during the dot-com bubble. First, management removed $97 million in expenses for interest, taxes, depreciation, and some other items to get to a metric it called *adjusted EBITDA* (earnings before interest, taxes, depreciation, and amortization). Then, it removed $15 million in noncash stock compensation expense, bringing the company to an adjusted cash EBITDA of *negative* $8 million. Close, but not all the way to profitability, management then removed a host of charges that it deemed one-time in nature, propelling the company to a positive $4 million in what it called *adjusted cash EBITDA less one-time items*. Bull's-eye!

It is easy to be skeptical about Global Crossing's three levels of pro forma, and it is hard not to laugh when looking at some of the "one-time" charges that the company removed. (See Table 13-1.) Last time we checked, expenses for "maintenance" were a normal cost of doing business and therefore should never be excluded from a pro forma calculation. Ditto for customer defaults (bad debts), employee retention bonuses, and routine regulatory charges. Do not be fooled into thinking these items will not recur just because management decides to present them as one-time in nature.

Table 13-1   Global Crossing's Adjusted Cash EBITDA Less One-Time Items

($ millions)	Q1, 3/07
Net income	(120)
Provision for income taxes	12
Other expense	6
Interest expense	29
Depreciation and amortization	50
Adjusted EBITDA	(23)
Noncash stock compensation	15
Adjusted cash EBITDA	(8)
One-time item: regulatory charges	5
One-time item: Asian earthquake	1
One-time item: customer defaults	2
One-time item: severance	1
One-time item: cash portion of retention bonus	3
One-time item: utility credit	(2)
One-time item: maintenance charge	2
Adjusted cash EBITDA less one-time items	4

Now You See It, Now You Don't

On its June 2007 earnings call, flash memory manufacturer Spansion proudly stated that EBITDA grew to $72 million from $61 million the quarter before. The following quarter, Spansion reported that EBITDA fell to $71 million; however, the company soothed concerned investors by claiming that EBITDA increased by $8 million if you exclude a one-time real estate gain received in the previous quarter. Conveniently, this one-time gain was not excluded from EBITDA when earnings were reported the previous quarter. So Spansion essentially included the one-time gain to help show strong

EBITDA growth in June, and then excluded the gain the next quarter to show strong EBITDA growth in September. You can't have it both ways!

Watch for Clever Games to Inflate EBITDA

Travel technology company Sabre Corporation found a clever way to inflate its reported EBITDA by excluding an important component of its cost structure. Sabre often makes up-front payments to travel agencies in order to induce them to use the company's travel reservation system; in 2016, these payments totaled $71 million. Because these up-front disbursements relate to multiyear contracts, the payments are capitalized and then amortized over the contract period. Since the costs hit the Income as an amortization expense, they are added back in the calculation of EBITDA. If EBITDA is meant to be a shorthand proxy for cash profitability, it's hard to think of a justification for permanently excluding this type of cost that is paid in cash each and every period.

SEC Cracks Down on Groupon's Misleading Operating Earnings Metrics

While Global Crossing, Spansion, and Sabre used interesting variations of EBITDA to make profits look more plentiful, other companies take it one step further—they create their own profitability metric. And that is exactly what Groupon did.

Recall in Chapter 4 that Groupon's much-anticipated 2011 IPO ran into some early headwinds when the SEC forced the company to restate revenues. That restatement resulted in a massive cut in revenue previously reported in every period from 2009 through June 2011 by over 50 percent. Separately, the SEC also forced Groupon to stop reporting what the agency considered a very misleading non-GAAP metric, consolidated segment reporting operating income (CSOI). In Table 13-2, we show that Groupon tried to trick investors into believing the company was profitable by eliminating several items from income from operations: (1) online marketing expenses, (2) stock-based compensation, and (3) acquisition-related expenses. The non-GAAP metric that Groupon used, adjusted CSOI, transformed the GAAP-based losses to gains.

Table 13-2. Groupon's Misleading Non-GAAP Metric

($ thousands)	Year Dec-09	Year Dec-10	Three Months Mar-10	Mar-11	27 Month Cumulative
Oper. income	(1,077)	(420,344)	8,571	(117,148)	(538,569)
Adjustments					
Marketing	4,446	241,546	3,904	179,903	
Stock comp	115	36,168	116	18,864	
Acquis. costs	–	203,183	–	–	
Total adjust	4,561	480,897	4,020	198,767	
Adj. CSOI	3,484	60,553	12,591	81,619	145,656

During the 27 months starting in January 2009, Groupon reported a cumulative GAAP-based operating loss totaling $536 million. However, the company wanted investors to instead use the misleading non-GAAP metric, adjusted CSOI, showing a cumulative profit of over $145 million. Fortunately, the SEC notified Groupon to stop using this misleading metric.

Pro Forma Earnings/Adjusted Earnings/Non-GAAP Earnings
What's in a name? That which companies call earnings, by any other name would smell as sweet . . . or so management would like you to think. Sometimes management insists that a foul-smelling "pro forma" or "adjusted" earnings metric (or any other earnings metric with a qualifying name) is a sweet and pure measure of earnings.

Pretending That Recurring Charges Are One-Time in Nature   You may recall that Peregrine Systems recorded bogus revenue and then tried to cover it up by fraudulently faking the sale of accounts receivable. Well, the company had so many bogus receivables that it also used pro forma tactics to hide the evidence of its chicanery. In addition to pretending to sell these receivables, Peregrine also took charges for these receivables, but it inappropriately classified those charges as nonrecurring and related to acquisitions. This classification gave Peregrine the cover to exclude these charges from its pro forma earnings presentation so investors would not be concerned (or at least those investors that always took the company at its word).

Whirlpool, one of the global leaders in large home appliances, reports a profitability metric called *ongoing earnings* that is meant to exclude the effects of nonrecurring and nonoperating items. One of the most common adjustments from GAAP earnings to "ongoing earnings" is restructuring charges that relate to a wide range of costs associated with the company's M&A, plant closures, layoffs, and asset impairments, among others. However, restructuring charges have been on Whirlpool's Income Statement in 23 of the past 27 years, hardly a "nonrecurring" cost! In October 2016, the SEC finally questioned the company's perennial exclusion of these costs.

3. Highlighting a Misleading Metric as a Surrogate for Cash Flow

Non-GAAP cash flow metrics are less common than non-GAAP revenue and earnings disclosures; however, they do exist. Sometimes companies create a pro forma cash flow metric to exclude a nonrecurring activity, such as a large litigation settlement. However, other times, companies may look to artificially enhance their cash-generation profile.

"Cash Earnings" and EBITDA Are Not Cash Flow Metrics
Companies sometimes present metrics like "cash earnings" or "cash EBITDA" (as we just saw with Global Crossing). Do not confuse these metrics with substitutes for cash flow! Many companies and investors alike believe that these metrics (as well as plain old EBITDA) are good surrogates for cash flow simply because the calculation includes the adding back of noncash expenses such as depreciation. As you surely know by now, a company's cash flow consists of much more than just net income plus noncash expenses. Calculating it in this way is just an abuse of using the indirect method of developing the Statement of Cash Flows (SCF) (refer to our discussion of cash flow presentation in the Part Three introduction). Ignoring working capital changes when calculating cash flow will provide you with a fictional portrait of a company's cash-generation abilities, in the same way that ignoring accruals for expenses such as bad debts, impairments, and warranty expenses will give you an illusory sense of profitability. In truth, metrics such as EBITDA and cash earnings are poor representations of performance.

Moreover, for capital-intensive businesses, EBITDA is often a misleading measure of performance and profitability because all the major capital costs run through the Income Statement as depreciation, and therefore they are excluded from EBITDA. Some companies abuse the investment community's acceptance of EBITDA and use the metric even though it is completely unwarranted.

Take, for example, the non-GAAP reporting at Gogo Inc., provider of in-flight Internet access. Gogo's non-GAAP adjusted EBITDA metric ignores some basic costs of delivering its in-flight services including the production and installation of network equipment and system software. Gogo treats these costs appropriately for GAAP purposes: they are capitalized on the Balance Sheet and depreciated through the P&L. However, since these expenses are categorized as "depreciation and amortization," they are eliminated from Gogo's non-GAAP adjusted EBITDA. No surprise that Gogo has been able to show positive adjusted EBITDA every year since its 2013 IPO despite deeply negative GAAP net income.

Non-GAAP Cash Flow Metrics May Be Put There to Confuse

In Chapter 10, "Cash Flow Shenanigan No. 1: Shifting Financing Cash Inflows to the Operating Section," we discussed how in 2000 Delphi Corp. improperly recorded a loan from the bank as the sale of inventory and in doing so boosted cash flow from operations by $200 million. Well, management at Delphi also liked to mislead investors by presenting tricky cash flow metrics. For example, Delphi routinely headlined its "Operating Cash Flow" in its Earnings Releases. No doubt, many people thought that Delphi was discussing its CFFO; however, this was not the case. "Operating Cash Flow" was actually Delphi's deceptively named surrogate for GAAP cash flow from operations. Since the name is so close to its GAAP compadre, you can imagine how many investors were confused into thinking that this pro forma metric was Delphi's actual CFFO. In truth, this surrogate barely resembled GAAP cash flow from operations. As shown in Table 13-3, it was calculated as net income *plus* depreciation and other noncash charges *minus* capital expenditures *plus* some huge mystery item labeled "other."

Table 13-3   Delphi's GAAP Cash Flow Versus Pro Forma Cash Flow, 2000

($ millions)	2000
Net income (GAAP)	1,062
One-time charge for in-process R&D	32
Depreciation and amortization	936
Capital expenditures	(1,272)
Other, net	878
"Operating Cash Flow" (non-GAAP)	**1,636**
Cash flow from operations (GAAP)	**268**
Free cash flow (GAAP CFFO less GAAP capital expenditures)	**(1,004)**

We mentioned earlier that Delphi's actual CFFO (as reported on the SCF) was $268 million, but its self-defined "Operating Cash Flow" (as presented in the Earnings Release) was $1.6 billion—an astonishing differential of almost $1.4 billion. Since this cash flow surrogate includes the impact of capital expenditures, it may be more relevant to compare it with Delphi's free cash flow (CFFO less capital expenditures) of *negative* $1.0 billion—bringing our differential to an outrageous $2.6 billion. (Oh, by the way, that $268 million in CFFO reported on the SCF was only $68 million if you exclude the sham sale of inventory that we discussed in Chapter 10.)

In 2003, Delphi was still up to the same tricks, but the company was now showing a reconciliation between its "Operating Cash Flow" and CFFO as reported on the Statement of Cash Flows. Delphi's "Operating Cash Flow" was $1.2 billion in 2003, versus $737 million in CFFO and *negative* $268 million in free cash flow. As shown in Table 13-4, the primary differences included routine operating uses of cash flow, including pension plan contributions, payments to employees, and a decline in the sales of accounts receivable.

Any serious investor who looked at this presentation would be aghast at seeing such normal operating expenditures excluded from the calculation of "Operating Cash Flow." The adage "Where there's smoke, there's fire" is very applicable when searching for shenanigans. Delphi's ridiculous cash flow surrogate deception was the smoke. The fraudulent revenue and cash flow was the fire.

Table 13-4   Delphi's GAAP Cash Flow Versus Pro Forma Cash Flow, 2003

($ millions)	2003
"Operating Cash Flow" (non-GAAP)	**1,220**
Pension contributions	(990)
Cash paid for employee and product line charges	(229)
Cash paid for lump-sum contract signing bonuses	(125)
Decrease in sales of accounts receivable	(144)
Capital expenditures	1,005
Cash flow from operations (GAAP)	737
Free cash flow (GAAP CFFO less GAAP capital expenditures)	**(268)**

Similarly, IBM showcased a free cash flow metric with an unusual and opportunistic definition. Free cash flow is a non-GAAP metric that is widely used and traditionally calculated as cash flow from operations minus capital expenditures. IBM adjusted this definition to also exclude changes in its financing receivables. This is problematic, since IBM's financing receivables are really just *long-term loans to its own customers*, in other words, accounts receivable. From 2010 to 2013, higher levels of financing to customers created a large drag on CFFO; however, IBM's tricky free cash flow metric made it seem as if these payments had been collected. In 2012 alone, the increase in financing receivables was nearly $3 billion, representing 16 percent of IBM's self-defined free cash flow.

What to Do When Non-GAAP Metrics Become Pervasive in an Industry?
Sometimes certain industries use non-GAAP metrics as the standard way to value companies or to calculate an appropriate dividend distribution to investors. Energy companies, structured as master limited partnerships (MLPs), stand out in eschewing GAAP-based numbers for non-GAAP ones.

With historically low interest rates since the 2008 financial crisis, investors have searched far and wide for securities offering an annual yield higher than the miserly interest on bonds. Wall Street took notice and began singing the praises of the high yields and tax-advantaged status of MLPs.

Houston-based Linn Energy quickly became a darling MLP for its ability to consistently grow its dividend payments. In 2012 the company paid investors $680 million in dividends, an increase of 15 percent from 2011. While impressive, these figures seem strange alongside the company's free cash flow, which fell by more than half a billion dollars to *negative* $694 million in 2012. How could the board have approved such a rich dividend payment when business required so much of Linn's available cash? The company actually had to borrow money in order to fund these payments. The answer lies in the way that Linn (and many other MLPs) reported their cash flow. The company emphasized "distributable cash flow"—this is a metric that has no standardized definition, but for Linn Energy it was derived from adjusted EBITDA, and it only took into account a portion of the company's capital expenditures. The methodology resulted in a much more favorable metric that was used to justify a higher dividend payment.

Table 13-5 shows Linn's GAAP and non-GAAP earnings and cash flow metrics, and Table 13-6 shows how Linn calculated "distributable cash flow" and the many costs that are not included.

Table 13-5   Linn Energy GAAP-Based and Non-GAAP-Based
Earnings and Cash Flow

($ thousands)	Fiscal 2010	Fiscal 2011	Fiscal 2012
GAAP-based metrics			
Net income	(114,290)	438,440	(386,616)
Calculate free cash flow			
CFFO	270,920	518,710	350,907
Capital expenditures	(223,033)	(629,864)	(1,045,079)
Free cash flows (FCF)	47,887	(111,154)	(694,172)
Acquisitions	(1,351,033)	(1,500,193)	(2,640,475)
FCF after acquisitions	(1,303,146)	(1,611,347)	(3,334,647)
Company's non-GAAP metrics			
Adjusted EBITDA	732,000	995,000	1,400,000
Distributable cash flow	450,400	570,600	663,757
Cash dividends paid	457,476	590,224	679,275
Coverage ratio	0.985%	0.967%	0.977%

Table 13-6 Linn Energy Non-GAAP Metrics Used to Determine Dividend Payout

($ thousands)	Fiscal 2010	Fiscal 2011	Fiscal 2012
Net income	(114,288)	438,439	(386,616)
Plus:			
Acquisition/divestiture	42,846	57,966	80,502
Interest expense	193,510	259,725	379,937
Depreciation/amortization	238,532	334,084	606,150
Impairments and losses	48,046	97,011	432,104
Losses (gains) on derivatives	300,284	(219,703)	256,379
Unit-based stock-comp	13,792	22,243	29,533
Exploration costs	5,168	2,390	1,915
Income tax expense	4,241	5,466	2,790
Adjusted EBITDA	**732,131**	**997,621**	**1,402,694**
Minus:			
Interest expense	(193,510)	(259,725)	(379,937)
Maintenance capital expenditures	(88,000)	(167,300)	(362,000)
Distributable cash flow (DCF)	**450,621**	**570,596**	**660,757**

You'll notice that Linn Energy deducted maintenance capital expenditures in arriving at distributable cash flow, while total capital expenditures on a GAAP basis were nearly double that amount. This follows an approach that some companies (and investors) take to consider capital expenditures in two distinct buckets: (1) *maintenance*—capital spent on existing facilities that do not increase capacity—and (2) *growth*—capital spent to expand the business at either existing facilities or new ones. Clearly, management has quite a bit of discretion in what it includes in each grouping. Table 13-7 shows how much Linn allocated to maintenance and growth. Naturally, the more Linn classifies as growth, the higher the DCF—as growth capital expenditures *are excluded in the calculation.*

Table 13-7   Linn Energy Allocation to Maintenance and Growth Capital Expenditures

($ thousands)	Fiscal 2010	Fiscal 2011	Fiscal 2012
Total capital expenditures	223,013	629,864	1,045,079
Maintenance capital expenditures	88,000	167,300	362,000
Growth capital expenditure	135,013	462,564	683,079
Percent of total expenditures classified as "growth"	60.5	73.4	65.3

The subsequent years proved to be quite challenging for Linn. First, the SEC raised questions about the company's calculations of the distributable cash flow. By the following year, the energy market had collapsed, causing Linn's business to fall on tough times. But following years of imprudently high dividends (paid largely with borrowing), Linn faced a severe cash crunch, leading to its 2016 bankruptcy filing. And with its $8.3 billion debt load, Linn earned the dubious distinction as the largest energy MLP bankruptcy.

Could investors have avoided suffering big losses from Linn's demise? We think so. Paying out enormous dividends while generating *negative* free cash flows was simply not a sustainable strategy—and should have been a strong warning sign. The fact that most shareholders were paying attention to a non-GAAP surrogate for free cash flow that didn't include many of the most significant costs of the business explained why the market had valued the company so richly, while more careful (and skeptical) investors would have stayed away.

Looking Ahead

In Chapter 14, we shift from key metrics that present an overly optimistic view of a company's performance to those metrics that mislead investors about a potentially imminent deterioration in the Balance Sheet and the company's economic health.

14

Key Metric Shenanigan No. 2: Distorting Balance Sheet Metrics to Avoid Showing Deterioration

As well as writing books, we also love reading them. We always make it a point to step into bookstores as often as possible, whether they're part of a mega chain like Barnes & Noble or the literary jewel of Portland, Oregon—Powell's Books. Once we're inside one of these places, it's hard not to notice the scores of self-help and diet books. They are everywhere. No doubt, we all yearn to look, feel, and be better at work, play, and all the other stuff. It's certainly a big business teaching people to feel better about their lives and to look fabulous.

Who knows if any of these plans really make us healthier or make us look any better? We do know, however, that upper management spends a great deal of time trying to make its Balance Sheets look great, even if they are loaded up with junk. This chapter highlights four techniques that struggling companies might use to convince investors that the company not only looks great but is in excellent health. Our hope is that these folks won't be as effective in fooling investors as the diet book authors are in persuading readers to trust their advice.

Techniques to Distort Balance Sheet Metrics to Avoid Showing Deterioration

1. Distorting accounts receivable metrics to hide revenue problems

2. Distorting inventory metrics to hide profitability problems

3. Distorting financial asset metrics to hide impairment problems

4. Distorting debt metrics to hide liquidity problems

1. Distorting Accounts Receivable Metrics to Hide Revenue Problems

Corporate executives understand that many investors review working capital trends carefully for signs of poor earnings quality or operational deterioration. They realize that a surge in receivables that is out of line with sales will lead investors to question the sustainability of recent revenue growth. To keep these kinds of questions at bay, companies may seek to distort the receivables numbers by (1) selling receivables or (2) converting them into notes receivable (both of which are discussed in this section) or (3) moving them somewhere else on the Balance Sheet (we address this later in the chapter).

Selling Accounts Receivable
In Chapter 10, "Cash Flow Shenanigan No. 1: Shifting Financing Cash Inflows to the Operating Section," we discussed how selling accounts receivable may be considered a useful cash management strategy, but an unsustainable longer-term driver of cash flow growth. Selling accounts receivable also serves another useful purpose: it lowers the days' sales outstanding (DSO) reported to investors (making it appear that customers have been paying

more quickly). Dishonest management can conceal a jump in DSO simply by selling more accounts receivable.

Let's refer to our discussion in Chapter 10 of Sanmina-SCI's stealth sales of receivables. After selling these receivables, the company highlighted a decline in DSO and an increase in cash flow from operations in its September 2005 quarterly results. Astute investors would have understood that it was the sale of receivables, not operational improvements, that drove DSO lower and CFFO higher. Such investors understand that the sale of receivables, in substance, represents a financing decision (that is, collecting cash due on customer accounts earlier). Therefore, the now lower accounts receivable balance naturally also results in a smaller DSO figure.

> **TIP**
>
> Whenever you spot a CFFO boost from the sale of receivables, also realize that by definition, the company's DSO *will have been lowered as well.*

Also recall how Peregrine recorded bogus revenue and then shamelessly faked the sale of the related bogus accounts receivable in order not to raise any alarms. Those receivables, obviously, went uncollected, and management became concerned that the bulging account balance would drive up DSO indefinitely—a clear warning for investors. By faking the sale of these receivables, Peregrine inflated its CFFO and removed the potential DSO red flag from investors' sights in one fell swoop.

The first examples of lowering receivables to improve DSO involved either selling them outright or faking the sale. Another way to hide accounts receivables is simply to reclassify them elsewhere on the Balance Sheet.

> **TIP**
>
> To calculate DSO on an apples-to-apples basis, simply add back sold receivables that remain outstanding at quarter-end for all periods.

Turning Accounts Receivable into Notes Receivable

Symbol Technologies' receivables had been growing rapidly because of aggressive revenue recognition and channel stuffing, surging to 119 days in June 2001 (up from 94 in March 2001 and 80 in June 2000). To avoid investor concerns, management engineered a cosmetic reduction in accounts receivable.

It was a pretty dirty trick, in our view. Symbol simply asked some of its closest customers to sign paperwork that would convert these trade accounts receivable into promissory notes or loans. Apparently, the customers acquiesced, since it made no difference to them; they owed the money either way. However, the new paperwork gave Symbol a convenient cover to move these accounts receivable to the notes receivable section of the Balance Sheet. In effect, Symbol waved a magic wand and, with the help of some compliant customers, "reclassified" these trade receivables to an account that was not as closely monitored by investors. It seems that Symbol's primary purpose for this reclassification was to lower its DSO and fool investors into believing that sales had been kosher and that customers had paid on time. And according to plan, DSO fell from the 119 days in June 2001 to 90 days the following period.

> **TIP**
>
> Investors should be as concerned when they see a *large decrease in DSO* (particularly following a period of rapidly rising DSO) as they are when they see a substantial increase in DSO.

Watch for Increases in Receivables Other Than Accounts Receivable UTStarcom pulled a similar switcheroo in 2004 by taking more payment in the form of "bank notes" and "commercial notes." Since UTStarcom chose not to classify these notes receivable as accounts receivable on the Balance Sheet (in fact, the bank notes were considered to be a subset of cash!), the company presented a more palatable DSO to investors, despite a severe deterioration in the business. Diligent investors could have spotted this improper account classification by reading UTStarcom's footnotes. As shown in the box, the company disclosed clearly that it had accepted a substantial amount of bank and commercial notes in place of accounts receivable.

UTSTARCOM'S JUNE 2004 FORM 10-Q

From Footnote 6 (Cash, Cash Equivalents and Short-Term Investments)

The Company *accepts bank notes receivable* with maturity dates between three and six months *from its customers in China* in the normal course of business. *Bank notes receivable were $100.0 million and $11.5 million at June 30, 2004 and December 31, 2003,* respectively, and have been included in cash and cash equivalents and short-term investments. [Italics added for emphasis.]

From Footnote 8 (Accounts and Notes Receivable)

The Company *accepts commercial notes receivable* with maturity dates between three and six months *from its customers in China* in the normal course of business. Notes receivable available for sale were *$42.9 million and $11.4 million at June 30, 2004 and December 31, 2003,* respectively. [Italics added for emphasis.]

Investors received another warning on UTStarcom's Balance Sheet: notes receivable surged, from $11 million in December 2003 to $43 million the following quarter. By now, it should be abundantly clear that identifying the reason for such a change is extremely important. If management cannot provide you with a plausible reason, assume that the company may be playing a game with accounts receivable and trying to hide otherwise bulging DSO.

Watch Out for Varying Company DSO Calculations   For the purposes of identifying aggressive revenue recognition practices, we suggest that investors use the ending (not the average) receivables balance when calculating DSO. Using average receivables works well for assessing cash management trends, but it works less well for trying to detect financial shenanigans. End-of-period balances are more representative of the revenue transactions that took place later in the period, which are more relevant in assessing revenue quality.

Accounting Capsule:
Days' Sales Outstanding

Days' sales outstanding is generally calculated as follows:

Ending receivables/revenue × number of days in the period
(for quarterly periods, 91.25 days is a normal approximation)

While we recommend using this calculation for DSO, you may encounter different calculations suggested by companies or texts. For example, some people believe that DSO should be calculated using average receivables over the period, as opposed to the ending balance of receivables that we suggest.

Since DSO is not a GAAP metric, there is no absolute definition for it. It is important, however, that the calculation reflect the analysis that you are trying to perform. For example, if you are assessing the likelihood that a company has accelerated revenue by booking a significant amount of revenue on the last day of the quarter, (i.e., stuffing the channel), it makes sense to calculate DSO using the ending balance of receivables rather than the average one. Similarly, if you are worried about the collectibility of receivables and you are evaluating a company's exposure, it is best to use the ending balance. However, if you wish to calculate the average time over which a company collects its receivables, you may want to use the average balance of receivables.

The bottom line is that for financial shenanigan detection purposes, we advise calculating DSO using ending balances, even if a company tells you otherwise.

Watch for Changes in a Company's DSO Calculation   Be especially wary if a company *changes its own DSO calculation* in a way that conceals deterioration, as Tellabs Inc. apparently tried to do in December 2006. Tellabs had been calculating DSO based on the ending receivables balance, but it then changed to using its quarterly average receivables balance. Since receivables surged in the quarter in which the change was made, the average receivables balance was naturally much lower than the ending one, allowing for a more favorable presentation of DSO on an earnings conference call with investors. As a result, Tellabs disclosed that DSO in December 2006 had increased by only 5 days sequentially (to 59 days from 54 days in the previous quarter). Had management made no changes in its calculation, Tellabs would have reported an increase in DSO of 16 days (to 82 days from 66 days the previous quarter). The change in the DSO calculation was mentioned in the same conference call. In this case, being aware of the change in calculation was the easy part; knowing it was a big deal was key for alert investors to realize that management was playing games and trying to hide its bulging receivables.

> **TIP**
>
> Astute investors should note a change in the calculation of DSO; when management changes how it computes operational metrics it is often attempting to hide some deterioration from investors.

2. Distorting Inventory Metrics to Hide Profitability Problems

Investors typically view an unexpected rise in inventory as a sign of upcoming margin pressure (through markdowns or write-offs) or falling product demand. Some companies with inventory problems seek to avoid this negative perception by toying with inventory metrics.

Covering Up a Cover-Up

You may recall from Chapter 4 that Symbol Technologies had overstated sales by offering customers very generous return rights. Moreover, some sales turned out to be completely bogus because customers had sent back products they never wanted, and based on a side agreement with Symbol, they could return them at any time and pay nothing. These returns became more than a minor nuisance, as they increased Symbol's inventory levels, a potential warning sign for investors. So as one cover-up often leads to another, Symbol created an "inventory reduction plan" designed to reduce inventory levels. The plan (as described by the Securities and Exchange Commission) included recording fictitious accounting entries to reduce inventory, leaving product deliveries on the receiving docks without recording them as inventory, and selling inventory to a third party but agreeing to repurchase it.

Watch for Inventory That Moves to Another Part of the Balance Sheet
Companies will sometimes reclassify inventory to a different account on the
Balance Sheet. Pharmaceutical giant Merck & Co., for example, in 2003
began reporting part of its inventory as a long-term asset, included in the
"other assets" line on the Balance Sheet. A footnote revealed that these oddly
classified inventories related to products that were not expected to be sold
within one year. In December 2003, the long-term portion of Merck's inventory
represented 13 percent of the total, and the next year, it jumped to 25 percent.
Investors should certainly have included these long-term inventory totals when
analyzing Merck's inventory trends. A sudden spike in long-term inventory war-
rants concern by investors.

Be Cautious About New Company-Created Metrics   Inventory balances at
mall retailer Tween Brands Inc. had been bloated in late 2006 and early
2007, and management correctly assumed that investors would be less than
overjoyed. Specifically, days' sales of inventory jumped to 60 days in the May
2007 quarter from 52 days the preceding year, marking the third consecutive
quarter of increase. Moreover, inventory per square foot (a non-GAAP metric often cited by Tween) increased by 18 percent.

To divert potential investor concerns about inventory, management began
highlighting a new metric: "in-store" inventory per square foot. In May
2007, Tween management claimed that the surge in inventory should not be
a source of worry because "in-store" inventory had increased only a modest
8 percent ($27 per square foot versus $25 last year). Despite the absurdity
of this new metric, Wall Street bulls were pleased; all they needed was an
explanation, no matter how weak.

Tween's explanation should have given astute investors pause on two
grounds. First, it would be completely inappropriate for Tween to simply
ignore inventory that it owned and included on its Balance Sheet but that
was not on store shelves. "Out-of-store" inventory qualifies as inventory and
has no less markdown risk than "in-store" inventory. Second, and even more
troubling, Tween tricked investors by providing an "apples-to-oranges" comparison of its inventory growth. Specifically, the $25 cited by management
as the prior year's *in-store* inventory per square foot reflected *total* inventory
per square foot. By definition, comparing the current year's in-store number

with the prior year's total number would understate inventory growth; of course, it was up only 8 percent! Since the in-store metric was new, the prior year's number was not previously disclosed, which made it difficult for investors to notice the inconsistency. However, diligent investors would have been *skeptical enough about the creation of a new inventory metric* at a time when inventory was increasing, and they would have questioned its usefulness as a measure of the company's health.

3. Distorting Financial Asset Metrics to Hide Impairment Problems

Financial assets (such as loans, investments, and securities) are significant sources of income for banks and other financial institutions. Therefore, assessing the "quality" or strength of these assets should be a key part of understanding the future operating performance of such companies. For example, it is crucial for investors to understand whether a bank's investment portfolio consists of risky, illiquid securities and to know if its loan portfolio is weighted toward dicey subprime borrowers.

Consider two banks that are identical in every way, except for the composition of their loan portfolios. One bank's loan portfolio consists entirely of loans to subprime borrowers, 20 percent of which have failed to pay their bills on time. The other bank's loan portfolio consists mainly of loans to prime borrowers, only 2 percent of which have failed to pay on time. It does not take a banking expert to realize that the second bank's operating performance will be steadier and that the first one will be more volatile.

Financial institutions will often present extremely helpful metrics that allow investors to understand the strength and performance of their assets. For example, a bank might report delinquency rates, nonperforming loans, and loan loss reserve levels. However, sometimes management dresses up or conceals important metrics that would show a deterioration in order to present itself in a more favorable light.

Watch for Changes in Financial Reporting Presentation

Consider the case of New Century Financial Corp., once the largest U.S. independent nonprime lender, whose risky mortgage lending culminated in its April 2007 bankruptcy. New Century kept its earnings afloat in September

2006 by *reducing* its loan loss reserve, instead of increasing it, despite facing higher delinquencies and bad loans. However, when it released its September 2006 earnings, the company was less than completely honest with investors about its reserve level. Most investors reading the Earnings Release came away thinking that New Century had raised its loan loss reserve.

Here's why. New Century realized that investors would be seriously spooked if they knew that the company had reduced its reserves while its subprime loan portfolio was souring and that this reduction was the primary driver of earnings. Indeed, analysts who followed New Century were monitoring the company's allowance for loan losses closely as the subprime market started to crack. So when the company released its September 2006 results, management quietly changed its reserve presentation.

Previously, New Century's Earnings Release had presented the loan loss reserve on a stand-alone basis. However, in September 2006, the company grouped the loan loss reserve with another reserve (allowance for real estate owned) and presented the two together as one unit (see the accompanying disclosure in the box). By combining the two reserves, New Century could say in its release that reserves increased from $236.5 million in June to $239.4 million in September. However, the number on which investors had previously been focused—the loan loss reserve—declined from $209.9 million to $191.6 million. The loan loss reserve fell because bad loans that had been written off (called *charge-offs*) had accelerated and New Century had failed to record a sufficient expense to refill the reserve; if it had done so, EPS in September 2006 would have been sliced to $0.47 from the $1.12 as reported.

By simply changing the presentation of a key metric, New Century was able to avoid signaling that asset quality had deteriorated, while also reporting higher earnings. This charade probably bought the company some time before its bankruptcy several months later. Astute investors who were monitoring not only the level of the loan loss reserve, but also the presentation, would have had a warning of the company's demise. Investors who missed the presentation change in New Century's Earnings Release, but read the 10-Q released several days later, would have seen the disaggregated loan loss reserve and had fair warning as well.

NEW CENTURY'S LOAN LOSS RESERVE DISCLOSURE

June 2006 Earnings Release

At June 30, 2006, the balance of the mortgage loan portfolio was $16.0 billion. *The allowance for losses on loans held for investment* was $209.9 million, representing 1.31 percent of the unpaid principal balance of the portfolio. This compares with 0.79 percent of the unpaid principal balance of the portfolio at June 30, 2005 and 1.30 percent of the portfolio at March 31, 2006. [Italics added for emphasis.] *September 2006 Earnings Release*

At September 30, 2006, *the allowance for losses on mortgage loans held for investment and real estate owned* was $239.4 million compared with $236.5 million at June 30, 2006. These amounts represent 1.68 percent and 1.47 percent of the unpaid principal balance of the mortgage loan portfolio, respectively. [Italics added for emphasis.]

Executives at New Century eventually got into trouble for their tactics. In 2009, the SEC charged New Century's former CEO, CFO, and Controller with securities fraud for misleading investors, alleging the company sought to assure investors that its business was not at risk and was performing better than its peers.

4. Distorting Debt Metrics to Hide Liquidity Problems

A company's cash obligations, such as debt payments, may have an impact on future operating performance as well. Large near-term debt obligations may prevent a company from funding its desired growth initiatives or, at worst, send it spiraling toward bankruptcy.

Europe's Enron

Parmalat Finanziaria SpA, the Italian-based dairy producer and one of the world's largest packaged-food companies, grew its business rapidly in the 1990s by aggressively acquiring food service companies around the world. Parmalat relied heavily on the debt markets to fund its shopping spree, borrowing at least $7 billion in various offerings between 1998 and 2003. As its business ran into serious problems, Parmalat began having trouble generating sufficient cash to pay down this debt. Moreover, top executives of this family-owned and family-dominated company began funneling hundreds of millions of dollars to other family businesses. Therefore, when bonds came due, Parmalat had a desperate need to issue new bonds and float equity offerings to raise enough cash to pay off the older debt.

Normally, investors would be reluctant to purchase new bonds and equity from a poorly performing company that was strapped with heavy debt obligations and had no cash. So to attract investors, Parmalat concocted a widespread scheme to fraudulently hide its debt and conceal bad assets. By dressing up its Balance Sheet, Parmalat fraudulently portrayed itself to investors as a company that was in robust economic health. In September 2003 (the quarter before the fraud was revealed), Parmalat's unreported debt amounted to an astonishing €7.9 billion. The company's net worth, reported to be €2.1 billion, was negative €11.2 billion—an inconceivable €13.3 billion overstatement!

The centerpiece of Parmalat's fraud seems to have been the company's use of offshore entities to hide fictitious or impaired assets, fabricate the reduction of debt, and create fake income. The scope of the fraudulent activities that Parmalat is alleged to have engaged in is quite amazing. SEC litigation against the company names a few, including forging the repurchase of its debt, faking the sale of bogus or uncollectible receivables, falsifying the payment of payables, recording fictional revenue, mischaracterizing debt as equity, disguising intercompany loans as income, and diverting company cash to various businesses owned by members of the CEO's family.

As usual, there were warning signs for perceptive investors to find. One key warning occurred in late October 2003 when Parmalat's auditors (Deloitte & Touche) wrote in an audit report that they were unable to certify certain transactions involving an investment fund called Epicurum, which later turned out to be one of these fraudulent offshore entities. These transactions were quite significant. Parmalat had recorded gains on a derivative contract just signed with Epicurum that *accounted for more than all Parmalat's €119.9 million in pretax earnings* in the first half of 2003. Moreover, these gains were revealed because of Parmalat's commenting on Deloitte's review report, but they had not previously been disclosed by Parmalat in its June 2003 Earnings Release.

Less than two weeks later, in early November 2003, Parmalat decided to formally respond to Deloitte's report in a very public manner. It issued four press releases over a span of three days seeking to clarify Deloitte's reasons for not signing off on its financial statements and also to explain its Epicurum investment in further detail. To be clear, Parmalat decided to refute its auditor in a public forum over a transaction with an obscure offshore entity that had accounted for all its recent earnings.

The late 2003 series of events at Parmalat is perhaps the reddest of red flags. As an investor, you should cringe when you see a company having a public disagreement with its auditor, particularly on a shady transaction of significant magnitude. Surprisingly, many investors in Parmalat did not feel that way. It was not until several weeks later that Parmalat's stock price plunged as the company defaulted on its debt.

Looking Ahead

This chapter completes the section on Key Metric Shenanigans. The next section of the book, Part Five, "Acquisition Accounting Shenanigans," introduces readers to the most complex companies to analyze—acquisitive ones—and how to navigate the many accounting tricks used by companies favoring an acquisition-driven strategy.

PART FIVE

ACQUISITION ACCOUNTING SHENANIGANS

> More value is destroyed by acquisitions than any other single action
> taken by companies.
>
> —ASWATH DAMODARAN, NYU FINANCE PROFESSOR

Finding new growth engines at a mature company can be challenging, and management generally takes one of two approaches: (1) develop new categories of products, services, or customers organically or (2) make acquisitions. In other words, "make or buy."

Success stories abound following either strategy, or combinations of both. Consider the smartphone market. Apple developed its megahit iPhone product internally. Since its release a decade ago, over a billion iPhones have been sold. Today, the smartphone generates about 60 percent of Apple's revenue. In contrast, Google became a formidable player in the smartphone space by acquiring Android for $50 million in 2005. According to information from a 2016 court deposition, since 2008, Android's software had generated well over $30 billion in revenue and $22 billion in profit for Google. So using different approaches, one an organic grower and the other through M&A, both Apple and Google scored big in the smartphone market.

Clearly, one big advantage of following the M&A path is timing. Unlike Apple, which spent many years developing the Apple iPhone, Google found a "plug-and-play" solution for its platform, getting its phone to market much more quickly than if it had built a comparable product internally.

But perhaps the biggest difference in outcomes between the organic growers and the acquirers relates to failure. As you might imagine, the failure rate for companies trying to discover, build, and market a new product is quite high. Think of it like oil drillers who know that the probability of hitting a gusher is low. So their thinking is generally to not "bet the farm" on a single drilling expedition, which could imperil the company. However, even if they fail to hit a wet well most of the time, spending to drill around an entire field can be quite profitable over the long run.

Acquisitions, by contrast, appear to provide a more attractive risk profile. After all, the acquired company presumably already has a track record in the marketplace and a base of business that can be measured. However, in some respects this is an illusion—in reality, the long-term success rate of acquisitions is quite low. Shareholders of AOL and Time Warner would agree. They learned this all too well in the megamerger of "new media" with "old media" in the $164 billion deal, with AOL shareholders owning 55 percent of the new company. The combined business crashed and burned over the next 18 months, reporting a hard-to-imagine $99 billion loss.

There are many reasons that acquisitions fail to live up to the hype. In our experience, three of them seem particularly resonant:

1. Widespread overconfidence in the magic of "synergies"
2. Reckless transactions motivated by intense fear or greed
3. Deals driven by artificial accounting and reporting benefits rather than business logic

1. Widespread Overconfidence in the Magic of "Synergies"

M&A deals often are pitched to investors with highly optimistic projections of cross-selling and cost-cutting opportunities. Consider the grand plan of United Airlines' parent, UAL, which in the 1980s sought to create a one-stop fly-drive-sleep behemoth that would take care of the most important needs of travelers. In just a two-year period, UAL CEO Richard Ferris spent $2.3 billion acquiring Hertz Car Rental and Westin and Hilton hotel chains. In 1987, Ferris changed the company name to Allegis to "reflect the broadened scope of the travel experience." Investors hated the new name (some mockingly calling it Egregious Corp.) and questioned the business strategy. The share price collapsed, and its CEO began looking for a new job.

Just as at UAL, Sears, the biggest retailer before Walmart, loved the concept of "cross-selling." So with its millions of customers, management believed that by creating a "financial supermarket," they could sell stocks, insurance, and homes after they acquired Dean Witter brokerage, Allstate insurance, and Coldwell Banker realty. Again, investors were baffled and unhappy with these confusing and costly acquisitions. One critic at Merrill Lynch mockingly asked, "Did consumers really want to buy socks and stocks under the same roof?" With investors giving an emphatic thumbs-down, Sears quickly began to sell off these companies.

2. Reckless Transactions Motivated by Intense Fear or Greed

We believe that many deals are driven by the human emotions of fear or greed. In the case of Valeant, for instance, CEO Michael Pearson's stock-based compensation (topping out if Valeant's share price appreciated an insane 60 percent annually) created huge incentives to grow the company at breakneck speed, making serial acquisitions the only logical strategy.

At Mattel in the late 1990s, CEO Jill Barad, fearful that her traditional toy business failed to provide sufficient growth opportunities, searched for a deal in the faster-growing software industry. At the same time, software entrepreneur Kevin O'Leary, founder of The Learning Company (TLC), was searching for a buyer of his business. TLC's business included a mishmash of around 60 mostly unprofitable educational software companies, all acquired in rapid succession over a few years, using its inflated stock or enormous amounts of debt. (Yes, this is the same Kevin O'Leary affectionately known as "Mr. Wonderful" on ABC's hit TV series *Shark Tank*.)

So when Mattel came knocking, O'Leary was eager to cash out. Mattel agreed to pay $3.7 billion in May 1999. Big mistake! Really big mistake! No sooner had the ink dried on the contract than Mattel started reporting disappointing results, largely from the TLC business. (In fact, on the day the deal was announced, Mattel's stock was pummeled, dropping $2 billion in market value in a single day.) The news kept getting worse as TLC reported losses totaling $206 million for the year, including $183 million in the fourth quarter alone. This caused Mattel to suffer an $86 million loss for the year and CEO Jill Barad to lose her job in February 2000. And less than one year after this ill-fated deal, Mattel had seen enough and basically gave TLC away for nothing, selling it to the Gores Group at a fire-sale price of $27 million! To add insult to injury, Mattel later wound up paying $122 million in class-action lawsuits filed by Mattel shareholders. Ouch!

3. Deals Driven by Artificial Accounting and Reporting Benefits Rather Than Business Logic

Part Five of this book focuses on artificial accounting and reporting used around the time of an acquisition and intended to inflate the performance and operating metrics of the acquiring company.

Comparing Acquisition Accounting Shenanigans to All Other Ones

Think about all the shenanigans we discussed earlier (Earnings Manipulation, Cash Flow, and Key Metric) as tricks designed to cover up some problem in the underlying business. Sometimes another layer of deception may help nefarious management teams to hide the original cover-up. That's where Acquisition Accounting (AA) Shenanigans can be used and can make detection of the underlying business problem that much more difficult. Consider the case of Olympus Corp., starting with management's decision to use an Earnings Manipulation (EM) Shenanigan to hide a business problem, only to later use an egregious AA Shenanigan to cover up the first accounting game.

Olympus ran a decades-long loss-hiding scheme in which it failed to record impairment charges for bad investments. Over the years, Olympus had invested in many enterprises, many of which turned out to be big money-losing investments. Rather than record disappointing impairment charges against income for these losses, management decided to maintain these investments at inflated values on the Balance Sheet. It was a textbook example of a technique described in Chapter 6, *failing to write down assets with impaired value*. As the oversized investment account on Olympus's Balance Sheet would likely raise questions by investors, management essentially made these losses disappear by shifting them into goodwill, under cover of an acquisition, then later shifting these losses to bogus nonconsolidated entities created by management.

In addition to serving as a cover-up of a typical accounting shenanigan, some AA tricks can be used to provide earnings benefits directly. Part Five, "Acquisition Accounting Shenanigans," shows various techniques often used to cover up business problems and other newly created schemes to trick investors.

Three Acquisition Accounting Shenanigans

ACQUISITION ACCOUNTING SHENANIGANS

AA Shenanigan No. 1: Artificially boosting revenue and earnings (Chapter 15)

AA Shenanigan No. 2: Inflating reported cash flow (Chapter 16)

AA Shenanigan No. 3: Manipulating key metrics (Chapter 17)

15

Acquisition Accounting Shenanigan No. 1: Artificially Boosting Revenue and Earnings

Acquisition Accounting Creates Distortions on the Financial Statements

One reason investors have difficulty in interpreting financial statements of acquisitive companies is because certain costs that typically should be reflected as expenses on the Income Statement are instead found on the Balance Sheet in *goodwill* or *intangibles*. Moreover, some cash outflows typically reflected as reductions in cash flow from operations are classified as *investing outflows* on the Statement of Cash Flows.

Thus, the first two manifestations of distortion (shifting operating costs *to* the Balance Sheet and shifting cash outflows *from* the Operations section to the Investing section) should be considered the *consequence* of the acquisition process, rather than an overt action by management to mislead. As such, we are not criticizing management; rather we are alerting investors to the inherently misleading information resulting from acquisition accounting conventions.

Shifting Operating Costs to the Balance Sheet

Consider two different companies in the drug industry. Company O grows organically, while Company A grows through acquisitions. Company O spends 15 percent of its $1 billion sales on R&D and charges to expense $150 million annually; in contrast, Company A spends only 3 percent of its $1 billion revenue on R&D, or a $30 million expense, as it acquires most of its new drugs through acquisitions. In comparing the results for the two companies, Company O will report a much smaller profit, as it must recognize $150 million as an expense. Company A, in contrast, would expense just the $30 million for the modest R&D spent, plus a relatively small amortization expense on the acquired intangible assets. However, over a five-year period, Company A will likely have *spent much more* than Company O to gain access to new drugs and to acquire entire companies. But under GAAP-based acquisition accounting conventions, most acquisition-related costs would not be expensed but rather would reside on the Balance Sheet, often with the lion's share shown as *goodwill* or *intangible assets*.

The key point is that acquisitive companies should logically report higher profits than organic growers, simply because certain necessary costs of growing their business (like R&D) have already been incurred by someone else and thus are not be charged as an expense against revenue.

Shifting Operating Cash Outflows to the Investing Section

As we will discuss in the next chapter, the same benefit received by the acquiring company on the Income Statement can also be seen on the Statement of Cash Flows. Specifically, cash paid to access products by acquisition would be reflected as a cash outflow in the Investing (and not Operating) section of the Statement of Cash Flows. This convention under acquisition accounting rules would make M&A-driven companies appear to generate much more operating cash flow than their organic peers. Again though, the M&A-driven companies will have a much larger cash outflow because of the much higher cost they pay to acquire an entire company.

Another important anomaly relates to the cash flow generated by an M&A-driven company. Recall that increases in working capital (i.e., rising inventory or receivables) would ordinarily be reflected as a reduction in cash flow from operations. However, if that working capital came from an acquisition, rather than organically, it would be reflected as a reduction in cash flow from investing activities (and not operations). Again, the acquisition accounting conventions would allow M&A-driven companies to appear to be bigger generators of operating cash flow, but this may be a mirage. (Chapter 16 shows a variety of tricks to inflate cash flow from operations during the acquisition process.)

The Sun Will Come Out Tomorrow

One of our favorite Broadway musicals, *Annie*, has a memorable song, "Tomorrow," sung by little Annie. The statement "The sun will come out tomorrow" expresses her hope for a very bright future. In much the same way, serial acquirers have mastered the art of convincing investors of a sunny future after a deal closes—no matter how cloudy the past. To increase the odds that the sun will indeed shine very brightly tomorrow on the newly merged company, the following Acquisition Accounting Shenanigans come in very handy.

The main objective in using AA Shenanigan No.1: Artificially Boosting Revenue and Earnings is to inflate the acquirer's revenue and profits after the deal closes.

Acquisition Accounting Techniques to Artificially Boost Revenue and Earnings

1. Inflating profits through tricks at a target company before a deal closes

2. Inflating profits by hiding losses at deal closing

3. Creating dubious new revenue streams after closing

4. Inflating profits by releasing suspicious reserves either before or just after closing

1. Inflating Profits Through Tricks at a Target Company Before a Deal Closes

Think back to the important themes we discussed in Part Two, "Earnings Manipulation Shenanigans." Unlike the first five EM shenanigans, which inflate current profits, EM Nos. 6 and 7 represent tricks to make *future periods* look sunny. And that's exactly the goal of the target and acquirer: to make the postclosing period beautiful. One way to accomplish this goal is to depress earnings in the period just before the deal—called the *stub period.*

Watch for a Slowdown in Revenue at the Target Prior to the Acquisition Close
Investors in Valeant would have found a very puzzling pattern if they had paid close attention to the revenues of the company's acquisition targets just prior to consolidation. In many of these cases, reported revenue at the target slowed down dramatically before the deal closed when compared with prior periods. No example, however, was more extreme than at Salix. Table 15-1 shows Salix's quarterly sales from 2013, 2014, and 2015. Notice a few interesting patterns in the numbers: (1) during the last three quarters of 2013, sales were virtually unchanged; (2) during the first quarters in 2014 (when Salix management was actively shopping the company), sales grew rapidly when compared with the same prior-year periods; (3) during the last quarter of 2014 and first one of 2015 (when Valeant was in the process of closing the acquisition), sales completely dried up; and (4) the last three quarters of 2015 (after Valeant acquired Salix), sales grew dramatically.

Table 15-1   Salix Quarterly Revenue, 2013 to 2015

| Year | Quarter ending ($ million) | | | |
	March	June	September	December
2013	203	235	239	238
2014	403	376	342	**13**
2015	**0**	313	461	497

Let's dig a bit deeper to make sense of these strange numbers and trends. Starting in 2014, Salix made a strong push to report terrific sales growth to maximize the price an acquirer would pay. Trying to spruce up the financial statements before a deal might be fairly common. But stuffing inventory to distributors that have no customers to buy those products goes a bit too far. Indeed, this aggressive channel stuffing caught the attention of the regulators and eventually cost the CEO and CFO their jobs.

But the accounting games were far from over. In the fourth quarter of 2014, for example, Salix reported almost no sales at all—a mere $13 million. So compared with the same quarter in 2013, sales declined an unbelievable 95 percent. How is that even possible? We can think of only two possible explanations: (1) the numbers are correct and Salix's business had completed imploded—very unlikely, as Valeant chose not to abort the deal—or (2) the numbers are rigged and Salix had intentionally refrained from booking any business during Q4 2014 to allow Valeant to include that revenue in the periods after the deal closed on April 1.

After the deal closed, Valeant booked a whopping $1.3 billion (or $424 million per quarter) in Salix product sales over the remaining three quarters of 2015. While we claim no "smoking-gun" evidence to prove inflated revenue at Valeant from spring-loading sales, the numbers in Table 15-1 look convincing.

Watch for Unusual Sources of Revenue at the Time of an Acquisition

Agreements between two parties just before they merge clearly lack an "arm's-length" element. Consider Krispy Kreme's nifty scheme to inflate revenue when it was about to reacquire one of its franchises in 2003.

Before the acquisition closed, Krispy Kreme sold doughnut-making equipment to this franchise for $700,000. As part of the deal, Krispy Kreme increased the amount that it would pay to acquire the franchise by the same $700,000 to cover the price of the equipment. This arrangement clearly had no real net economic impact, so no revenue should have been recorded. Krispy Kreme, however, did not see it that way, and so it recorded the sale of equipment as revenue rather than as an offset to the increased franchise purchase price. Not surprisingly, this ruse helped Krispy Kreme maintain its streak of consistently exceeding Wall Street expectations.

Target Company Takes Large Expense Write-off During Stub Period

With the goal of deflating earnings during the stub period, companies not only refrain from reporting all their sales, but can also take big write-offs during the period. Specifically, a company might write off assets causing the stub period to be burdened with expenses that otherwise would have been charged to the newly merged company. It is simple to execute. The target company simply announces a write-off to streamline its operation in advance of the two companies merging.

2. Inflating Profits by Hiding Losses at Deal Closing

As we discussed in Chapter 6, Olympus Corporation pumped billions into money-losing investments to accelerate sluggish growth at the company. The company chose to keep the assets at full cost on the Balance Sheet, against the wishes of its auditor. As the amounts grew to an uncomfortably large amount, Olympus knew it had to find another trick to make the balance in its investment account disappear.

In October 2011 when Olympus fired its newly appointed CEO, Michael Woodford, it was revealed that the company had been operating a *tobashi* scheme (a scheme that makes problems "fly away," in Japanese) in which $2 billion was said to have been siphoned off to cover bad investments made up to 20 years before.

Around 2008, Olympus had bought three companies and paid far more than they were worth, according to Woodford. This inflated price (totaling 30 percent of the deal value) was labeled "fees to a middleman." Woodford pointed out that the cut for investment bankers typically would be 1 to 2 percent, so the $674 million paid on the $2 billion deals likely was a payment to cover losses and move the investments off the Balance Sheet to an unconsolidated related-party entity.

When Woodford, who was responsible for considerable business across Europe, noticed this shenanigan in 2008, he attempted to tender his resignation over the "strange" European acquisitions. He was given plausible reassurances and promoted to run Olympus's entire European business. Over the next few years, Woodford was promoted to COO and eventually became the chief executive officer. As he then became aware of the true nature of these and other accounting tricks at the company, he made the board aware of his deep concerns. Unfortunately, rather than investigate the prior executives, the board fired Woodford. Shortly thereafter, the fraud was revealed.

3. Creating Dubious New Revenue Streams After Closing

Both buyers and sellers of businesses have great flexibility in structuring a deal to create dubious future revenue streams. For example, assume Buyer Ben wants to purchase Seller Sam's business, and they come to terms on a price of $5 million, which is the fair market value of the company. Buyer Ben then says to Seller Sam, "I will instead pay you $6 million (rather than the $5 million), provided you also agree to pay me a $1 million licensing fee next year." This change has no real economic impact to either Buyer Ben or Seller Sam, but the change in structure allows Ben to show $1 million more in revenue in the year following the acquisition. Seriously, this type of non-sense actually does happen.

Watch for Either a Buyer or Seller Creating an
Unrelated Nonrecurring Revenue Stream

Occasionally, we see either a buyer or seller of a business cleverly create a recurring revenue stream by bundling a seemingly unrelated agreement into the acquisition accounting.

One clever scheme to create revenue out of thin air, using the cover of an acquisition, was employed by FPA Medical (FPAM). In 1996, FPAM paid $197 million to nursing home operator Foundation Health to purchase a group of medical practices. As part of the acquisition, however, FPAM guaranteed that Foundation's patients would receive continued and uninterrupted access for the next 30 years. In exchange, Foundation (the seller) agreed to pay FPAM $55 million in rebates over two years. As FPAM received the $27.5 million payment each year, it recorded these amounts as sales revenue. As we thought through the essence of this transaction, we considered it quite aggressive to record any revenue for the transaction. In real economic terms, FPAM paid $197 million and received $55 million rebate over two years, resulting in a net acquisition cost of $142 million and zero revenue on this deal.

Turning the Sale of a Business into a Recurring Revenue Stream

Some companies will sell a manufacturing plant or a business unit to another company and, at the same time, enter into an agreement to buy back product from that sold business unit. Like the FPAM-Foundation deal, when cash is flowing in two directions, opportunities abound for playing games regarding how the flows are classified.

Consider the November 2006 deal between semiconductor giant Intel and fellow chip manufacturer Marvell Technology Group. Intel agreed to sell certain assets to Marvell. At the same time, Marvell agreed to purchase a minimum number of semiconductor wafers from Intel over the next two years.

In studying the footnotes to the financial statements of both companies, we learned that Intel priced this business below market value (presumably booking a smaller gain on that sale), but it was made whole as Marvell agreed to later purchase wafers at *above market prices* (thereby creating a new and inflated recurring revenue stream). In short, Intel used a shenanigan that resulted in shifting some of the one-time gain related to an asset sale to increase its recurring revenue from selling a product to a customer.

Question the Management of the Acquirer When Changing Accounting Practices of a Target Inflate Profits

While the first AA Shenanigan showed how the target company could play games to aid the acquirer, the acquiring company still has a lot of cards it can play to inflate profits *after* the deal closes. Recall that in Chapter 3 we discussed the accounting change made just after Valeant acquired Medicis. In the first quarter after the deal closed, Valeant changed the revenue recognition policy for Medicis so that sales would be recognized sooner, thereby inflating Valeant's revenue and profits. Medicis sold through its distributor, McKesson, which then sold to its customer, the physicians. Medicis historically used the more conservative "sell-through" approach, that is, booking no sales until the distributor sold to the physicians. To goose sales at the Medicis unit after the deal closed, Valeant had Medicis immediately switch to the more aggressive "sell-in" approach and started recognizing sales much earlier—when product was sent to the distributor. Not surprisingly, this brazen change in revenue recognition caught the attention of the SEC, which notified the company in a formal letter and asked it to explain any reasons for this change.

4. Inflating Profits by Releasing Suspicious Reserves Either Before or Just After Closing

During the closing process of a deal, a variety of new opportunities are created for management to provide an artificial boost to income at a later point. Management can include taking a charge for layoffs or projected legal payments and later releasing part of these reserves back into income as management deems such payments will be much less than first anticipated (the quintessential example of this shenanigan is CUC, profiled in Chapter 1). The acquirer can also set up a bigger-than-necessary reserve for contingent consideration payments that might be paid to the owners of the target company, then later release some of the reserves back into income when they are deemed unnecessary.

Releasing Deal-Related Reserves When Contingency Payments May Be Payable
Let's assume you buy a business paying $60 million and later might have to pay an "earn-out" for as much as another $40 million if the acquired business achieves certain agreed-upon targets. That $40 million would be recorded as a "contingent consideration liability" on the Balance Sheet. Say, one year later, the business performs *below* expectations and the expected payout drops to $30 million. You must make an accounting entry reducing (debiting) the contingent consideration reserve and reducing (crediting) operating expenses, which results in a $10 million increase to earnings. On the face of it, the outcome seems illogical. You *increase* your profits when the business you bought *underperforms*. From an accounting perspective, however, the reduction of the future earn-out is considered a gain.

If a company wants to play games with its contingent consideration reserve, it is quite easy to do. Both inflating the initial fair market value of the total estimated payments to be made and later asserting that the acquired business is performing poorly (and little or no future payments will be made), management, like a master magician, can take out its wand and create profits out of thin air.

Watch for Big Gains from Reductions of Contingent Consideration Liability
Apparel manufacturing giant Li & Fung materially boosted its operating income during the first six months of 2012 by lowering an acquisition-related contingent consideration liability from potential earn-out payments. This simple management decision resulted in a $198 million gain (51 percent of its operating profit) during the six-month period. Investors should have raised concerns about the disappointing performance of the acquired businesses, because the reduction in the contingent liability indicated that certain of the acquired businesses must have missed performance targets set by Li & Fung as of the acquisition date.

Looking Forward

Chapter 15 demonstrated how managers, under the cover of an acquisition, can cleverly inflate profits and trick investors. The following chapter shows how managers can use the acquisition structure and flexibility to inflate reported cash flow from operations.

16

Acquisition Accounting Shenanigan No. 2: Inflating Reported Cash Flow

The Friday after Thanksgiving is generally considered the unofficial start of the holiday shopping season. Traditionally, it is one of the biggest shopping days of the year, if not *the* biggest. The day has long been called "Black Friday" since many people are hopeful that it will be the day when retailers move "into the black" (accounting slang for "turning a profit") for the year. Every time Black Friday approaches, retailers are quick to remind us of all the holiday shopping we need to do. They offer huge sales and fill the airwaves and newsprint with "Shop 'til You Drop" advertisements trying to lure us into their stores.

Tyco and WorldCom seemed to adhere to the "Shop 'til You Drop" mantra quite literally; however, they were buying entire businesses, and their holiday season ran all year long for many years. In the late 1990s and early 2000s, both companies went on lavish shopping sprees, acquiring business after business to fuel impressive performance. Organic growth at Tyco and WorldCom was much weaker than investors realized, though, as the companies hid their problems by acquiring oodles of companies and futzing with the accounting to show impressive results. They shopped and shopped—until the exposure of their massive accounting frauds caused them to drop like a ton of bricks.

Throughout their shopping sprees, both companies satiated investors and quashed naysayers by consistently reporting strong cash flow from operations. However, this cash flow was not a sign of operational strength at all. Rather, it came mainly from a liberal use of AA Shananigan No. 2: Inflating Reported Cash Flow.

In this chapter, we will discuss three techniques by which Tyco, WorldCom, and other companies use acquisitions and disposals to enhance and flatter CFFO.

Acquisition Accounting Techniques to Artificially Boost Cash Flow from Operations

1. Inheriting operating inflows in a normal business acquisition

2. Acquiring contracts or customers rather than developing them internally

3. Boosting CFFO by creatively structuring the sale of a business

1. Inheriting Operating Inflows in a Normal Business Acquisition

The cash flow shifting tricks in this chapter have many similarities to the ones we discussed in Chapter 11; they represent shifts between the Operating section and other sections. However, in this chapter, we focus solely on shifts that are related to acquisitions and disposals. The first two techniques in this chapter involve shifting cash outflows from the Operating section to the Investing section, as shown in Figure 16-1.

Rabidly acquisitive companies such as Tyco and WorldCom often report impressive CFFO quarter after quarter. Faced with the opacity that is inherent whenever multiple sets of financial statements are suddenly combined, investors in these types of companies often rely more heavily on CFFO generation as a sign of business strength and earnings quality. Unfortunately, heavy reliance on CFFO for acquisitive companies is ill-advised because of a deep, dark secret that companies want to hide from investors.

Figure 16-1 Shifting Cash Outflows from Operating Activities to Investing Activities

	Operating Activities	**Investing Activities**	**Financing Activities**
Inflows	Customer collections Interest collections Dividend collections	Investment sales Plant/equipment sales Business disposals	Bank borrowings Other borrowings Stock issuance
Outflows	Vendor payments Employee salaries Tax payments Interest payments	Capital expenditures Investment purchases Property purchases Business acquisitions	Loan repayments Stock repurchases Dividend payments

This secret concerns an accounting quirk (read "loophole") that enables acquisitive companies to show strong CFFO every quarter *simply because they are acquiring other businesses.* In other words, the mere act of acquiring a company provides a benefit to CFFO. How can this be true? Well, it's a peculiar side effect from the accounting rules that segregate cash flows into three sections. The quirk is quite simple and easy to understand.

Imagine you are a company that is getting ready to make a business acquisition. When you pay for the acquisition, you do so without affecting CFFO. If you buy the company with cash, the payment is recorded as an *investing outflow.* If you offer stock instead, there is, of course, no cash outflow.

As soon as you gain control of the company, all the ins and outs of the acquired business become a part of the combined company's operations. For example, when the newly acquired company makes a sale, you record that sale on your Income Statement as revenue. Similarly, when the newly acquired company collects cash from a customer, you record that collection on your Statement of Cash Flows (SCF) as an operating inflow. Think about the cash flow implications of this situation. For one, you could generate a new cash flow stream (the acquired business) without any initial CFFO outflow. In contrast, companies that seek to grow their business *organically* would generally first incur CFFO outflows to build the new business.

Additionally, now that you have inherited the receivables and inventory of the acquired business, you can generate an unsustainable CFFO benefit by rapidly liquidating these assets (that is, by collecting the receivables and selling the inventory). Normally, accounts receivable result from past cash expenditures (e.g., cash paid to purchase or manufacture the inventory sold). In other words, a cash inflow from collecting a receivable comes only after you have had a cash outflow to generate that receivable. When you acquire a company, however, and inherit its accounts receivable, the cash outflows involved in generating those receivables were recorded on the acquired company's books prior to the acquisition. This means that when you collect these receivables, you will be receiving an *operating cash inflow* without ever having recorded a corresponding *operating cash outflow*. The same is true with inventory. The proceeds received from selling inventory inherited in an acquisition will be recorded as an operating inflow even though no operating outflow ever occurred.

Think of it this way: cash spent to purchase inventory and other costs related to the sale *occurred before the acquisition*, and when you close on the deal, you obviously must pay the seller for inventory, receivables, and so on, but those outflows are reflected in the Investing section. Then, after the deal closes, you collect all that delicious cash from customers and show it as inflows in the Operating section. By liquidating and not replenishing these assets (i.e., keeping the acquired business's inventories at a lower level), you can show an unsustainable benefit to cash flow. Brilliant! In an acquisition context, cash outflows never hit the Operating section, yet all the inflows do.

To be fair, when companies inherit working capital liabilities (such as accounts payable), then the acquirer will be on the hook for paying off the seller's vendors and the cash paid will be an operating cash outflow. However, most acquisitions involve companies that *have positive net working capital* (more receivables and inventory than accounts payable).

Accounting Capsule:
The Impact of Acquisition Accounting on CFFO

A quirk in the accounting rules gives many companies a benefit to CFFO just for acquiring a company. When a company grows organically, naturally, it incurs CFFO outflows (payments for creating and marketing products) to create CFFO inflows (receipts from customers). However, a company that grows by acquiring other businesses would classify some CFFO outflows regarding working capital differently on the SCF. In short, since the entire acquisition price (including working capital of the target company acquired) would be included in the CFFI (cash flow from investing) section of the SCF, naturally, CFFO would be artificially inflated.

To understand why, realize that cash spent to acquire another business runs through the Investing section of the Statement of Cash Flows (of course, stock issued for an acquisition does not impact the SCF at all). As a result, when buying another business, companies inherit a new stream of cash flows without having to incur a CFFO outflow. Moreover, by liquidating the working capital of the acquired business, a company can provide itself with an unsustainable CFFO boost. These accounting nuances are why companies that grow through acquisitions often appear to have stronger CFFO than companies that grow organically.

It is important to realize that because this CFFO boost is simply an artifact of required acquisition accounting, even the most honest companies will benefit from inflated CFFO after an acquisition. Moreover, this boost may cause "quality of earnings" measures (such as comparisons of CFFO to net income) to improve, particularly if a company does not engage in any Earnings Manipulation Shenanigans at the time of the acquisition.

Serial Acquirers Receive This CFFO Boost Repeatedly

So far, we have established that by their very nature, acquisitions serve to boost CFFO. Consider the impact at companies that make numerous acquisitions every year, serial acquirers like Tyco and WorldCom. Many investors criticize serial acquirers for being able to produce revenue and earnings growth only inorganically by "rolling up" acquisitions.

These "roll-ups" often reject this criticism and point to their CFFO as proof that they are running the acquired businesses well and exploiting synergies. Many investors believe this hype because they fail to understand the lesson you just learned: stronger reported CFFO is merely an accounting side effect from acquiring numerous companies each year.

Putting the "Con" in Conglomerate

For some companies, these pure boosts to cash flow are seemingly not enough. They want to squeeze even more juice out of these acquisitions. Consider the following scenario, based on allegations in legal proceedings of Tyco's behavior during the acquisition process.

Imagine that you work in the accounting department of a company that just announced that it was being bought by a serial acquirer. The acquisition has not officially happened yet, but it is a friendly takeover with lucrative terms, and the deal is likely to close before the end of the month. The new owners want to start coordinating operations.

In walks one of the finance executives from the acquirer. He calls a meeting with the team and discusses some logistics that he says will help the transition go more smoothly. He points to a pile of checks—payments from customers that you had planned to deposit later that day. "You see all those checks? I know you normally deposit them at the end of the day, but let's hold off on that for now. Put them in the drawer, and we'll deposit them in a few weeks. And let's call up our biggest customers and tell them that they can hold off on paying us for a few weeks. I know that sounds odd, but this will score us some points and ensure that they stay loyal through the transition.

"And you see that pile of bills? I know you normally wait until the deadline approaches to pay them; however, let's pay them down ASAP. In fact, see if you can prepay any vendors or suppliers—I'm sure those folks would be willing to take our money and perhaps even give us a discount. We certainly have enough cash in the bank; let's put it to good use."

The day after the acquisition closes, the executive returns. "Now that we are one company, it's time to go back to normal business procedure. Deposit those checks immediately and start collecting from customers. And stop paying those bills early—let's wait until we get closer to the deadline."

Think about the cash flow implications of this scenario. The target company's CFFO was abnormally low in the weeks leading up to the acquisition because of abandoning collection efforts and paying down bills rapidly. However, once the acquisition closed, there were an unusually large number of receivables to collect and an unusually small number of bills to pay. This causes CFFO for your division to be abnormally high in the period immediately after the acquisition.

The finance executive had a trick up his sleeve. His reasons for abandoning collection efforts and prepaying vendors had little to do with engendering goodwill. He concocted this scheme to boost the CFFO of the combined company in the first quarter after the acquisition. Granted, the effect of this benefit would be short-lived; however, the executive knew that the scheme could continue if the company kept rolling up more and more acquisitions each quarter.

Tyco: The Mother of All Roll-Ups

This scenario is similar to allegations of what happened behind the scenes when Tyco made its acquisitions. And Tyco made *a lot* of acquisitions. From 1999 to 2002, Tyco bought more than 700 companies (not a typo) for a total of approximately $29 billion. Some of these acquisitions were large companies; however, most of the businesses acquired were small enough that Tyco considered them "immaterial" and chose to disclose nothing at all about them. Imagine the impact that this game could have with 700 companies worth a combined $29 billion! It should come as no surprise, then, that Tyco was able to generate strong CFFO over these years, as shown in Table 16-1. But it certainly was not from a booming business!

Table 16-1 Tyco's Cash Flow from Operations (from Continuing Operations)

($ millions)	FY 1999	FY 2000	FY 2001	FY 2002
Cash flow from operations	3,550	5,275	6,926	5,696

Treat CFFO Differently for Acquisitive Companies   Since acquisitions create an unsustainable boost to CFFO, investors should not blindly rely on CFFO as a barometer of performance. Use free cash flow *after* acquisitions to assess cash generation at acquisitive companies. Table 16-2 shows that Tyco recorded negative free cash flow after acquisitions each year, despite reporting positive CFFO; this was a warning that operating cash flow was not what it appeared to be.

Table 16-2   Tyco's Free Cash Flow After Acquisitions (from Continuing Operations)

($ millions)	1999	2000	2001	2002
Reported cash flow from operations	**3,550**	**5,275**	**6,926**	**5,696**
Subtract: Capital expenditures	(1,632)	(1,704)	(1,798)	(1,709)
Subtract: Construction in Progress	—	(111)	(2,248)	(1,146)
Free cash flow	**1,918**	**3,460**	**2,880**	**2,841**
Subtract: Acquisitions	(5,135)	(4,791)	(11,851)	(3,709)
Free cash flow after acquisitions	**(3,217)**	**(1,331)**	**(8,971)**	**(868)**

> **TIP**
>
> "Free cash flow after acquisitions" is a useful measure of cash flow when analyzing serial acquirers. This metric can easily be calculated from the Statement of Cash Flows: CFFO *minus* capital expenditures *minus* cash paid for acquisitions.

Review the Balance Sheets of Acquired Companies   If these documents are available, then absolutely review them. Doing so should help you gauge the potential inherent working capital benefits. It may be difficult to be precise in this analysis; however, you often will be able to make an assessment that is within the "ballpark" of the benefit. Companies often disclose the Balance Sheets of larger acquisitions and sometimes an aggregate Balance Sheet for smaller ones in their footnotes. If the acquired company had publicly traded stock or bonds, you can probably obtain a Balance Sheet from public records.

2. Acquiring Contracts or Customers Rather Than Developing Them Internally

In the previous section, we discussed how acquisitions, by their very nature, provide a boost to CFFO. This benefit results not from illegitimate accounting maneuvers, but rather from quirky accounting rules. We witnessed Tyco abusing the rules by quietly snapping up hundreds of small companies and finding ways to squeeze even more CFFO out of these acquisitions.

In this section, we take a step into more nefarious terrain and explore how companies use the acquisition accounting loophole for nonacquisition situations to shift normal operating cash flows to the Investing section.

Among the hundreds of businesses Tyco owned was an electronic security monitoring provider. Home security monitoring was a fast-growing industry in the 1990s, and Tyco's ADT division proved to be among the most popular brand names. Tyco generated new security systems contracts in two ways: through its own direct sales force and through an external network of dealerships. The dealers allowed Tyco to outsource a portion of its sales force. They were not on Tyco's payroll, but they sold security contracts, and Tyco paid them about $800 for every new customer.

Oddly, Tyco executives did not view these $800 payments to dealers to be normal customer solicitation costs, as the economics would suggest. Instead, they deemed these payments to be a purchase price for the "acquisition" of contracts. Thus, after the dealer presented Tyco with many contracts and received payment, Tyco curiously accounted for these "contract acquisitions" in the same way that it accounted for normal business acquisitions: as investing outflows.

Given how deeply the acquisition mentality was engrained in Tyco's culture and DNA, you can almost picture the confusion among its executives. Almost. These customer solicitation costs resemble normal operating expenditures much more closely than they resemble business acquisitions. As a result, it makes more sense for them to be recorded on the Statement of Cash Flows in the same way that Tyco's internal sales force commissions are recorded: as operating outflows. By classifying these operating outflows in the "acquisitions" line in the Investing section, Tyco found a convenient way to overstate CFFO. *And the company didn't stop there!*

From Aggressive Accounting to Fraud

By turning the Investing section into a hidden dumping ground for customer solicitation costs, Tyco aggressively and creatively twisted the accounting rules. But the company still wanted more. So it concocted a new scheme to inflate CFFO (and earnings) even further, and in so doing, it crossed the line from aggressive accounting to fraud. The SEC charged that from 1998 to 2002, Tyco used a "Dealer Connection Fee Sham Transaction" to fraudulently generate $719 million in CFFO. Here's how it worked:

For every contract Tyco purchased from a dealer, the dealer would be required to pay an up-front $200 "dealer connection fee." Of course, the dealers would not be happy about this new fee, so Tyco raised the price at which it would purchase new contracts by the same $200—from $800 to $1,000. The net result caused no change in the economics of the transaction—Tyco was still paying a net of $800 to purchase these contracts from dealers.

However, Tyco did not see it that way. After all, the company would not have created the ruse unless management felt the tactic would be beneficial in the end. Tyco now recorded a $1,000 investing outflow for the purchase of these contracts and an offsetting $200 as an operating inflow. Essentially, Tyco created a bogus $200 CFFO inflow by depressing its investing cash flow. (See Table 16-3.) Over the course of five years and hundreds of thousands of contracts, this was quite a contribution to CFFO!

Table 16-3   Tyco's Creative Classification of Net Payments to Dealers

	Original	Sham	Tyco's SCF
Tyco purchases contract from dealer	$800	$1,000	Investing outflow
Dealer pays "connection fee" to Tyco	—	($200)	Operating inflow
Net payment by Tyco to dealer	$800	$800	—

3. Boosting CFFO by Creatively Structuring the Sale of a Business

In the previous two sections, we showed how companies use acquisitions to shift cash *outflows* from the Operating section to the Investing section of the SCF. In this next section, we discuss the flip side of that coin: how companies use disposals to shift cash *inflows* from the Investing section to the Operating section, as shown in Figure 16-2.

Recording CFFO for Proceeds from the Sale of a Business

In 2005, Softbank structured an interesting two-way arrangement with fellow Japanese telecom company Gemini BB. Softbank sold its modem rental business to Gemini, and simultaneously, the companies entered into a "service agreement" in which Gemini would pay Softbank royalties based on the modem rental business's future revenue. At the time of the sale, Softbank

Figure 16-2 Shifting Cash Inflows from Investing Activities to Operating Activities

	Operating Activities	Investing Activities	Financing Activities
Inflows	Customer collections Interest collections Dividend collections	Investment sales Plant/equipment sales Business disposals	Bank borrowings Other borrowings Stock issuance
Outflows	Vendor payments Employee salaries Tax payments Interest payments	Capital expenditures Investment purchases Property purchases Business acquisitions	Loan repayments Stock repurchases Dividend payments

received ¥85 billion in cash from Gemini, but Softbank did not consider the entire amount to be related to the sale price of the business. Instead, Softbank decided to split the cash received into two categories: ¥45 billion was allocated to the sale of the business, and ¥40 billion was deemed to be an "advance" on the future royalty revenue stream. (You may recall the earnings boost that this transaction provided, as discussed in EM Shenanigan No. 3 in Chapter 5.)

The economic reality of this situation seems to be that Softbank sold its modem rental business for ¥85 billion. However, the way it structured the transaction seemingly allowed Softbank to exercise discretion in its presentation of cash flow. Rather than recording an ¥85 billion *investing* inflow from the sale of the business, Softbank recorded (1) a ¥45 billion *investing* inflow from the sale of the business and (2) a ¥40 billion *operating* inflow from the "advance" on future revenue. This ¥40 billion boost to CFFO represented 69 percent of Softbank's ¥57.8 billion in CFFO for the full year.

Watch for New Categories on the Statement of Cash Flows   Investors could easily have spotted Softbank's CFFO boost just by looking at the Statement of Cash Flows. Look at Table 16-4, and note that a new line item surfaced in 2006—a ¥40 billion "increase in deferred revenue." This Statement of Cash Flows disclosure (together with the magnitude of its impact on CFFO) would be reason enough for astute investors to dig deeper.

Table 16-4   Softbank's Statement of Cash Flows, 2005–2006

(¥ millions)	2005	2006
Pretax earnings	(9,549)	129,484
Depreciation and amortization	66,417	80,418
Other noncash gains, net	(115,659)	(136,455)
Increase in trade receivables	(15,854)	(23,333)
Increase in trade payables	2,373	4,331
Increase in deferred revenue	—	**40,000**
Increase in other receivables	(70,813)	(9,865)
Increase (decrease) in other payables	97,096	(26,774)
Cash flow from operating activities	(45,989)	57,806

Sell the Business, but Keep Some of the Good Stuff

Tenet Healthcare is a company that owns and operates hospitals and medical centers. In recent years, Tenet has sold some of its hospitals to improve its liquidity and profitability. It often played a neat little CFFO-enhancing trick when structuring the sale of these hospitals—it sold *everything but the receivables*.

Let's discuss how this works. Think of each hospital as being its own little business, with revenue, expenses, cash, receivables, payables, and so on, just like any other company. Before putting a hospital up for sale, Tenet strips the receivables out of the business. In other words, if a hospital has, say, $10 million in receivables, Tenet keeps the rights to those receivables and puts the rest of the business up for sale. This, of course, lowers the eventual sale price of the hospital by about $10 million, but Tenet couldn't care less, as it recoups that amount when it collects the receivables.

What are the implications about cash flow? Well, normally all proceeds from selling a hospital would be recorded as an investing inflow (just like the sale of any business or fixed assets). But by stripping out the receivables prior to the sale, Tenet lowers the sale price (and the investing inflow) by $10 million. However, the company will soon collect the $10 million from its former customers, and here's the nice part: all the proceeds will be reported as an operating inflow, since it is related to the collection of receivables. This trick allowed Tenet to shift the $10 million inflow from the Investing to the Operating section.

This game would have been spotted by those diligent investors who read Tenet's financial reports. As presented below, the company clearly disclosed in its March 2004 10-Q that it planned to keep $394 million in receivables related to the sale of 27 hospitals.

TENET'S DISCLOSURE ABOUT THE SALE OF HOSPITALS, 3/04 10-Q

Because *we do not intend to sell the accounts receivable* of the asset group, except for one hospital, these receivables, less the related allowance for doubtful accounts, have been included in our consolidated net accounts receivable in the accompanying condensed consolidated Balance Sheets. At March 31, 2004, *the net accounts receivable for the hospitals to be divested aggregated $394 million.* [Italics added for emphasis]

Buy the Business, but Not Any of the Bad Stuff

In the last section, we showed how Tenet inflated its future operating cash flows by cleverly structuring a sale of a business—by selling everything *except* the receivables. Well, a buyer of a business can also inflate its cash flows in much the same way; that is, by buying everything *except* the payables. And that is exactly the ploy used by Treehouse Foods in early 2016 when it bought Private Brands for $2.7 billion. Ordinarily in this type of acquisition, Treehouse would have assumed the assets and liabilities of Private Brands on the day the deal closed. However, in this case, the acquisition *specifically excluded accounts payable* for nine of Private Brands' manufacturing facilities. These obligations were essentially carved out of the acquisition, resulting in a higher purchase price corresponding with higher net assets. Following the consolidation, Treehouse's operating cash flow benefited from cash collections of the working capital assets that had been acquired, and conveniently did not incur the natural offset of these benefits, as it didn't hold the associated accounts payable. Very clever, indeed.

Buy Controlling Interest in a Business,
but Use Restricted Cash to Hide Outflows

When Whirlpool acquired a controlling interest in Chinese appliance manufacturer Hefei Sanyo, the company segregated cash into a restricted account to cover the working capital and ongoing research and development needs of that business. Over the next few years the liquidity needs of Hefei Sanyo (renamed Whirlpool China) were funded from the restricted cash account. Like most companies, Whirlpool's Statement of Cash Flows provided a reconciliation to the beginning and ending balances of ordinary (unrestricted) cash, so the payments from the separate account had no adverse impact on reported operating or free cash flow.

Fuzzy Line Between Operating and Investing Outflows

Sometimes acquisitions create a murky situation making it difficult to distinguish between investment activities and operating activities. This is particularly true when the acquired business was previously owned by partners/employees who are to remain involved in operations on an ongoing basis. MDC Partners provides a good example. This New York City–based advertising agency grew in large part by acquiring smaller agencies, closing several deals each year. Typically, only part of the acquisition price would be paid up front, with significant portions structured as earn-outs and paid over time. Since the company mainly acquired partnerships, the ongoing earn-out payments were directed to existing workers and likely represented a big portion of their annual income. Whether such payments are strictly "capital payments" or in some part more like compensation is hard to determine and can be quite subjective. In all cases, though, the payments are reflected as a reduction of cash flow from financing activities, and they enrich employees without having any adverse effect on reported operating or free cash flow.

Looking Ahead

The next chapter covers AA Shenanigan No. 3: Manipulating Key Metrics and completes our discussion on acquisition accounting tricks.

17

Acquisition Accounting Shenanigan No. 3: Manipulating Key Metrics

Academic research has long supported the claim that most acquisitions destroy shareholder value. Management must therefore work very hard to convince investors of the merits of a deal. That's where AA Shenanigan No. 3: Manipulating Key Metrics comes in handy to portray a business combination in a very favorable light. As Key Metric Shenanigans have become much more pervasive in recent years, there has been an uptick in misleading non-GAAP metrics used by the most acquisitive companies.

Inflating Sales Growth at the Core Business

When analyzing acquisitive companies, investors often have a difficult time separating organic revenue growth in the legacy business from revenue growth in the acquired company. A major obstacle is that organic revenue growth is not a measure defined by GAAP, thereby allowing management to come up with its own calculation (or not disclose organic growth at all). Naturally, management would like investors to believe that its core business is strong, so investors must be extra vigilant when interpreting company-defined measures of organic growth.

Determining Representative Sales Growth Rates Following an Acquisition

When evaluating a company that completes an acquisition, it's important to recognize the impact of the deal on reported revenue, and assess what the growth rate would have been absent the transaction. The results of the acquired business are included on a GAAP basis from the moment the transaction closes, so naturally reported sales growth will be artificially boosted. There are several ways that investors can correct for this distortion and arrive at a more accurate understanding of the real underlying growth rate of the business.

In many cases the acquirer will provide a footnote disclosure that shows sales on a "pro-forma" basis, which includes the results from recently acquired businesses, along with the legacy businesses, from the beginning of the prior-year period. This can be a very useful disclosure, as it provides the year-over-year growth rate of the business units that now comprise the company. In other cases, the acquirer may disclose the contribution of the target company to overall revenue post-consolidation. This too is a useful disclosure, as it provides the reader with enough information to calculate what reported results would likely have been absent the transaction.

In the presence of a significant acquisition we recommend reading through each of the available disclosures, and crunching the numbers, in order to parse out the underlying growth rates of the legacy business, the acquired business, and the combined business.

Look for Strange Definitions of Organic or Pro Forma Sales Growth

Affiliated Computer Systems (ACS) had an odd way of presenting its organic growth, or what it called "internal growth." Rather than simply excluding all revenue from acquired businesses when calculating internal growth, ACS calculated a fixed amount to remove based on the acquired business's revenue for the previous year. (See ACS's disclosure below.) This meant ACS could include in its own internal growth any large deals that the acquired company booked just before the acquisition.

> ### ACS'S INTERNAL REVENUE GROWTH DEFINITION, MARCH 2005 EARNINGS RELEASE
>
> Internal revenue growth is measured as total revenue growth less acquired revenue from acquisitions and revenues from divested operations. Acquired revenue from acquisitions *is based on pre-acquisition normalized revenue of acquired companies.* [Italics added for emphasis]

To illustrate, let's hypothetically assume that ACS acquired a company on January 1, 2005. In 2004, that target company had generated $120 million in revenue ($30 million per quarter). In the weeks before the acquisition, the target company also closed a large deal that would bring in an additional $10 million in revenue each quarter beginning in 2005.

Now assume that in March 2005 (the first quarter after the acquisition), the target company generates $40 million in revenue as expected (the normal $30 million plus $10 million from the new contract). ACS, when calculating its own March 2005 internal revenue growth, logically should exclude this entire $40 million because none of it would have been included in ACS's revenue absent the acquisition. However, ACS's calculation allows the company to treat the new $10 million contract as part of its own "internal" growth. As a result, ACS's internal revenue growth would improperly benefit from revenue that came from the acquired company's business. Clearly, this is not an apples-to-apples comparison.

> **TIP**
>
> Scrutinize the organic growth calculation of acquisitive companies, as it may include revenue that spilled over from the target company.

Raise Your Antennae When Key Metrics Include Acquired Revenue Streams

Usually same-store sales metrics exclude the effects of new stores; however, when Starbucks went about acquiring regional licensees beginning in 2004, it brought existing stores into the comp base immediately. As a result,

Starbucks calculated same-store sales using a different universe each quarter—hardly a comparable metric. If Starbucks had been purchasing its strongest licensees, this acquisition activity would have had a positive impact on same-store sales performance, thereby misleading investors about the company's underlying sales growth.

As discussed in Chapter 13, comparing same-store sales with average revenue per store is a helpful way to identify inorganic changes in the same-store sales metric. In 2006, Starbucks's same-store sales trend began diverging from its revenue per store trend. The gap widened in 2007, and in September 2007, Starbucks reported that U.S. traffic had fallen for the first time ever. When same-store sales in the United States turned negative in December, Starbucks announced it would no longer disclose same-store sales, stating that it would "not be an effective indicator of the Company's performance."

Look Out for Acquisitions of Companies with Competing Products

Sometimes a company will acquire a competitor in order to wind down a competing product and move the target's customers onto the acquirer's platform. This may be a good business strategy, but it could wreak havoc with organic growth metrics. For example, 3D printer manufacturer 3D Systems acquired competitor Z-Corp in 2012 and quickly announced that it would discontinue some of Z-Corp's products. Naturally, Z-Corp's revenue fell after being acquired, and 3D Systems reported strong organic growth. Any revenue growth that 3D Systems derived from legacy Z-Corp customers should not be considered organic.

Highlighting Inflated Earnings

Acquirers often incur substantial deal-related costs (legal, investment banking, integration, etc.) and have much leeway regarding classification of these costs as one-time in nature and segregating them below the line. That is, management might guide investors to ignore such costs and only consider normal recurring operating costs. In theory, it may sound sensible to ignore one-time costs, as by definition, they should not be there next year.

However, for companies that do deal after deal, such costs are absolutely *recurring* and a regular part of the cost structure. Additionally, companies doing many deals and incurring many write-offs often cross the proverbial line and improperly shift some normal recurring operating costs (selling, R&D, administration, etc.) below the line into the nonrecurring category.

Be Skeptical When GAAP Earnings Materially Lag "Adjusted Earnings"

A good rule of thumb to assess legitimacy of a non-GAAP metric is to compare it with the corresponding GAAP-based metric. So if the non-GAAP "adjusted earnings" tracked closely to GAAP-based net income, we consider the non-GAAP equivalent as legitimate. Of course, if the non-GAAP metric continually produced "A-plus" results and the GAAP-based equivalent produced "D-minus" results, investors should reject the non-GAAP metric.

Consider the metrics posited by Valeant highlighting its "stellar" performance under the metric "cash earnings." Valeant generated a four-year total (2013–2016) GAAP-based net income of *negative* $2.7 billion, but the company boasted a cumulative non-GAAP "cash earnings" of *positive* $9.6 billion—a staggering differential of over $12 billion. With the non-GAAP metric lagging the GAAP-based equivalent by such a large amount (and one a profit and the other a loss), investors should reject the non-GAAP metric as woefully misleading.

In Figure 17-1, we show Valeant's reported GAAP versus non-GAAP profits for the 16 quarters covering 2013 through 2016. Notice that in most quarters, GAAP-based net income was either negative or very close to zero. One exception, however, was Q4 2014, shown as the highest bar right in the middle of the chart, with GAAP-based net income approaching $500 million. That figure, however, should have a big asterisk, since it includes the one-time $287 million pretax gain on the sale of its stake in another business (Allergan). Clearly, Valeant's gain should be considered one-time in nature, so the chasm between GAAP and non-GAAP earnings would be even greater than the $12 billion differential.

Figure 17-1   VRX NI Versus Cash Earnings, 2013–2016, by Quarter

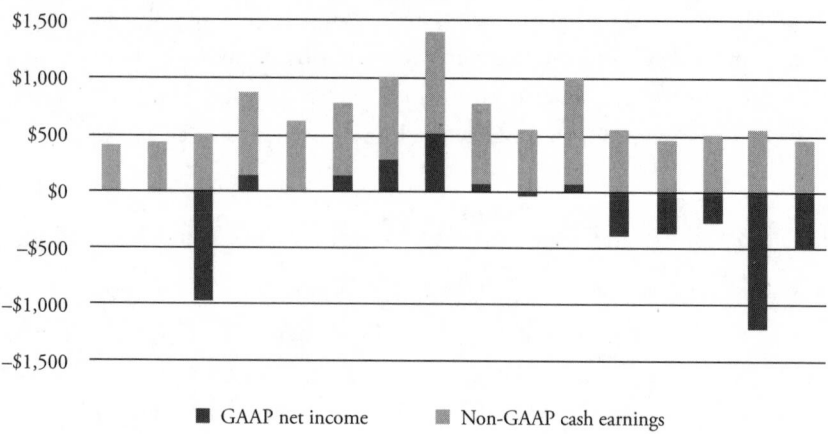

■ GAAP net income   ■ Non-GAAP cash earnings

Looking Forward

Part Six includes two chapters that tie everything together. Chapter 18 shows the unraveling of three prominent companies, each of which used a variety of shenanigans to fool investors. Chapter 19 discusses key elements of the forensic mindset and offers 10 takeaway lessons that will help you become a better investor.

PART SIX

PUTTING IT ALL TOGETHER

Congratulations! You have scaled the fourth and final shenanigan mountain. In Chapter 18, we look at three storied companies whose accounting shenanigans turned them into some of the largest corporate debacles in recent years. Then in our closing chapter, "The Forensic Mindset," we reflect on the most important issues and questions to keep in mind as you voyage through financial statements.

18
The Unraveling

Until now, *Financial Shenanigans* has mainly focused on describing a variety of accounting tricks and how investors could have spotted them. Companies using such tricks to hide business problems sometimes collapse in a spectacular fashion, creating large losses for investors. We refer to this meltdown as the unraveling.

This chapter highlights three companies that employed a variety of shenanigans to hide business problems from investors but eventually imploded as the accounting scandals were revealed. The first two companies profiled have had a long history of success (Hertz Global Holdings and Toshiba Corporation). The third company profiled is a relative newcomer, but had a spectacular rise and fall in less than a decade (Valeant Pharmaceuticals).

Hertz

Background and History

Founded in 1918, Hertz has been a leader in the car rental business for a century. For many years, it was owned by large publicly traded companies including RCA, UAL, and until late 2005, Ford Motor Company. In June of 2005, Ford announced plans to spin out Hertz in an IPO, but several months later, a trio of private equity firms (Carlyle, Clayton Dubilier & Rice, and

Merrill Lynch Private Equity) made an offer to buy the entire company. In December of 2005, the trio paid $15 billion for Hertz in a heavily leveraged transaction. In this fast-moving drama, not even seven months later, the trio filed to take Hertz public, which resulted in a November 2016 IPO. As a "last hurrah" before the IPO, the private equity sponsors took a new $1 billion loan to pay themselves a special dividend in the same amount. After the public offering, the trio continued to hold a controlling interest in Hertz.

The Years as a Public Company

Hertz was hit severely during the 2008 financial crisis, and its stock price plummeted to $1.56 during its darkest days. Over the subsequent years, its business slowly recovered, and revenue began rising in 2010 and each year through 2013. With the company seemingly in fine shape, the trio sold their remaining stake in early 2013.

By early autumn, the first signs of possible trouble for investors blew in with the September 23 announcement that Hertz's longtime CFO, Elyse Douglas, would leave just one week later for "personal reasons." A few things about Ms. Douglas's decision seemed odd: the *timing* and the *reason*. No doubt, seasoned executives regularly leave jobs for better ones or even to spend more time with family. But they almost never give just a single week's notice. Also, late in the year just when the finance team should be getting the year-end results ready for the auditors is a terribly troublesome time to leave a company—particularly on such short notice. More warning signs followed in quick succession._

When the new CFO, Thomas Kennedy, arrived, he must have found the accounting to be a mess. The first evidence of his concerns appeared when Hertz filed a Non-Timely (NT) 10-K on March 3, 2014, requesting an extension to file its Annual Report. As reason for the delay, Hertz cited that certain adjustments were needed to correct previously issued financial state-ments—but indicated that *no material impact was expected*. Indeed, Hertz was able to file its 2013 10-K on March 19, but ominously, it contained a footnote titled "Correction of Errors," indicating that wholesale errors had been found in its financial statements for 2011, 2012, and 2013.

> **TIP**
>
> When first signs point to accounting problems, don't take management's assurances at face value. Initial disclosures by management usually "sugarcoat" the problem.

The warnings grew louder and more ominous with the May 13 announcement of another late filing (the first quarter of 2014) with these disclosures:

> Errors were identified relating to Hertz's conclusions regarding the capitalization and timing of depreciation for certain non-fleet assets, allowances for doubtful accounts in Brazil, as well as other items. Hertz continued its review and recently identified additional errors related to allowances for uncollectible amounts with respect to renter obligations for damaged vehicles and restoration obligations at the end of lease facilities.

But amazingly, just six days later, Hertz felt comfortable enough to release its Q1 2014 financial statements. But then, on June 3, 2014, Hertz reversed itself again and told investors that its 2011–2013 financial statements could no longer be relied upon. Hertz also announced that its auditor, PwC, would be amending its internal control report and most likely rendering an adverse opinion on Hertz's internal controls as of December 31, 2013.

Perhaps just to calm the frayed nerves of investors (who understandably were quite concerned), Hertz management released some preliminary restatements, shaving pretax profits from 2011 by $19 million and from 2012 by just $9 million. At that point, some value-oriented investors, no doubt, became interested in acquiring a stake in Hertz, as it looked dirt cheap and the reported restatements *appeared not to be material*—just 1.9 percent lower than first reported numbers, across the three years. (The $28 million haircut reduced only minimally the reported pretax profits of $1.4 billion reported.) Moreover, respected and influential investor Carl Icahn had acquired a 12 percent stake in Hertz and received three seats on the board of directors.

While some investors began scooping up shares at seemingly bargain prices, prudent investors would have been concerned that initial management estimates of restatements tend to be woefully wrong and almost always turn out to be much worse than first reported. Indeed, the actual results at Hertz would be much worse than management first suggested, as the *revised* error was not the originally reported $28 million—not even close.

Investors had to wait in limbo for over a year before receiving the corrected financial statements. It was not a good period for Hertz as the stock price continued to dive and longtime chairman and CEO Mark Frissora was ousted from the company. Finally, in July 2015, Hertz completed its restatement and provided details of its accounting transgressions. The restatement cut a whopping $349 million from pretax profits, including $235 million for the years 2011 through 2013.

The restatement revealed that Hertz had used a variety of accounting gimmicks to conceal its deteriorating underlying performance. Most shenanigans used by Hertz fit into three Earnings Manipulation groupings: (1) EM Shenanigan No. 1: Recording Revenue Too Soon; (2) EM Shenanigan No. 4: Shifting Current Expenses to a Later Period; or (3) EM Shenanigan No. 5: Employing Other Techniques to Hide Expenses or Losses. As you recall, when management uses EM No. 1, revenue would be inflated; and when it uses EM No. 4 or No. 5, expenses would be deflated. In all cases, however, profits would be inflated.

Hertz's unraveling continued even after its large restatement as persistent business problems drove down revenue and profits. The restatement provided investors with a brand-new picture of the business. After years of analyzing false numbers, investors were now able to see Hertz's true economic reality. And they became aghast at what they saw. Hertz's stock price continued to tank, and by February 2016, it was down nearly 75 percent from its peak just a year and a half earlier.

TIP

When a company is in the process of correcting past accounting errors, smart investors will stay away until they have the chance to analyze the company's true performance. There is a good chance that the corrected numbers and underlying business performance will be worse than expected.

Toshiba

Background and History

Toshiba traces its roots to the founding of Tanaka Engineering in 1875. In 1939, through an earlier merger, the company took on the name Toshiba. It grew into an impressive conglomerate, with diverse businesses including Energy and Infrastructure, Community Solutions (elevators, lighting, and HVAC), Healthcare Systems and Services, Lifestyle Products and Services, and others. Toshiba encompasses over 600 consolidated subsidiaries and generates annual sales exceeding $44 billion in fiscal 2017.

Recent History of Problems and Accounting

The year 2015 was a nightmare for Toshiba, as news of a long-term accounting scandal cut the share price in half. The first shoe to drop came on April 3, 2015, when the company disclosed it would convene a "Special Investigation Committee" to conduct an internal investigation into certain accounting matters. In particular, the investigation would focus on the company's use of percentage-of-completion revenue recognition accounting on past infrastructure contracts. This was an incredibly scary announcement, yet the market showed only mild concern. Shares fell just 5 percent from ¥512 to ¥487 and actually began to rebound by the end of the month.

Astute investors would have seen this announcement as a major warning sign. News of an internal accounting investigation, particularly one focused on revenue recognition, should never be taken lightly. It is a sign that accounting problems exist and likely are significant. While the scope and magnitude of the issues may be unknown, it is wise to assume they will be worse than imagined. Rather than hoping for the best, investors would be better off sitting on the sidelines.

As we just learned with Hertz, management often sugarcoats its initial disclosures about accounting problems. The onset of an internal investigation likely means there will be more bad news. If the accounting issue being investigated was minor, it would have been settled without need for a major investigation.

On May 8, 2015, one month after the special committee was formed, Toshiba disclosed that the revenue recognition issues were even worse than initially thought. Given the seriousness of the situation, Toshiba changed the composition of its committee members to be solely composed of "fair and impartial outside experts, who do not have any interests in the company." This troubling news sent the stock down another 17 percent to ¥403.

On July 20, 2015, Toshiba's investigation committee announced preliminary findings that shocked investors: Toshiba would be forced to lower its previously reported profits going back seven years to fiscal year 2008, by a staggering $1.2 billion (¥152 billion). The following day, its president, Hisao Tanaka, resigned in disgrace, as he called the scandal "the most damaging event to our brand in the company's 140-year history."

Toshiba's stock price continued to tank, and by September, the committee released its complete report and the numbers were even worse than the preliminary findings. Amazingly, the restatements in profits covered all years from 2008 to 2014, which spanned the reign of three separate CEOs. The cumulative overstatement of pretax profits approached $1.9 billion (¥225 billion). The largest restatements occurred in 2011 and 2012, and the most substantial amounts related to (1) inflating revenue by improperly applying percentage-of-completion accounting, (2) stuffing inventory channels on transactions in the PC business, and (3) failing to take charges for impairment and depreciation. By December 2015, Toshiba's stock had fallen to ¥215, down 60 percent from its March 2015 peak.

Valeant Pharmaceuticals

Background and History

Although founded in 1960, the story of Valeant's meteoric rise and fall began in 2007, when Valeant hired the management consultancy McKinsey & Company to help jump-start growth in the business. The McKinsey team, led by Michael Pearson, advised a radical strategy—cutting internal R&D and pursuing growth through acquisitions and price increases. Apparently, Pearson impressed Valeant's board, and in early 2008 he was recruited to serve as the company's CEO. Over the next seven years, Valeant made scores of acquisitions, taking on an enormous amount of debt to finance the deals. All the while, Valeant's core business registered only tepid organic growth, and the company regularly posted GAAP-based net *losses*. But Valeant used a variety of misleading non-GAAP metrics to convince investors that Pearson's strategy was going well.

Unlike the more infamous and widely known accounting frauds, the Valeant story really is that of a relatively small company that a decade ago had delusions of grandeur and set out to become one of the five largest pharmaceutical companies in the United States. And Pearson's plan to do so was very unorthodox; it would shun the drug discovery and other R&D spending that was commonplace in the industry and instead rely on buying established companies with proven drugs and existing customers. Once part of Valeant's drug portfolio, the company could then materially increase prices as an additional driver of sales growth. Investors cheered them on as Pearson watched the value of his personal stock holdings rise to an astounding $3 billion by the summer of 2015. When the stock peaked in August 2015, Valeant's market value hit $90 billion (an almost unimaginable climb from around $2 billion when Pearson became CEO in February 2008). By the spring of 2017, Valeant's market value crash-landed back to around $3 billion, wiping out $87 billion in equity value.

While many investors were caught flat-footed when the market value began to collapse, warning signs were everywhere. Perhaps most obviously, to execute on its strategy Valeant would need to secure a steady supply of attractive acquisition targets at reasonable prices. Moreover, the volume of deals would have to expand each year to supply meaningful growth to its increasing revenue base. In the best of circumstances, this would have been an unsustainable strategy; however, Valeant's unusual choice of targets made perpetual growth through M&A even less likely.

Merger with Biovail

In 2010, after several previous failed overtures to consummate a deal, Valeant and Canadian-based Biovail agreed to merge, enabling U.S.-based Valeant to be taxed at a very low 5 percent Canadian rate (rather than the U.S. rate of 35 percent) and move its headquarters to Quebec, Canada.

Biovail had been founded by Eugene Melnyk, and both Biovail and Melnyk had scrapes with regulators and the courts. For example, in March 2008 the SEC sued Biovail and some of its former officers, charging that they were *"obsessed with meeting quarterly earnings guidance, repeatedly overstated earnings and hid losses to deceive investors and create the appearance of achieving earnings goals."* Biovail settled the litigation by paying $10 million. Its problems continued, and in February 2009, Biovail settled with the Ontario Securities Commission after representatives admitted to making false statements and engaging in illegal conduct. Melnyk was subsequently banned from senior roles at public companies in Canada for five years and penalized $565,000 by the Canadian authorities. He also settled with the SEC and agreed to pay over $1 million in fines.

> ### RED FLAG
>
> Valeant certainly was aware of the sordid history of Biovail before it closed on the deal in September 2010, when it still had time to walk away. Unfortunately, when management is driven to constantly do deals to grow (and to drive up the share price), "trivial details" like the unethical culture at Biovail and its history of unethical and illegal behavior may be overlooked by management. Thoughtful investors, however, should never overlook a culture of unethical business or financial reporting practices.

Also, as discussed in Chapter 11, Biovail inflated its cash flow from operations (in the period before the Valeant merger) by acquiring certain drug rights through noncash transactions. Specifically, rather than paying cash at the time of the sale, Biovail compensated the sellers by issuing a note—essentially, a long-term IOU under which the company would pay cash *in the future*. Since no cash changed hands at the time of the sale, there was no impact on the Statement of Cash Flows. And as Biovail paid down the notes over time, the cash payments were presented on the SCF as the repayment of debt—that is, a financing outflow. Thus, using this clever two-step technique, the normal reduction in cash flow from operations for acquiring the drug rights was shifted to cash flow from financing—thereby inflating Biovail's CFFO.

Sure enough, investors, either unaware or unconcerned with Biovail's history, cheered on news of the merger as the share price spiked and continued rising in the months following the deal.

Acquisition of Medicis

Two years after merging with Biovail, in December 2012, Valeant closed on its next major deal, Medicis. Like Biovail, Medicis also had a well-known history of accounting problems, particularly overstating revenue by improper recording of sales returns. The company had been sanctioned, and its auditor Ernst & Young had been charged with conducting ineffective audits that failed to surface and correct those issues. During the period just before the acquisition, Medicis' sales slowed—seemingly so that they could be booked under Valeant ownership and help show additional growth. As detailed in Chapter 3, Valeant then changed Medicis' accounting policies to recognize more revenue earlier in the selling process to increase reported sales even further.

In addition to these accounting issues, several other warning signs emerged, including (1) former Medicis CEO Jonah Shacknai complaining about substantial friction with Valeant executives and low morale of his team; and (2) Valeant announcing a $100 million charge-off related to its decision to fire hundreds of sales personnel at the Medicis unit.

Acquisition of Bausch & Lomb

In early 2013, just a few months after the Medicis deal, Pearson was ready to do a much bigger one. An intriguing opportunity arose when the private equity firm Warburg Pincus (WP) filed registration documents with the SEC to take Bausch & Lomb (B&L) public. Pearson pounced on this opportunity to buy B&L outright, and WP decided to pull the offering and instead sell the company to Valeant. Following what had become a pattern, Bausch & Lomb too had serious accounting scandals in its recent history.

Investors were giddy when news of Valeant's offer to buy B&L came out, as Valeant's share price shot up over 20 percent over two days on volume more than 15 times the normal daily trading volume. Warburg Pincus had acquired a controlling stake of B&L through a leveraged buyout in 2007, putting up $1.7 billion in equity. So, when Valeant offered $8.7 billion to acquire the business, it was a windfall for Warburg and its limited partners. Less obvious was why it would be a good deal for Valeant investors, since the business had anemic growth, poor profitability, and mountains of debt;

however, by focusing on non-GAAP results Pearson was able to excite share-holders and the share price.

CONCERNS OF A COMPANY SOLD BY A PRIVATE EQUITY FIRM

As you know by now, we are no big fans of an M&A-driven approach because so much can (and often does) go wrong. But when the seller has been a long-time owner (and ideally, the founder), we can breathe a sigh of relief knowing that the business probably was built carefully, with a solid foundation, and often with a goal of being built to last.

Things get more complicated when the seller has a very short-term horizon, like a leveraged buyout firm. The goals of such firms are to benefit themselves and their limited partners by flipping the acquisition and maximizing their gain. They often do so by (1) putting little equity into the investment, using mainly debt; (2) paying themselves special dividends, even if it means loading more debt on the Balance Sheet of a portfolio company; (3) making further acquisitions adding yet more debt; and (4) cutting "discretionary" costs, such as R&D, which may help short-term earnings but make long-term success more uncertain.

The substantial borrowing by B&L during the Warburg Pincus reign left the company heavily leveraged. Just two months before Valeant acquired B&L in August 2013, studious analysts might have been aghast seeing the debt level swell to $4.2 billion, up 26 percent in just the prior six months. During that period, the shareholders' equity plummeted from around $800 million to only $8.4 million, and the cash flow from operations sank from *positive* $78.8 million in the 2012 period to *negative* $114.5 million in 2013. Clearly, the suddenly exploding debt coupled with sinking cash flow should have given pause to any potential prudent acquirer. But, of course, Valeant certainly would not be considered a prudent acquirer and *had to* continue doing deals to create the illusion of being a successful company.

Failed Hostile Deals Leave a Bitter Taste for Investors

In addition to acquisitions that closed, Valeant faced several unsuccessful campaigns; these episodes were damaging to the company and perhaps put it on a faster course for its eventual collapse.

In 2011, Valeant made an aggressive play for Cephalon, a U.S. biopharmaceutical company, offering $5.7 billion. When Cephalon pushed back to say, "not interested," Valeant became much more aggressive, threatening to go to Cephalon's board and nominate its own slate of board members.

> **Commentary:** This should have been viewed by investors as an important warning sign as Valeant had turned from doing only "friendly" deals to occasional "hostile" ones. Pearson was beginning to show his cards. He seemingly became more desperate to do another large deal and refused to take no for an answer. A second reason for concern was the apparent indifference toward employees of the target company, since Valeant planned to fire many and appeared interested only in obtaining the new drugs and customers from the target company. We sense that executives at Valeant cared little about maintaining culture and values fostered at newly acquired companies; that should be a flashing red flag for investors.

The second, and more consequential hostile offer took place in 2014, involving both Allergan and an activist hedge fund manager, Bill Ackman.

Six Months That Changed Everything for Valeant—for the Worse

After years of successfully maintaining a low profile, in 2014 Valeant became a household name and constantly found itself the subject of both financial and mainstream media reports. The company had formed an unorthodox "partnership" with Bill Ackman to facilitate another hostile acquisition, and for its largest target yet, Allergan. Ackman's fund, Pershing Square Capital ("PSC") accumulated a significant equity stake in Allergan and used its influence to try to convince the target's board and institutional investors to agree to Valeant's offer. Ackman even launched its own public marketing campaign for the deal to help push it through. As this went on, more media outlets began questioning the ethics of the Ackman partnership and whether it violated insider trading rules, and lawsuits ensued. In late December 2017 the lawsuit with Allergan was settled, mandating Ackman's Pershing Square hedge fund to pay $194 million and Valeant an additional $96 million, subject to court approval. This negative attention, alongside an already contentious hostile campaign, began to cast Valeant as desperate for a large acquisition at any cost.

Things only got worse when Allergan definitively rebuffed Valeant's final, mostly stock offer, raising fundamental questions about Valeant's unorthodox business model. Not only did the upward momentum in Valeant's share price come to a screeching halt during the six months of battling for Allergan, but more important, rumblings about its reputation, unusual business model, and aggressive accounting practices grew louder. And journalists who had hardly covered Valeant a year prior began probing the company's business practices looking for a bigger story.

Acquisition of Salix Pharmaceuticals, Valeant's Biggest and Most Flawed Acquisition

Valeant was badly bruised in its failed hostile takeover of Allergan in 2014, but ultimately found another big target in early 2015, and acquired Salix Pharmaceuticals on April 1. Not surprisingly, this was another troubled company, just working its way through a major accounting scandal.

Salix Pharmaceuticals was founded in 1989, and in more recent years has been headquartered in Raleigh, North Carolina. The company develops and sells drugs and medical devices to prevent and treat gastrointestinal disorders. The year 2014 was a busy one for Salix on the M&A front, starting with its January acquisition of Santarus for $2.6 billion. During much of the year, Salix was in talks with several suitors to sell itself, but that came to a screeching halt when disclosures about its own accounting problems were revealed in the autumn. The end of the year proved quite tumultuous, with both Salix's CEO and CFO leaving under a dark cloud and a new suitor (Valeant) entering the bidding.

Beginning on November 7, 2014, three class action lawsuits were filed against Salix, alleging accounting fraud. The company had *already* restated its audited financial statements for 2013 and its unaudited quarterly reports for each of the three quarters in 2014. It was abundantly clear that the company had played fast and loose with its accounting to dress up the business for sale. For some strange reason, these aggressive accounting practices seemed to be of little concern for Valeant.

Let's think about this for a moment. Why would someone be interested in buying this company when the acquirer likely would be responsible for a potential huge legal liability? Even if you could get comfortable with the legal exposure, concerns about the culture and ethics loomed large. Putting aside both the legal exposure and the culture/ethical issues at Salix, you still would have no clue of the real health and performance at the company because the *numbers were rigged.*

Others Had a Look, but Walked Away

About six months before Valeant approached Salix about a deal, several other suitors had been sniffing around, and at least one put a substantial offer on the table. That was until the accounting issues became known. Ironically, it was Allergan that had offered Salix as much as $205 per share in cash, valued at $13 billion. But when its management found serious accounting issues in October 2014, Allergan reportedly withdrew its offer and walked away from the negotiating table.

The fallout from the accounting problems cost both CEO Carolyn Logan and CFO Adam Derbyshire their jobs, as shareholders took a 35 percent haircut in value when the fraud was revealed.

Without much regard for these issues, on April 1, 2015, Pearson completed the $11 billion transaction, and just as in the case of prior mergers, the news was welcomed by investors and Valeant's share price surged again.

Restatements and Warning from the Auditor of Internal Control Weakness

On March 2, 2015, almost a month before Valeant closed on the deal, Salix filed its 10-K for 2014, along with the restated financial statements for 2013 and each of the three quarters of 2014. Included in the filing was the auditor's assessment of the internal controls at Salix:

> Management has identified material weaknesses in controls related to product returns and communications between trade relations and accounting/finance to record agreed-upon returns by trade personnel; controls for recognition of revenue for sales to customers with FOB

destination shipping terms; controls to comply with established policies and procedures to obtain, evaluate, review, and approve agreements with customers; and controls around classification of balances within the consolidated financial statements.

Translating to plain English: the controls to ensure accurate financial reporting stunk and a lot of things could go wrong. Indeed, they already had! In Q4 2013, Salix improperly booked $14.4 million of sales that should have been recorded in Q1 2014. Additionally, Q1 profits were inflated as the company had underreported its "reserve for product returns" by reporting $8.7 million when it should have been $16.9 million—again inflating sales. In Q2 2014, Salix made a suspicious $7.5 million payment to a wholesaler (that is a customer) and treated that payment as a marketing expense, rather than as a reduction to gross revenues. Then in Q3 2014, Salix had just one final quarter to "juice" its revenue before inking a deal, so it tried not to miss that opportunity by posting $15.2 million in sales that really belonged in Q4. Again, none of this information seemed to dampen Valeant's desire to close the deal.

The Valeant Balloon Bursts

When Valeant announced its offer to acquire Salix in February 2015, its investors were elated. The share price immediately jumped $25 in a single day from $173 to $199. Over the next five months, Valeant's share price continued shooting straight up, hitting its all-time peak of $263 on August 5, valuing the company at $90 billion. With each acquisition, its GAAP-based losses intensified, but the profitability metric that management focused on, "cash earnings," grew and compounded.

The tide began to turn against Valeant by late August, as allegations of price gouging were leveled against several pharmaceutical companies. The following month, Democratic presidential candidate Hillary Clinton spooked the pharmaceuticals industry with an ominous tweet saying, "Price gouging like this in the specialty drug market is outrageous. Tomorrow I'll lay out a plan to take it on." As a result, investors started worrying about the government broadly cracking down on pricing at drug companies and depressing profits. Clinton's tweet helped push Valeant's share price back down to $229 (Figure 18-1).

Figure 18-1   Valeant Share Price, 2/1/2008 to 12/31/2016

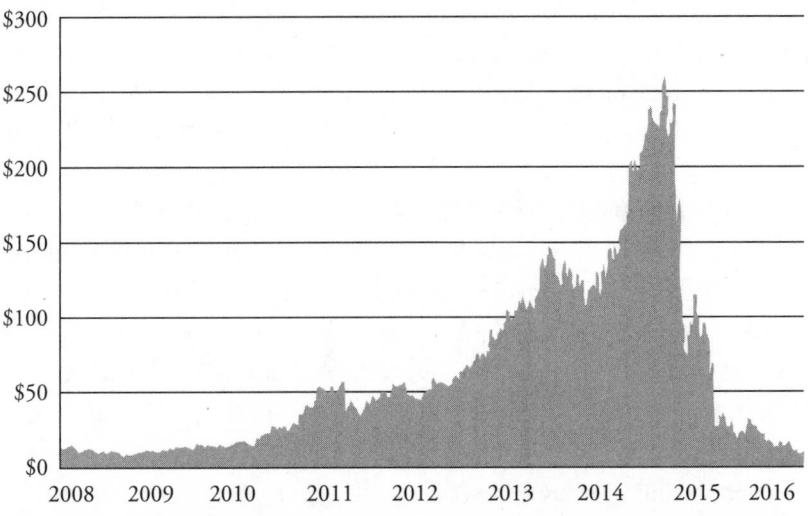

Date	Market Cap (in millions)	Price	Event
2/1/2008	$2,132	$13.24	Pearson becomes CEO
9/30/2010	$7,395	$25.05	Biovail merger closes
12/11/2012	$17,654	$59.23	Medicis acquisition closes
8/7/2013	$32,549	$97.59	Bausch & Lomb acquisition closes
4/24/2014	$44,833	$134.42	Ackman stake in AGN revealed
4/1/2015	$67,903	$197.39	Salix acquisition closes
8/5/2015	$89,989	$262.52	Valeant hits peak price/market value
9/21/2015	$78,498	$229.00	Hillary Clinton tweets about pharma price gouging
10//19/2015	$57,074	$163.83	Initial reports exposing Philidor
10/30/2015	$32,172	$93.77	Valeant announces it will cut ties with Philidor
2/29/2016	$22,450	$65.80	Valeant announces it is under SEC investigation
3/15/2016	$11,433	$33.51	Valeant cuts revenue forecast and delays filing
3/21/2016	$9,888	$28.98	Pearson steps down as CEO
3/13/2017	$4,212	$12.11	Ackman sells VRX position
4/12/2017	$3,298	$8.51	Decline of 96 percent from peak

Over the next three months, Valeant had a giant target on its back, and criticism came from all directions. In October, a group of investigative journalists published an exposé revealing a shady and fraudulent relationship with a mail-order pharmacy named Philidor Rx. Valeant's share price went into a free fall, dropping to under $90 by late November. Many "believers" who thought the sell-off was overdone tried to make a quick buck on a "depressed" situation, but only succeeded in catching a falling knife.

In March 2016, Pearson was ousted as CEO and the board accused former CFO (and current board member) Howard Schiller of engaging in "improper conduct." The SEC was investigating the company for fraud, and investors continued to lose faith. The unraveling accelerated throughout 2016 and early 2017 as Valeant's business fell apart and all the debt raised to finance its bad acquisitions came back to haunt the company. By April 2017, with former executives under criminal investigation for fraud, Valeant's share price crash-landed below $9, an incredible decline of 96 percent from its summer 2015 peak.

Important Lessons from the Valeant Story

Valeant was destined to collapse because its financial representations falsely portrayed a fast-growing, prosperous company, when in reality, its numbers were embellished by accounting gimmickry. Astute investors understood that while it was impossible to know the exact catalyst that would spark the unraveling, they knew the downfall would be inevitable, no matter how big the balloon inflated. The Clinton tweet and Philidor findings were the incendiary events that ignited the unraveling. While there was no way to predict that these specific events would be the proverbial "straws that broke the camel's back," without them, something else surely would have sparked Valeant's ultimate unraveling.

Looking Ahead

In our concluding chapter, we weave through the many lessons in this book (and our experience from the last quarter century) and present 10 of the most important lessons to help you detect shenanigans and dramatically improve your investment performance.

19

The Forensic Mindset

In the quarter-century since publishing the first edition of *Financial Shenanigans*, we have identified many accounting tricks hidden in corporate filings and shared our analysis with thousands of professionals and students. In discussing our findings (and what led us to them), we often are asked how we spotted these shenanigans when others, evaluating the same documents, failed to see them. Is it that we work so much harder or are more clever than other analysts? We think not. Rather, we believe our success stems from starting with a very different mindset—a forensic one. This approach incorporates qualities of skepticism, curiosity, and humility and mixes them with a deep understanding of human behavior and principles of fair play.

In the following pages, we summarize key elements of the forensic mindset that will keep you focused on key issues and questions and help you to detect accounting gimmicks and fraud in financial statements.

1. Skepticism Is a Competitive Advantage

In many ways, capital markets are designed to circulate good news. Financial services firms on the buy side and sell side, and corporate issuers themselves, typically make more money when share prices rise. Corporate issuers are incentivized to announce good news, sell-side firms to spread such news, and investors to believe it. This dynamic is part of what occasionally creates

---

APPLYING THE FORENSIC MINDSET

1. Skepticism is a competitive advantage.

2. Pay close attention to changes—always ask "why?" and "why now?"

3. Look past "accounting problems" to see if business problems are being covered up.

4. Pay attention to corporate culture and watch for breeding grounds of bad behavior.

5. Never blindly adopt the company's profitability framework.

6. Incentives matter: pay close attention to how executives are compensated.

7. Even in financial disclosures: location, location, location.

8. Like in golf, every shot counts.

9. Patterns of behavior provide a reliable signal.

10. Be humble and curious, and never stop learning.

---

asset bubbles and boom/bust cycles. Investors who can remain objective and skeptical, while the herds echo and amplify each other's excitement, have a better chance of profiting from the more blatant disconnects from reality.

Between 1995 and 2000, Enron's revenue had grown from under $10 billion to over $100 billion, a feat never achieved so quickly before at an American company. Management had become deified as some of the smartest people in commerce. Yet, Enron operated in a mature and heavily regulated industry, and hardly generated any accounting income or cash flow at all. The few skeptics who noticed and questioned the improbable sales-growth pattern were able to see that the business was a house of cards.

2. Pay Close Attention to Changes—Always Ask "Why?" and "Why Now?"

Many of the insights highlighted in this book came from noticing some important *change* (changes in accounting practices, policy disclosures,

Balance Sheet trends, key metrics, customer payment terms, executive departures, auditors, etc.). In most cases involving a change, management, wearing rose-colored glasses, dreamt up flattering and seemingly rational explanations to convince investors not to be concerned. All too often, however, we find these explanations to be irrelevant, boilerplate, or beside the point. For example, accounting policy changes are often attributed to a desire to follow the practices of peers, higher inventory is explained by the need to build product ahead of sales, and executive departures are explained by a wish to spend more time with their families, and so on. Asking "why" the change happened is an important question, but an even more insightful one is "why now?" What prompted the change to be made at that particular point in time? Asking "why now?" often leads investors to probe deeper into how results would have looked absent the change.

In Chapter 3, we discussed a very consequential change in revenue recognition at Ulvac, a Japanese semiconductor manufacturer. The company's choice to begin using percentage-of-completion accounting was an unusual and aggressive move; however, the "why now?" factor is what makes interpreting the change so powerful. Absent the change in accounting, the financial statements would have revealed that Ulvac's business actually was imploding, not improving as the reported numbers misleadingly showed.

3. Look Past "Accounting Problems" to See if Business Problems Are Being Covered Up

When questions arise about a company using inappropriate accounting practices, investors tend to view those issues solely as "accounting problems" that need to be investigated and eventually remediated (usually with the help of a big-four accounting firm). The financial press reinforces this by focusing on technical rules that have been violated, the significance of the violations, and who within the organization is believed to be responsible. While these are all important issues, we believe it more important for investors to focus on this question: "To what extent have these incorrect applications of accounting served to hide problems in the business?"

When Hertz announced that it would restate several years of financial statements to correct for inappropriate accounting, the press asked these predictable questions: What was the nature of the problems? Who was responsible? This shaped discussions common among investors who talked about the company's "accounting issues overhang." Remarkably little attention was paid to why Hertz had been fast and loose with its accounting, and what it meant about the real health of the business. As a result, investors were surprised when after the restatement dust finally cleared, the business was significantly less profitable than was previously understood.

4. Pay Attention to Corporate Culture and Watch for Breeding Grounds of Bad Behavior

The shenanigans profiled in this book are not representative of normal corporate behavior; rather, they reflect outlier actions of more aggressive and dishonest executives. They are also typically not just discrete choices of bad actors, but rather, the result of an environment and context that made those choices more probable. As we discussed in Chapter 2, certain characteristics at a company provide the breeding grounds for bad behavior. Weak checks and balances, an autocratic CEO, and a culture of meeting targets at all costs are among the elements that increase the risk of shenanigans.

The missive of Joe Nacchio, former CEO of Qwest Communications, to his sales team serves as a prime example of a win-at-all-costs culture that comes from the top: "The most important thing we do is meet our numbers. It's more important than any individual product. . . . We stop everything else when we don't make the numbers." This culture pushed Qwest employees to cut corners whenever necessary to make the numbers, and even engage in outright fraud.

5. Never Blindly Adopt the Company's Profitability Framework

In press releases, earnings calls, and investor presentations, company executives often take advantage of opportunities to report results in the most impressive and flattering light. In addition to reporting the required GAAP profits, management often discusses such non-GAAP metrics as its "EBITDA," "underlying business profit," "adjusted earnings," or many other variants. In some cases, these alternative metrics provide a valuable supplement to the GAAP-based figures; however, in many cases they leave out important aspects of the business's cost structure. Even if certain metrics become industry standards, investors must consider how well they actually reflect the full economics of the business.

Linn Energy, for example, focused investors on its "distributable cash flow" in order to justify ever-increasing dividend payouts. That metric was based on a vague management distinction between "growth-oriented" capital expenditures and other payments considered to be "maintenance-oriented." In many cases, such distinctions are arbitrary or intentionally misleading, resulting in inflated headline figures being presented by management.

When evaluating a non-GAAP profitability metric, we recommend stopping to consider what question it is that the measure answers, and then assess whether the question itself is a worthwhile one. In the case of Linn Energy's distributable cash flow, the question the metric provided would seem to answer is "How much cash flow was generated by the company's assets, excluding all expenditures that management considers to be associated with expansion activities?" Upon articulating the question, it might become apparent that it is not a very useful one, since management's assessment of capital expenditures by category (growth vs. maintenance capital) is entirely subjective, and in many cases, the distinctions are without meaningful differences.

6. Incentives Matter: Pay Close Attention to How Executives Are Compensated

Conventional wisdom espoused by compensation experts (and accepted by investors) is that management compensation should be directly tied to performance. Mediocre performance should yield mediocre compensation (or termination), and fantastic performance should be rewarded with a handsome compensation package. Naturally, performance is measured relative to established targets. Pay close attention to these targets, as they will inevitably shape management's strategy for the business.

When Valeant's board set the CEO's incentive compensation plan, the most significant financial performance metric specified was "cash earnings per share." This metric was calculated to exclude all expenses associated with

M&A activity, including restructuring, integration, and impairment costs, as well as the amortization expense associated with the acquired assets. Based on these targets, the most efficient way to maximize the underlying bonus would be to make large acquisitions using cash, *at any price*—since doing so would certainly improve cash earnings per share. Had the board instead designated a performance target based on a more inclusive measure of profitability (such as GAAP net income), the company would likely have pursued a very different strategy.

7. Even in Financial Disclosures: Location, Location, Location

Earnings Releases, annual and interim financial reports, and other regulatory filings are comprised of a combination of required disclosures and voluntary content, including additional information and commentary. Naturally, companies can highlight the most positive information in their Earnings Releases and quarterly investor presentations, which are broadly disseminated and read, and bury necessary but unflattering disclosures in the back pages of regulatory filings where few readers will find them. For this reason, we always read through these documents in their entirety, and our skeptical antennae are most engaged in sections of the filings that are too technical or boring for most readers. When we come across concerning information that seems relevant to the health of the business in these back sections (often in small type), we can be reasonably confident that we have discovered disclosures that management was trying to hide from investors. These are often the most valuable inputs.

In Chapter 7 we discussed the unusual boost to Under Armour's earnings in the fourth quarter of 2016, when the company reversed a $48 million charge (previously accrued as bonus compensation) back into the Income Statement. This action artificially lowered reported SG&A expense, making profitability look stronger in the quarter. Interestingly, the only mention of this reversal was made deep in the company's 10-K filing in a footnote to a completely unrelated table that detailed the business's seasonality patterns. Clearly this was a disclosure that management was trying to bury.

8. Like in Golf, Every Shot Counts

Golf stands apart from any other widely played spectator sports in this country. Unlike tennis, soccer, or basketball, in golf every shot is extremely meaningful. Professionals play 72 holes in a four-day tournament, and the player needing the fewest strokes wins. If you have a few terrible holes, you may still win, but every shot you take will count in your final tally. And that is how the game of accounting and financial reporting works under GAAP, as well. Companies that regularly encourage investors to ignore certain expenses or outflows are asking for a "mulligan" (a free shot). Those should only be accepted in very rare cases.

In Chapter 5, we discussed how for over a quarter century, Whirlpool consistently excluded its annual restructuring charges when presenting non-GAAP earnings, presumably on the grounds that such expenses were not part of the company's normal operations. Similarly, product recalls, litigation, M&A integration, and other expenses are all part of the cost of doing business. To pretend they are not is tantamount to cheating on the golf course—but with far worse consequences!

9. Patterns of Behavior Provide a Reliable Signal

We have long been fans of Nobel laureate Richard Thaler, a pioneer of behavioral finance. He has developed very useful theories about why investors consistently make seemingly irrational decisions, and he suggests how to avoid problematic biases.

About 15 years ago, Howard spoke at an investment conference in Chicago, immediately after Thaler had presented his research. Howard capitalized on Thaler's presentation adding that while Thaler's research had succeeded in profiling the predictable *behavior of investors*, our work focuses on profiling the predictable *behavior of corporate executives*. Indeed, investors attuned to executives' patterns of behavior can benefit knowing that these patterns tend to persist. For example, a CFO who uses aggressive accounting methods at one company is apt to do the same at a subsequent company. Moreover, if one Balance Sheet metric signals that the firm has "stuffed its sales channel" full of inventory, investors should look for similar trends in the company's history to see if a revenue shortfall followed similar aggressive behavior in the past. While forensic analysis is more art than science, you will find that many relationships and patterns have reliable persistence.

10. Be Humble and Curious, and Never Stop Learning

As we completed this special twenty-fifth anniversary edition of *Financial Shenanigans*, it became clear how much we had learned since the original edition. We are curious people by nature, and always look for opportunities to learn new things. Also, we are fortunate to be surrounded by teammates and clients and who are similarly motivated to crack complicated problems and acquire new skills and expertise. As we have become credentialed "gurus" in the field of forensic accounting, we keep humble, keenly aware that the learning curve ahead remains steep, with much to learn from everyone around us. We also appreciate the importance of recognizing when we have made a mistake and learning from it. Most important, we come to the office every day expecting to work hard, figure out how to solve difficult problems, learn something useful, and teach others something valuable.

Concluding Thoughts

This fourth edition of *Financial Shenanigans* updates investors with lessons gleaned from our examination of many deceptive financial reporting practices employed during the last quarter century. Since we published the original edition of *Financial Shenanigans*, corporate management has continued to concoct new ways to manipulate its financial reports to inflate its share price and other compensation-related metrics. And, looking to the future, as management works to create newfangled tricks, diligent investors must continue to learn to detect these new financial shenanigans.

> *What has been will be again, what has been done, will be done again; there is nothing new under the sun.* (Ecclesiastes 1:9)

Corporate financial scandals have been around for as long as corporations and investors themselves. Dishonest management has preyed on unsuspecting investors, and it is time for such investors to redouble their efforts to be alert for such financial shenanigans so that they can protect themselves.

Since shenanigans at their most basic level represent management's attempt to put a positive spin on a company's financial performance and economic health, our universal message is that investors should assume that the urge to exaggerate the positive and hide the negative will never disappear. And where temptation exists, shenanigans often follow.

Index

Acknowledgments

In writing this book we drew on insights from our research over the past 25 years. We owe a tremendous amount of credit and gratitude to our colleagues, past and present, whose curiosity, investigative spirit, smarts, and passion helped to advance the field of forensic accounting. We are especially proud of the work of our team at Schilit Forensics, including Aquiba Benarroch, Lucy Guo, Elie Himmelfarb, Kate Konetzke, Rebecca Lebwohl, Tom Skoglund, Sydney Traub, and Andrea Willette. Working shoulder to shoulder with such an exceptionally talented, kind, and fun group has made working a pleasure. We are also ever grateful to our clients who have entrusted us to stand as a line of defense against avoidable losses in their portfolios.

We are also deeply grateful for the love and support of our families:

To Diane, my amazing wife of 37 years, your love and support has been the bedrock in every achievement. To Jonathan, Suzanne, and Amy, your father could not be any prouder. And to the next generation of Schilit shenanigan-busters (Levi, Micah, and Grace), Grandpa is expecting that you also will make a wonderful contribution to the world for the next century.

—Howard

To my wife Andrea, who strengthens and inspires me every day with her brilliance, benevolence, and endless love. To our four beautiful children: Shira, Orli, Lev, and Rina; who inspirit and enlighten me with their curiosity, kindness, and enthusiasm. And to my parents, Vicki and Arthur, my daily models of devotion and integrity.

—Jeremy

To Talia, I am forever grateful for your love, support, inspiration, and encouragement. To Yakira, Nadav, Lior, and Noam for your good questions, insights, and contagious giggles. To my parents, Larry and Marlene for giving me a strong foundation and education, and for always encouraging my curiosity.

—Yoni

About the Authors

Dr. Howard M. Schilit, PhD, CPA is a pioneer in the field of detecting accounting manipulation in corporate financial reports. He is the founder and CEO of Schilit Forensics, an expert forensic accounting research consultancy serving institutional investors. Previously he founded and led the Center for Financial Research and Analysis (CFRA), a forensic accounting research publisher. Before establishing CFRA, Howard was an accounting professor at American University for seventeen years. He has been a leading spokesman before the U.S. Congress, regulators, and global media outlets on issues relating to accounting gimmicks and the early warning signs of business deterioration in public filings. Howard holds a doctorate in accounting from the University of Maryland. He lives in Key Biscayne, FL, and Bethesda, MD.

Jeremy Perler, CFA, CPA is a globally recognized expert in forensic accounting investment research. He is a partner at Schilit Forensics, a forensic accounting research consultancy serving institutional investors. Previously, Jeremy was a forensic accounting analyst for Coatue Management, a global long/short equity hedge fund; Director of Research for CFRA; and auditor for PricewaterhouseCoopers. In addition, he serves on the Standing Advisory Group of the PCAOB, and he previously served on the FASB's Financial Accounting Standards Advisory Council (FASAC). Jeremy is a CFA charterholder, and holds a BBA and Master of Accounting from the University of Michigan Ross School of Business. He lives in White Plains, NY.

Yoni Engelhart, CFA is a globally recognized expert in forensic accounting investment research. He is a partner at Schilit Forensics, a forensic accounting research consultancy serving institutional investors. Previously, Yoni worked as an Investment Principal at Partners Capital, a private investment office; Product Management Specialist at Wellington Management Company; and Senior Analyst, Director of Quantitative Research, and Director of Business Strategy at CFRA. He has been a guest lecturer at Harvard, Stanford, Columbia, Wharton, University of Chicago, and many other top business schools. Yoni is a CFA charterholder, and holds a BS from the University of Maryland, and an MBA from Harvard Business School. He lives in Brookline, MA.